Practical RHEL AI

Designing, Deploying and Scaling AI Solutions with Red Hat Enterprise Linux

Luca Berton

Apress®

Practical RHEL AI: Designing, Deploying and Scaling AI Solutions with Red Hat Enterprise Linux

Luca Berton
Amsterdam, The Netherlands

ISBN-13 (pbk): 979-8-8688-1900-1 ISBN-13 (electronic): 979-8-8688-1901-8
https://doi.org/10.1007/979-8-8688-1901-8

Copyright © 2026 by Luca Berton

This work is subject to copyright. All rights are reserved by the Publisher, whether the whole or part of the material is concerned, specifically the rights of translation, reprinting, reuse of illustrations, recitation, broadcasting, reproduction on microfilms or in any other physical way, and transmission or information storage and retrieval, electronic adaptation, computer software, or by similar or dissimilar methodology now known or hereafter developed.

Trademarked names, logos, and images may appear in this book. Rather than use a trademark symbol with every occurrence of a trademarked name, logo, or image we use the names, logos, and images only in an editorial fashion and to the benefit of the trademark owner, with no intention of infringement of the trademark.

The use in this publication of trade names, trademarks, service marks, and similar terms, even if they are not identified as such, is not to be taken as an expression of opinion as to whether or not they are subject to proprietary rights.

While the advice and information in this book are believed to be true and accurate at the date of publication, neither the authors nor the editors nor the publisher can accept any legal responsibility for any errors or omissions that may be made. The publisher makes no warranty, express or implied, with respect to the material contained herein.

Managing Director, Apress Media LLC: Welmoed Spahr
Acquisitions Editor: Divya Modi
Editorial Assistant: Gryffin Winkler

Cover designed by eStudioCalamar

Cover image designed by Pixabay

Distributed to the book trade worldwide by Springer Science+Business Media New York, 1 New York Plaza, New York, NY 10004. Phone 1-800-SPRINGER, fax (201) 348-4505, e-mail orders-ny@springer-sbm.com, or visit www.springeronline.com. Apress Media, LLC is a Delaware LLC and the sole member (owner) is Springer Science + Business Media Finance Inc (SSBM Finance Inc). SSBM Finance Inc is a **Delaware** corporation.

For information on translations, please e-mail booktranslations@springernature.com; for reprint, paperback, or audio rights, please e-mail bookpermissions@springernature.com.

Apress titles may be purchased in bulk for academic, corporate, or promotional use. eBook versions and licenses are also available for most titles. For more information, reference our Print and eBook Bulk Sales web page at http://www.apress.com/bulk-sales.

Any source code or other supplementary material referenced by the author in this book is available to readers on GitHub. For more detailed information, please visit https://github.com/Apress/Practical-RHEL-AI.

If disposing of this product, please recycle the paper

For my son Filippo, the joy of my life.

Table of Contents

About the Author xi

About the Technical Reviewer xiii

Acknowledgments xv

Introduction xvii

Chapter 1: Introduction to RHEL AI 1

AI in Enterprise 1

    Red Hat 2

    Why RHEL AI 3

    Use Cases 4

Artificial Intelligence 6

    Predictive AI 8

    Generative AI (GenAI) 8

    Agentic AI 10

    Artificial General Intelligence (AGI) 11

Red Hat AI 11

    Red Hat Enterprise Linux for AI 12

    OpenShift AI 14

    Red Hat AI Inference Server 17

Real-World Applications 17

    Healthcare 18

    Finance 19

    Manufacturing 20

    Retail 21

TABLE OF CONTENTS

    Telecommunications 22

    Government and Defense 23

Conclusion 24

Chapter 2: Setting Up RHEL AI 25

RHEL AI Version 25

Core Features 27

    Command-Line Tool 27

    GPU Acceleration Support 28

    System Requirements 29

    Download 30

    License 32

    Trial Activation 33

    Repositories 34

Bare Metal 36

    GUI Installation 37

    Automated Kickstart Installation 37

Cloud Providers 40

    Amazon Web Services 40

    Microsoft Azure 45

    Google Cloud Platform 51

    IBM Cloud 55

Verifying RHEL AI 60

GPU Support 60

    Verifying GPU Acceleration 61

Additional Storage 62

Governance Framework 64

Conclusion 65

TABLE OF CONTENTS

Chapter 3: Exploring Core Components 67
Introduction 67
    Knowledge Distillation 67
    Four-Step InstructLab 69
    The InstructLab Workflow 74
Core iLab Components and Architecture 74
Downloading and Managing Large Language Models (LLMs) 75
Configuring and Customizing Our AI Environment 76
Model Training and Uploading 77
Serving Models for Inference 77
Chatting with Models and Securing Access 78
Conclusion 80

Chapter 4: Advanced Features of RHEL AI 81
Introduction 81
    Training and Inference 82
    Leveraging GPU Acceleration 83
    Cloud Services for Scalable AI 93
    Automating RHEL AI 96
    Security and Compliance 101
    Ansible Automation 106
Conclusion 113

Chapter 5: Developing Custom AI Applications 115
Introduction 115
    Create a Custom AI Model 115
AI Design Document 116
    Provision the Right Infrastructure 118
    Bootstrap InstructLab 119
    Baseline Model 121
    Curate Domain Knowledge (Taxonomy) 127

TABLE OF CONTENTS

Synthetic Data Generation (SDG) 130
Serving, Chatting, and Integrating 136
Extend RHEL AI with Third-Party Libraries and Tools.. 138
Conclusion 142

Chapter 6: Monitoring and Maintenance 143

Introduction 143
Observability.. 143
Real-Time Monitoring 151
Service Reliability Goals 154
Red Hat AI Inference Server 155
Diagnose and Troubleshoot 159
GPU Telemetry 162
Monitoring and Reliable Rollouts in RHEL AI 168
Conclusion 176

Chapter 7: Use Cases and Best Practices 179

Introduction 179
Retrieval-Augmented Generation 179
Real-World Analogy 181
Brain Surgery.. 181
Librarian 182
RAG vs. Retraining 183
Use Case 185
Vector Database 186
RAG 189
REST API 190
LangChain 193
Third-Party Integrations 196
Accelerate Training 197
Training with DeepSpeed on NVIDIA A100 198
Training with FSDP on AMD MI300X or Mixed Hardware............................. 199

TABLE OF CONTENTS

Tune vLLM 199
Bring Our Own Teacher 201
Automate with Ansible 202
Custom Image Layers 204
GPU Profiles 205
Updates and Maintenance 206
Storage 206
Preflight Checklist 207
Troubleshooting Quick Reference 208
AI Agents 210
Model Registry 212
    Open-Source and Self-Hosted 213
    Cloud-Provider Registries 214
    Specialist SaaS/Enterprise 215
Frequently Asked Questions 216
Conclusion 218

Chapter 8: Future Trends in RHEL AI 219
Introduction 219
    Disclaimer 219
Explainable AI (XAI) 219
    Native SPDX Lineage 221
Edge AI 228
    Edge-Optimized Profiles 229
    Container-Native Update-of-Weights (UoW) 229
Governance and Ethics 231
    Runtime Attestation 231
    Differential Privacy 233
Agentic AI 234
Quantum AI 234

ix

TABLE OF CONTENTS

Hybrid AI 236

Sustainable Development 237

Conclusion 239

Chapter 9: Community and Support 241

Introduction 241

Official Support Channels 241

    InstructLab Community Collaboration Spaces 242

Training Resources for RHEL AI 244

Certifications 245

    Red Hat Certified Engineer (RHCE) 245

    Red Hat Certified Specialist in OpenShift Administration 246

    AI and Data Science Learning Paths 246

    External Certifications 246

Contributing to the Open-Source Community 247

Webinars, Workshops, and Conferences 248

    Hands-On Workshops 248

    Conferences 249

    Happy Hacking! 250

Conclusion 250

Index 251

About the Author

Luca Berton is a seasoned AI automation and DevOps expert with more than 18 years of experience in IT, specializing in cloud infrastructure, machine learning platforms, and enterprise-scale automation. He has led major AI and automation initiatives for financial institutions such as JPMorgan Chase, Société Générale, ABN Amro, and BPCE, designing GPU-accelerated Kubernetes/OpenShift AI clusters and optimizing CI/CD pipelines for regulated environments.

Luca is the creator of the popular Ansible Pilot project and author of several best-selling technical books, including *Ansible for Kubernetes by Example* and *Hands-on Ansible Automation*. A former Red Hat engineer, he has made significant contributions to the open-source ecosystem, particularly in enhancing Ansible's capabilities for cloud and AI workloads.

Widely recognized for his teaching and community leadership, Luca regularly shares his expertise through courses on Coursera, Pluralsight, and Educative and speaks at global tech conferences on topics ranging from MLOps to infrastructure automation.

About the Technical Reviewer

 **Kenneth Hitchcock** currently works as a senior architect with over 25 years of experience in IT. He has spent the last 15 years predominantly focused on Red Hat products, certificating himself as a Red Hat Architect along the way. Originally from Durban, South Africa, he now lives in England, where he hopes to not only continue inspiring all he meets but also to continue improving himself and the industry he works in.

Acknowledgments

To my son, family, and friends, who make life worth living and whose support and encouragement make this work possible.

To all whom I've worked with over the years and shared any ideas for this book. Thank you for the knowledge you've shared.

Introduction

Artificial intelligence is no longer a research and development side project—it is the foundational system of modern business. Whether automating claims processing, discovering new medicines, or defending cloud borders in real time, AI determines who wins the next decade. Yet, most enterprises still struggle with the same frustrations: toolchains that break between development and production, GPU clusters that behave like cats on a hot tin roof, and governance officers who appear the day after a model goes astray. Red Hat Enterprise Linux AI (RHEL AI) was built to turn that chaos into disciplined velocity, allowing you to fine-tune models on Friday and ship them to production on Monday. This book, *Practical RHEL AI*, is your field guide to doing precisely that—securely, repeatably, and at scale.

RHEL AI combines the rock-solid pedigree of Red Hat Enterprise Linux with an opinionated AI stack that integrates DeepSpeed, vLLM, InstructLab, and GPU drivers, allowing you to spend time designing solutions, not searching for the right CUDA wheel. With it, a small team can stand up a private ChatGPT clone, wire it into Grafana for drift alerts, and sleep soundly knowing SELinux is still on duty.

I draw on 18 years of experience automating highly regulated environments at JPMorgan Chase & Co., Société Générale, and BPCE. If you've watched one of my Ansible screencasts, you already know my style: pragmatic, vendor-neutral, and allergic to hand-waving. My mission with this book is simple—hand you a reproducible recipe for building AI services that auditors, SREs, and CFOs will all sign off on. By the final page, you will be able to

- Install and harden a GPU-accelerated RHEL AI cluster in any hybrid cloud
- Generate synthetic data, fine-tune Granite or Mixtral models, and serve them through an OpenAI-compatible API
- Automate monitoring, drift detection, and CI/CD so models evolve without surprise regressions
- Map cutting-edge trends—explainable AI, edge AI, AI governance—to concrete RHEL AI features you can deploy next quarter

INTRODUCTION

If you are an AI engineer, DevOps lead, or architect tasked with "making GenAI real," keep this book next to your terminal. Each chapter includes runnable examples, so you can translate theory into commits the same day.

How This Book Is Structured

Chapter 1: Introduction to RHEL AI
We begin with the *why*: the business drivers behind RHEL AI and the architectural pillars that distinguish it from roll-your-own Python stacks—security, reproducibility, and hybrid cloud reach. You will spin up your first RHEL AI image and tour the built-in InstructLab CLI that powers the rest of the book.

Chapter 2: Setting Up RHEL AI
Next comes groundwork. Hardware sizing tables help you pick between A100, H100, or MI300X GPUs; Kickstart snippets automate bare metal installs; and cloud templates launch ready-to-train images on AWS, Azure, or GCP. By the chapter's end, you will have a GPU node that passes the ILAB system info with flying colors.

Chapter 3: Exploring Core Components
Here, we dissect the "four-step" InstructLab workflow—crafting YAML skills, generating synthetic data, fine-tuning, and serving models—and see how cache folders, taxonomy trees, and model registries fit together. You will walk away understanding exactly where every checkpoint and JSONL file lives on disk.

Chapter 4: Advanced Features of RHEL AI
Performance junkies, rejoice. DeepSpeed ZeRO-3, MiCS communication scaling, FP8 inference, and NVMe offload are demystified with benchmark tables that show real numbers on H100 and MI300X silicon. Flip a single flag in your ds_config.json and watch the time-to-train drop by 40%.

Chapter 5: Developing Custom AI Applications
Turning models into revenue means aligning them with domain knowledge. This chapter teaches you to write a one-page capability statement, translate it into taxonomy seeds, and run the curate → generate → train → serve loop. End-to-end examples cover underwriting classification and multilingual chatbots, complete with Ansible playbooks for CI.

Chapter 6: Monitoring and Maintenance
AI without observability is a ticking time bomb. You will wire GPU thermals, cgroup pressure, vLLM latency buckets, and MMLU drift scores into a single Grafana lens, then define SLOs that map directly to SLIs like P95 ≤ 80 ms. The result is an on-call playbook your SREs will actually trust.

Chapter 7: Use Cases and Best Practices
From retrieval-augmented generation to edge-deployed sentiment analysis, we distill field patterns into decision tables: when to retrain vs. when to retrieve, which vector store to pick, and how to inject policy-as-code gates. Each pattern includes Terraform or OpenShift manifests you can fork on Friday afternoon.

Chapter 8: Future Trends in RHEL AI
Regulations tighten, GPUs evolve, and explainability moves from "nice to have" to a contract clause. This forward-looking chapter forecasts attribution pipelines baked into the ilab model evaluate, SPDX lineage for every weight, and carbon-aware scheduling. You will leave with a road map that keeps your platform ahead of audits and silicon curves alike.

Chapter 9: Community and Support
Finally, we plug you into Red Hat's lifeline: enterprise SLAs, weekly InstructLab Discord calls, community taxonomies, and contributor sprints. Learn how to open a support ticket, file a pull request, or present your custom skill at the next summit—and never feel alone in production again.

Ready to Build AI That Ships?
The pages ahead are opinionated, hands-on, and battle-tested. They assume you would rather see a snippet than a slide and that uptime, security, and debuggability matter as much as model quality. If that sounds like your reality, crack open your terminal, provision a GPU, and turn to Chapter 1. *Practical RHEL AI* is about to make enterprise AI boring—in the best possible way—so your team can focus on delivering features that matter. Let's build something remarkable.

CHAPTER 1

Introduction to RHEL AI

Artificial intelligence is reshaping the digital landscape, and enterprises are eager to adopt AI technologies that are powerful but in a secure, scalable, and compliant way. This chapter introduces RHEL AI—a platform built on the reliable Red Hat Enterprise Linux foundation—to streamline AI development and deployment in enterprise environments. We explore the motivations behind RHEL AI, its architecture, key capabilities, and provide step-by-step guidance for setting up our first AI-enabled system. By the end of this chapter, you will understand how RHEL AI empowers organizations to operationalize AI initiatives with confidence.

AI in Enterprise

Artificial intelligence (AI) is no longer confined to academic research or experimental applications; it has become an essential component of enterprise information technology. Whether facilitating predictive analytics, real-time decision-making, process automation, or customer engagement, AI is driving transformative change across various industries. Nevertheless, the development of AI systems that are secure, scalable, maintainable, and compliant with enterprise standards continues to present significant challenges.

Red Hat Enterprise Linux (RHEL) AI exemplifies a pinnacle of trust and innovation, providing a unified platform to develop, deploy, and manage intelligent applications. It leverages the established reliability of RHEL, coupled with integrated AI tools, frameworks, and best practices, to operationalize machine learning (ML) and deep learning (DL) within a modern IT infrastructure.

This chapter explores the strategic importance of RHEL AI, its fundamental architecture, detailed installation procedures, and methods of integration within real-world enterprise environments.

CHAPTER 1 INTRODUCTION TO RHEL AI

Red Hat

Following the inception of Linux in 1991, Red Hat's journey commenced in 1993 with its founding, driven by an ambitious objective: to introduce open-source software to the global community. During an era dominated by proprietary systems, Red Hat prioritized collaboration, transparency, and community engagement. This vision materialized with the release of Red Hat Linux in 1995, one of the pioneering Linux distributions to attain commercial success while adhering to open-source principles.

A significant milestone was reached in 2002 with the focus on the enterprise market through the launch of Red Hat Enterprise Linux (RHEL). It introduced a subscription-based model integrating open-source software with enterprise-level support, thereby establishing a foundation for open-source software within corporate information technology environments. RHEL swiftly established itself as a benchmark for reliability, security, and lifecycle management, paving the way for future innovations by Red Hat.

In subsequent years, Red Hat expanded its scope beyond Linux to encompass hybrid cloud, virtualization, and containerization. The acquisition of JBoss in 2006 augmented its application platform portfolio, and the 2014 introduction of OpenShift, Red Hat's Kubernetes-based container platform, positioned the company as a leader in cloud-native computing. These milestones exemplify Red Hat's consistent ability to anticipate technological trends and to align open-source communities with business and enterprise needs.

Red Hat's commitment to open source extended beyond product development. The company became one of the foremost corporate contributors to the Linux kernel and other pivotal projects such as Ansible, Ceph, Fedora, and Podman. Through governance, funding, and support for developers, Red Hat contributed to the vitality of the global open-source community while ensuring that innovation remained accessible.

In 2019, IBM acquired Red Hat for $34 billion, marking a landmark event in the technology sector. The acquisition did not signify a departure from Red Hat's open-source principles but was instead a strategic initiative to enhance its influence in cloud computing and artificial intelligence technologies. IBM was committed to maintaining Red Hat's independence and open model, allowing it to persist as a neutral leader within the broader ecosystem. This partnership amplified Red Hat's engagement in artificial intelligence, particularly through collaborative efforts in open hybrid cloud infrastructure, AI workloads, and foundational model development.

Presently, Red Hat continues to serve as a cornerstone of the open-source movement. It has effectively navigated decades of technological transformations without compromising its fundamental values. From its nascent Linux distributions to AI-compatible platforms, its contributions have shaped the way open-source software is developed, adopted, and trusted—empowering a global community of developers and enterprises to innovate collaboratively.

Why RHEL AI

In the AI landscape, companies face pressure to innovate while ensuring security, scalability, and reliability. Red Hat's focus on AI grew with the 2023 launch of Red Hat Enterprise Linux AI (RHEL AI), its first dedicated AI product. It offers a bootable container optimized for AI development, training, and inference, with tools like InstructLab, DeepSpeed, and vLLM, plus immediate GPU acceleration. This move expands Red Hat's open-source AI efforts, enabling developers to build and deploy large language models on transparent infrastructure. Since May 2025, Red Hat has also launched the llm-d project, a Kubernetes-native large language model inference framework. RHEL AI combines AI capabilities with Red Hat's reliable foundation, focusing on confident, efficient, and enterprise-grade model creation.

A primary reason to select RHEL AI is its emphasis on security. Red Hat's long-standing reputation for delivering secure and reliable infrastructure extends to its AI solutions. RHEL AI includes features such as SELinux-based access control, regular security updates, container integrity checks, and components designed for compliance. For organizations operating within regulated industries or managing sensitive data, this level of security is not optional; it is essential.

Performance also constitutes a vital aspect of the RHEL AI experience. Since version 1.4 of RHEL AI, it is specifically engineered to support demanding AI workloads, particularly large-scale model training and inference. It supports NVIDIA GPUs, including the latest A100 and H100 series, as of the current writing, and integrates robust AI frameworks such as DeepSpeed, FSDP, and vLLM. This configuration enables developers and data scientists to attain exceptional speed and efficiency when training or deploying large language models (LLMs), supported by hardware acceleration and software optimization.

A noteworthy feature of RHEL AI is the inclusion of InstructLab, a versatile AI toolkit that simplifies the customization and deployment of LLMs. With the built-in ilab command-line interface, users can create synthetic data, develop skill taxonomies, train models on custom data, and serve these models for real-time inference or chat-based applications. InstructLab streamlines complex AI tasks into manageable steps, facilitating rapid iteration and scalable deployment.

RHEL AI also demonstrates flexibility in deployment. Whether operating on bare metal servers, private data centers, or across major public cloud providers, RHEL AI is designed to be platform-independent. It supports Amazon Web Services, Microsoft Azure, Google Cloud Platform, and IBM Cloud, enabling organizations to deploy once and scale efficiently. This hybrid and multicloud approach ensures that AI infrastructure integrates seamlessly with existing architectures, rather than necessitating complete redesigns.

Red Hat's strength lies in its enterprise support system, with tools for automation, monitoring, and lifecycle management under RHEL AI. Automation, proactive monitoring, and dedicated support streamline operations. The open-source ethos combines community innovation with enterprise stability, fostering confident innovation. RHEL AI is impacting diverse sectors with AI applications like chatbots, virtual assistants, and analytics, promoting faster, trustworthy development. Choosing RHEL AI signifies a move toward responsible, scalable AI, enabling smarter innovation, quicker deployment, and better security in a growing AI landscape.

Use Cases

The true impact of Red Hat Enterprise Linux AI (RHEL AI) becomes evident when its robust features are employed to address practical challenges across diverse industries. By facilitating advanced analytics, intelligent decision-making, and automation, RHEL AI assists organizations in developing tailored AI solutions that not only satisfy complex business requirements but also uphold enterprise standards concerning security, scalability, and compliance.

In the healthcare industry, RHEL AI is being used to improve how medical professionals interact with information. Large language models trained on private clinical data allow organizations to create assistants that can summarize complex medical documents and provide intelligent triage support for patient symptoms. These models respect privacy and compliance requirements while enhancing both the speed and accuracy of clinical workflows.

CHAPTER 1 INTRODUCTION TO RHEL AI

In financial services, RHEL AI is helping institutions streamline compliance, reporting, and fraud detection. Natural language processing (NLP) models built on RHEL AI can automate the generation of financial reports and scan documents for regulatory compliance. Meanwhile, traditional machine learning models, such as those developed with scikit-learn, can be used to identify anomalies and fraudulent activities in transaction data, all within a secure and auditable environment.

The manufacturing industry is also benefiting from AI powered by RHEL AI. Predictive maintenance models help manufacturers reduce downtime by detecting equipment failures before they happen. AI-enabled edge devices, integrated into the production line, can inspect product quality in real time, ensuring consistent output without manual checks. Additionally, RHEL AI supports the development of operator-assistive systems, including voice-activated workflows, making human–machine interaction more natural and efficient on the factory floor.

Across these sectors, the flexibility of RHEL AI allows businesses to create AI solutions that are deeply integrated into their operations. Whether in hospitals, financial firms, or manufacturing facilities, RHEL AI speeds up innovation while offering the control and support needed for enterprise use. It turns AI's potential into real, measurable results.

With the exponential growth in data and compute needs, organizations are no longer asking *if* they should integrate AI—but *how*. RHEL AI provides a consistent, flexible foundation for building, deploying, and scaling AI solutions across on-premise, cloud, and hybrid environments.

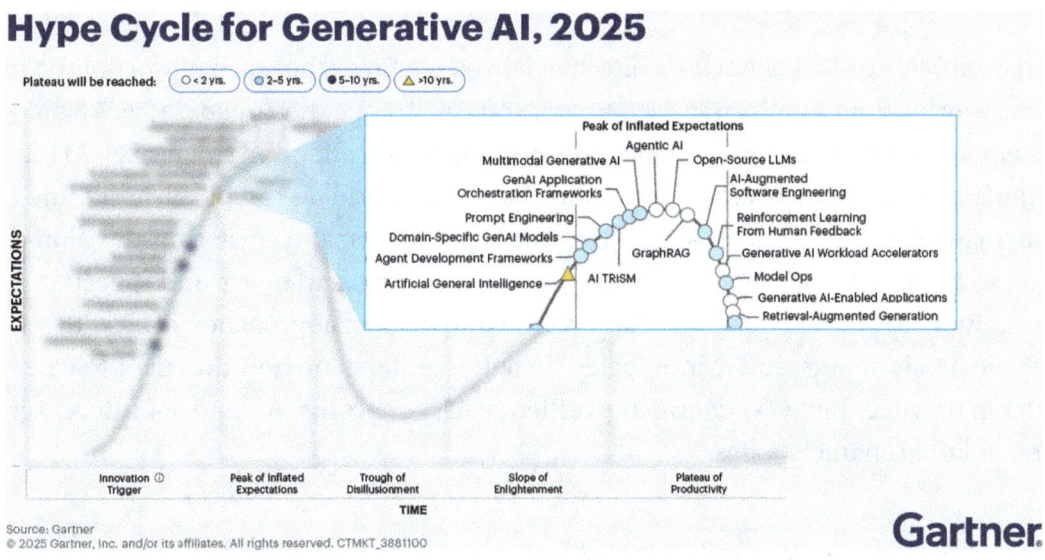

Figure 1-1. *Gartner Hype Cycle for Artificial Intelligence 2025*

CHAPTER 1   INTRODUCTION TO RHEL AI

According to IDC, global expenditure on artificial intelligence-centric systems reached $154 billion in 2023 and is projected to increase to $300 billion by 2027, reflecting a compound annual growth rate (CAGR) of 18.3%. Gartner[1] anticipates that by 2028, over 95% of enterprises will have implemented generative AI models or APIs in production, representing a significant increase from the current rate of less than 5% in 2023, as depicted in Figure 1-1.

Key industry-specific projections include

- **Manufacturing**: 25% year-over-year growth in AI spending, mainly in predictive maintenance and quality assurance

- **Healthcare**: Projected 22% year-over-year growth, driven by imaging diagnostics and AI-assisted clinical decision support

- **Finance**: 19% year-over-year growth, focusing on fraud detection, risk modeling, and customer service automation

- **Public Sector**: 17% year-over-year growth as governments adopt digital transformation and automation

By 2028, AI will account for more than 10% of enterprise IT budgets globally, underscoring its strategic importance.

Artificial Intelligence

AI has rapidly evolved, branching into specialized subfields that each play a unique role in the way machines understand, generate, and act. Among these, generative AI and the emerging field of agentic AI have garnered significant attention since 2025. AI refers to the broad discipline of creating systems that can perform tasks typically requiring human intelligence. These tasks include data classification and clustering, decision-making and predictions, natural language understanding, and image and speech recognition. Artificial intelligence has evolved into distinct approaches, each with different goals, inputs, and technologies. To better understand how these approaches differ in practice, Table 1-1 contrasts **predictive AI**, **generative AI**, and **agentic AI** across their defining characteristics.

---

[1] https://www.gartner.com/en/articles/hype-cycle-for-genai

Table 1-1. *Type of AIs*

Feature	Predictive AI	Generative AI	Agentic AI
Purpose	Perception, prediction	Content generation	Autonomy and decision execution
Input	Structured/ unstructured	Prompts or patterns	Goals and environment state
Output	Classifications, actions	Text, images, code	Actions, plans, API calls
Core Technology	ML, DL, statistics	Transformers, LLMs	LLMs + tools + orchestration
Example Tools	Scikit-learn, XGBoost	GPT, DALL·E, Stable Diff.	AutoGPT, LangChain, Ansible AI
Human Involvement	High	Moderate	Low (semi-autonomous)

These distinctions are not merely theoretical; they have tangible implications for the manner in which enterprises adopt and incorporate artificial intelligence. Gaining insight into the specific roles of each type of AI offers essential context for understanding how platforms such as RHEL AI facilitate organizations in progressing from intelligence to creativity and ultimately toward autonomy. Why it matters in the enterprise:

- **AI** powers business intelligence and automation.
- **Generative AI** transforms content workflows and enhances human creativity.
- **Agentic AI** is the future of self-healing infrastructure, intelligent operations, and autonomous decision systems.

In platforms like **RHEL AI**, we're seeing these domains converge:

- LLMs are deployed for GenAI use cases (e.g., documentation, ticket summarization).
- Agentic frameworks are emerging through integrations with tools like **Ansible**, enabling proactive remediation and autonomous DevSecOps workflows.

Understanding the distinction between predictive AI, generative AI, and agentic AI is crucial for selecting the right tools for the right problems. While AI provides intelligence, generative AI adds creativity, and agentic AI introduces autonomy.

Each level builds on the previous—forming a stack that enables smarter, faster, and more capable enterprise systems.

Predictive AI

Predictive AI systems are typically goal-driven and trained using data. Examples include

- Email spam filters
- Fraud detection models
- Antivirus
- Predictive maintenance algorithms
- Recommendation engines

AI can be rule-based (traditional), statistical (machine learning), or neural network-based (deep learning), encompassing both narrow AI (task-specific) and general AI (theoretical, humanlike cognition).

Generative AI (GenAI)

Generative AI is a subset of AI focused on creating new content—text, images, audio, video, or code—based on training data. Rather than classifying data, GenAI outputs new data.

Key characteristics:

- Uses foundation models (e.g., GPT, DALL·E, Stable Diffusion)
- Works with unsupervised or semi-supervised learning
- Trained on large-scale datasets
- Learns patterns and probabilities to generate original outputs

Examples:

- ChatGPT for text generation
- GitHub Copilot for code suggestions
- Midjourney for image creation

RHEL AI empowers organizations to deploy and fine-tune large language models (LLMs) for domain-specific applications, thereby accelerating the adoption of generative AI within enterprise environments. By offering tools for secure, scalable model tuning and deployment—such as synthetic data generation (SDG) and taxonomy-driven skill injection-RHEL AI streamlines the process of delivering customized digital experiences and automating knowledge-intensive tasks. Key use cases facilitated by RHEL AI:

- **Customize Domain-Specific LLMs with InstructLab (SDG ➤ Train ➤ Evaluate)**: RHEL AI's workflow lets us generate synthetic data, fine-tune, and evaluate models to fit our organization's language/tasks.

    Typical outcomes: Better task accuracy for our jargon, processes, and policies.

- **Taxonomy-Driven "Skills" and "Knowledge" Injection**: Author YAMLs to add capabilities/knowledge that guide SDG and tuning, then validate them before training.

- **Model Serving and Enterprise Assistants (Chat)**: Stand up a service and interact via chat for help-desk bots, operator copilot UX, or internal assistants.

- **Model Lifecycle Management**: Initialize our environment, download vetted models (including Granite 3.1 v2 variants), and keep both platform and models updated using the supported update paths.

- **Data Augmentation for ML Pipelines**: Use synthetic data generation to expand scarce domain examples and feed downstream training.

- **On-Prem GPU Acceleration for Training/Inference**: Plan deployments with documented accelerator support (e.g., NVIDIA H200, GH200 Tech Preview, AMD MI300X) and hardware sizing guidance.

- **Consistent Installation and Environment Bring-Up**: Install via the bootable container image across supported targets to create a reproducible, supportable AI stack.

- **Enterprise Support/Lifecycle Planning**: Align upgrades and support windows with the published RHEL AI lifecycle policy for GA, full-support, and EOL dates.

Additionally, RHEL AI supports data augmentation to enhance machine learning pipelines with synthetic data.

Agentic AI

Agentic AI, or autonomous agents, goes one step beyond generative capabilities by coupling generation with decision-making, planning, and action.

Key characteristics:

- Operates as a software agent with autonomy
- Possesses a memory, planning module, and goal-oriented behavior
- Capable of self-correction and continuous learning
- Can call external tools, APIs, or scripts

Examples:

- **AutoGPT**: Iteratively sets and refines goals
- **LangChain Agents**: Perform multi-step tasks via tool invocation
- **Red Hat Ansible Automation + LLM**: AI agent triggering automated remediation

Business use cases:

- Automated troubleshooting in IT (AIOps)
- Intelligent DevOps pipelines (code, test, deploy)
- Procurement agents for dynamic supplier negotiation
- AI-powered robotic process automation (RPA) with decision loops

Agentic AI is interactive, adaptive, and continuous, making it ideal for closed-loop enterprise systems.

Artificial General Intelligence (AGI)

Artificial General Intelligence (AGI) refers to a hypothetical form of artificial intelligence that possesses the ability to understand, learn, and apply knowledge across a broad spectrum of tasks at a level comparable to or exceeding human intelligence. Unlike narrow artificial intelligence, which is specialized for specific domains such as image recognition or language translation, AGI would be capable of general reasoning, abstract thinking, and autonomous decision-making in unfamiliar situations without task-specific programming. While current technologies—including large language models and agentic AI—demonstrate increasingly sophisticated behaviors, genuine AGI remains an aspirational objective. Achieving AGI presents significant technical challenges along with profound ethical, social, and governance implications for humanity.

Red Hat AI

Red Hat AI is a portfolio of products and services that accelerates the development and deployment of AI solutions across hybrid cloud environments.

- RHEL AI is a foundation model platform for building and customizing large language models using open-source tools, synthetic data generation, and Red Hat's Granite models.

- Red Hat OpenShift AI is an enterprise-grade MLOps platform that enables collaborative development, deployment, and management of AI/ML models at scale across hybrid and edge environments.

- Red Hat AI Inference Server is a lightweight, containerized solution that optimizes large language model serving with technologies such as continuous batching, tensor parallelism, and paged attention, reducing latency and cost.

Together, these products in the Red Hat AI portfolio empower organizations to build, fine-tune, deploy, and scale predictive and generative AI workloads efficiently across diverse infrastructures.

CHAPTER 1   INTRODUCTION TO RHEL AI

Red Hat Enterprise Linux for AI

RHEL AI is a set of layered capabilities on top of RHEL, specifically designed to simplify and standardize AI development and operations (AI/ML-Ops). It includes

- **Prepackaged AI tools** for model training, inference, and evaluation
- **Support for industry-standard frameworks** like TensorFlow, PyTorch, and scikit-learn
- **Integration with GPU acceleration**, enabling high-performance deep learning workloads
- **Deployment options across infrastructure** like bare metal, cloud (AWS, Azure), and edge devices
- **Enterprise-grade security and support**, including SELinux, RBAC, and compliance policies

RHEL AI builds on the robustness of the RHEL operating system while optimizing for AI workflows—ensuring that developers, data scientists, and system administrators can collaborate effectively on building intelligent systems.

RHEL AI offers a powerful, enterprise-ready platform tailored to meet the performance, security, and scalability needs of modern AI workloads. At its core is a set of performance optimization features, including kernel-level tuning and driver enhancements specifically designed for AI processing. It supports GPU-accelerated model training via NVIDIA CUDA and AMD ROCm and integrates machine learning toolkits with preconfigured defaults to streamline performance tuning. The platform delivers a comprehensive toolchain, providing access to industry-standard libraries such as TensorFlow, PyTorch, and scikit-learn for model development, as well as Pandas, NumPy, and Dask for efficient data manipulation and preparation. To accelerate deployment, RHEL AI includes pre-built, containerized environments optimized for rapid prototyping and scalability.

Security and compliance are first-class citizens in RHEL AI, featuring hardened enterprise-grade protections including SELinux, role-based access control (RBAC), and comprehensive auditing. It supports out-of-the-box compliance with regulatory standards relevant to sectors such as healthcare, finance, and government. RHEL AI also natively integrates with Red Hat Ansible and OpenShift, enabling secure and automated deployment pipelines across development and production environments.

Designed for hybrid scalability, RHEL AI can be deployed flexibly across bare metal, virtual machines, private and public cloud infrastructure, as well as edge environments.

As artificial intelligence adoption grows across enterprises, Red Hat offers two distinct platforms tailored to different stages of the AI lifecycle: Red Hat Enterprise Linux AI (RHEL AI) and Red Hat OpenShift AI. While both platforms share foundational technologies such as the Granite LLMs and InstructLab, they cater to very different user needs and operational scales.

RHEL AI is a Linux-based platform designed to lower the barriers to entry for AI development. It provides a lightweight, secure environment for experimenting with AI models, fine-tuning foundation models via InstructLab, and running workloads on modest hardware—including CPU-only systems.

The platform integrates seamlessly with Red Hat Enterprise Linux and includes powerful CLI tools (`ilab`) for managing models, generating synthetic data, fine-tuning, and evaluation. It supports custom model development with open-source frameworks such as TensorFlow and PyTorch and can run locally with or without GPU acceleration.

A key feature of RHEL AI is its YAML-based taxonomy system, which lets users define and extend skills and knowledge hierarchies. This approach reduces the need for dedicated MLOps teams, making it especially useful for developers, sysadmins, and researchers who want to prototype and iterate quickly before scaling up.

At the core of RHEL AI is InstructLab, an open-source project that redefines how large language models (LLMs) are built and extended. Unlike traditional approaches that rely on proprietary data and closed ecosystems, InstructLab enables collaborative, community-driven development.

Contributors can add new skills and knowledge directly to shared models without forking or branching, ensuring transparency and accessibility. Submissions use licensed, non-proprietary datasets and can typically be created in 10–20 minutes.

The strength of InstructLab lies in its simplicity and openness. By allowing both technical and nontechnical contributors to participate, it makes LLM development more inclusive, transparent, and sustainable—transforming AI from a specialized discipline into a shared, community-driven process.

CHAPTER 1 INTRODUCTION TO RHEL AI

OpenShift AI

OpenShift AI, formerly known as Red Hat OpenShift Data Science, is an enterprise-grade platform built on OpenShift Kubernetes for organizations ready to scale AI into production.

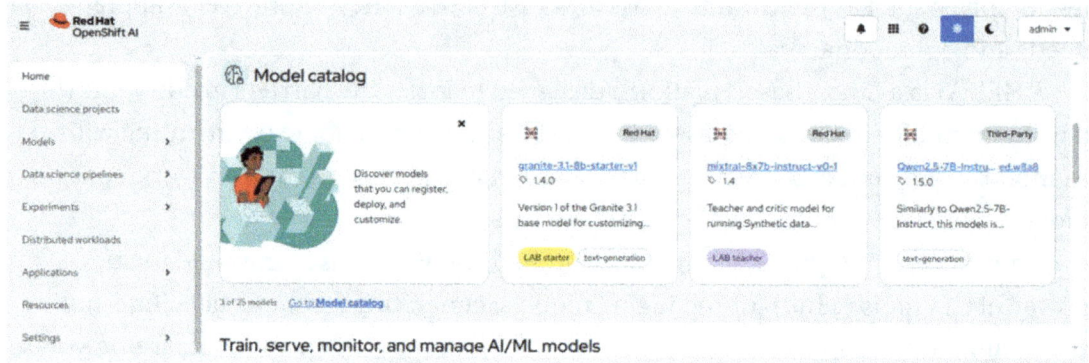

Figure 1-2. OpenShift AI interface

It offers robust support for the entire AI/ML lifecycle with full MLOps capabilities, including experiment tracking, model versioning, and automated deployment. Designed for hybrid and multicloud environments, OpenShift AI enables collaborative workflows among data scientists and ML engineers, supported by real-time monitoring, CI/CD pipelines, and integrated security. Its key features include seamless integration with GitOps, Prometheus, Grafana, and NVIDIA AI Enterprise, along with optimized performance on GPU-backed infrastructure and multiuser support for large-scale, team-based AI development. It is ideal for organizations needing a production-grade platform to deploy, manage, and scale AI workloads across environments. Figure 1-2 shows the OpenShift interface and how to integrate with the Jupyter Notebook application.

CHAPTER 1 INTRODUCTION TO RHEL AI

Table 1-2. RHEL AI vs. OpenShift AI feature comparison

Feature	RHEL AI	OpenShift AI
Target User	Developers, IT pros starting with AI	Enterprises scaling AI in production
Infrastructure	Single node or edge device	Kubernetes-based hybrid cloud
Model Management	Local fine-tuning and testing	Full MLOps (CI/CD, versioning, monitoring)
GPU Acceleration	Supported	Strongly integrated and optimized
Use Case Fit	Prototyping, education, edge AI	Production-grade AI, model ops, collaboration

A financial institution, for example, might begin with RHEL AI to prototype fraud detection models in a controlled local environment. This allows teams to test ideas, fine-tune models, and validate approaches without heavy infrastructure requirements. Once those models prove effective, they can be promoted to OpenShift AI, where they benefit from large-scale deployment features such as versioning, monitoring, and role-based access across hybrid cloud environments.

Rather than competing, the two platforms are designed to complement each other. RHEL AI serves as the entry point—ideal for experimentation, lightweight customization, and development close to existing RHEL systems. OpenShift AI extends that work into production, delivering the orchestration, governance, and scalability required for enterprise workloads.

OpenShift AI architecture, managed by a cluster-resident control plane, oversees the lifecycle, tenancy, quotas, and placement of models. It translates desired configurations like models, versions, and SKUs into operational inference services that are securely isolated via OpenShift RBAC and namespaces. The workload layer is powered by llm-d,[2] offering predictable latency and scalability across nodes and GPUs. It reimagines how LLMs run natively on Kubernetes, integrating key open-source technologies such as Kubernetes Gateway API Inference Extension,[3] NVIDIA Dynamo (NIXL[4]) KV Transfer

---

[2] https://llm-d.ai
[3] https://gateway-api-inference-extension.sigs.k8s.io
[4] https://developer.nvidia.com/blog/nvidia-dynamo-accelerates-llm-d-community-initiatives-for-advancing-large-scale-distributed-inference

CHAPTER 1   INTRODUCTION TO RHEL AI

Library, and DeepEP[5] Mixture of Experts (MoE). It connects with Red Hat AI Inference Server, supporting vLLM on CUDA/ROCm/TPU images, enabling faster and more cost-effective inference. The integrated API gateway provides stable, versioned endpoints—compatible with OpenAI embedding, completion, and Llama Stack options—creating a platform for RAG, agents, safety, evaluations, and tool integrations, leveraging open-source technologies like docling.[6] The gateway also features per-tenant authentication, rate limiting, request and response logging hooks, and policy enforcement, including standardized tool access for agents via the Model Context Protocol (MCP[7]) for centralized governance. Red Hat offers a curated collection of models and MCP in the catalog to reduce integration risks and improve performance-per-watt and efficiency. The registry and pipelines enable lineage tracking, approval gates, and rollback options, along with reusable pipeline components and support for Bring Your Own (BYO) Argo workflows. Deployment strategies like blue/green or canary are managed at the gateway through versioned routes. Observability metrics follow SRE standards, using OpenTelemetry to monitor TTFT, tokens per second, queue depth, and GPU health, complemented by dashboards that support enterprise monitoring, chargeback, showback, and inference Service-Level Agreements (SLAs). Additionally, GPU-as-a-Service (GPUaaS) employs NVIDIA MIG slicing and Kueue bin-packing with fair-share scheduling, optimized for resource utilization across diverse training and inference workloads. The AI Hub and Generative AI Studio offer separate platform and application functions, accelerating the transition from concept to pilot projects. The Model-as-a-Service (MaaS) feature introduced in OpenShift AI 3.0 provides an internal, governed method for deploying models as APIs—on-premises, in public clouds, or in sovereign environments—without transmitting sensitive data externally. MaaS utilizes built-in metering and policy controls, allowing teams to maintain sovereignty while preserving development velocity.

In short: use RHEL AI for flexibility and simplicity at the edge or during early exploration, and switch to OpenShift AI when enterprise-grade reliability and scale are needed.

---

[5] https://github.com/deepseek-ai/DeepEP
[6] https://www.docling.ai
[7] https://modelcontextprotocol.io

Red Hat AI Inference Server

Red Hat AI Inference Server is a containerized, enterprise-grade platform for deploying and optimizing inferencing with large language models (LLMs) across diverse hardware accelerators, including NVIDIA CUDA, AMD ROCm, Google TPU, and IBM Spyre. Built on the upstream vLLM engine, the latest version 3.2, at the time of writing this book, introduces performance enhancements like speculative decoding, CUDA graph optimization, improved memory throughput, and expanded quantization techniques (FP8, MXFP4, NVFP4), along with support for cutting-edge models such as Llama, Gemma, and Qwen. This release also introduces the Red Hat AI Model Optimization Toolkit, which enables fine-grained compression strategies, Mixture of Experts (MoE)[8] support, and integration with OpenShift Container Platform for scalable and cost-efficient LLM deployment.

Real-World Applications

Organizations across industries are already harnessing the power of RHEL AI in production:

- **Healthcare**: Enhancing diagnostics with medical image classification using deep learning
- **Finance**: Detecting fraud in real time with machine learning pipelines deployed on secure RHEL instances
- **Manufacturing**: Predictive maintenance using time-series analysis of sensor data
- **Government**: Secure AI workloads for document classification and public service automation

Case studies show that RHEL AI not only accelerates time-to-value for AI projects but also reduces infrastructure complexity and improves governance.

---

[8] https://www.ibm.com/think/topics/mixture-of-experts

CHAPTER 1 INTRODUCTION TO RHEL AI

Healthcare

At a large hospital network, radiologists faced growing backlogs as imaging volumes surged. Reviewing thousands of MRI scans and chest X-rays each week not only slowed diagnostic turnaround times but also risked missing subtle anomalies hidden in massive datasets. By deploying RHEL AI, the hospital's data science team built and fine-tuned deep learning models specifically for medical imaging. With GPU-accelerated training and inference pipelines, these models could rapidly process large batches of images—identifying potential tumors or abnormalities with a level of speed and consistency impossible for manual review alone. The results were transformative. Diagnostic turnaround times dropped significantly, giving clinicians faster insights for critical cases. Accuracy improved as AI-assisted analysis caught early indicators that might otherwise be overlooked. And because RHEL AI builds on SELinux-based enterprise security, the platform supported HIPAA compliance requirements, ensuring that sensitive patient data was protected throughout the workflow. What began as a technology pilot quickly became a clinical asset—freeing radiologists to focus on complex cases while improving both patient outcomes and operational efficiency.

Example Stack: TensorFlow + CUDA on RHEL AI + Ansible for automated deployments

Use Case: Medical imaging with AI

Example: *Boston Children's Hospital*[9] leverages AI models running on Red Hat OpenShift and RHEL to support radiology workflows and improve pediatric diagnostic accuracy.

Technology Stack: TensorFlow, NVIDIA CUDA, Red Hat OpenShift, RHEL AI

Enterprise value:

- Faster diagnostics and reduced clinical workload
- Integrated security and HIPAA compliance
- Enables AI deployment in hybrid cloud with OpenShift

---

[9] https://www.redhat.com/en/about/press-releases/red-hat-works-advance-radiology-through-ai

Finance

A global financial services provider faced the challenge of monitoring millions of transactions per second across digital and in-branch channels. Traditional rule-based fraud detection systems struggled to keep pace with evolving attack patterns, often flagging too many false positives while still missing sophisticated threats. By adopting RHEL AI, the institution's data science team built and deployed machine learning models capable of detecting anomalies in real time. These models continuously adapted to new fraud behaviors through synthetic data generation and fine-tuning pipelines, ensuring they stayed ahead of emerging risks. With secure deployment across hybrid cloud environments, the models integrated seamlessly with the existing core banking infrastructure without disrupting operations. The impact was immediate: fraudulent transactions were flagged and blocked before funds were lost, saving millions in potential damages. Compliance teams benefited from explainable AI (XAI) features, which provided transparent insights into why transactions were flagged—an essential capability for regulatory audits. Most importantly, customers gained confidence that their accounts and payments were protected, reinforcing trust in the institution's services.

Example Stack: Scikit-learn + OpenShift AI + Grafana for monitoring

Use Case: Anomaly detection in digital payments

Example: *DenizBank*[10] uses Red Hat technologies, including RHEL and OpenShift, to support AI workloads in fraud prevention systems that analyze transactions in real time.

Technology Stack: Scikit-learn, OpenShift AI, Kafka, Grafana

Enterprise value:

- Millisecond-level fraud detection
- Built-in explainability for regulatory compliance
- Secure pipeline from model training to deployment

---

[10] https://www.redhat.com/en/blog/denizbank-drives-ai-innovation-red-hat-openshift-ai

CHAPTER 1   INTRODUCTION TO RHEL AI

Manufacturing

In a modern manufacturing plant, even a single equipment failure can halt production lines and cost millions in lost output. Maintenance teams traditionally relied on scheduled service intervals or reacting after breakdowns occurred—approaches that often led to unnecessary downtime or unexpected failures.

With RHEL AI, the factory's engineers connected industrial IoT sensors across key machinery and began streaming time-series data into machine learning models trained to detect early warning signs of failure. These models continuously analyzed vibration patterns, temperature changes, and other operational signals to predict when equipment would need servicing.

Instead of waiting for machines to fail or over-servicing them too early, maintenance could now be scheduled proactively at the optimal time. This shift not only reduced unplanned downtime but also extended the life of expensive equipment. Because RHEL AI supports air-gapped deployments, the solution was implemented directly within the operational technology (OT) environment, ensuring both performance and security without exposing sensitive systems to external networks.

The outcome: Maintenance costs dropped by as much as 30%, equipment uptime improved, and production schedules became more predictable—turning maintenance from a cost center into a driver of efficiency and resilience.

Example Stack: PyTorch + Dask + Red Hat Enterprise Linux on edge gateways

Use Case: Machine learning for equipment failure prediction

Example: *Hitachi, Ltd.*[11] uses Red Hat OpenShift AI to operationalize AI across IT and OT environments, including predictive maintenance in manufacturing. By building on Red Hat's hybrid cloud platform, Hitachi supports over 250 internal AI projects, enhancing system development and real-time asset monitoring across industrial operations.

Technology Stack: PyTorch, Red Hat OpenShift AI, Red Hat Enterprise Linux, Dask, Podman

Enterprise value:

- Avoids costly unplanned downtime

---

[11] https://www.redhat.com/en/about/press-releases/red-hat-empowers-hitachi-ltd-evolve-ai-driven-enterprise-red-hat-openshift-ai

- Ensures AI governance and cross-functional scalability
- Enables real-time inference and system optimization in edge and enterprise environments

Retail

In a competitive retail landscape, delivering the right product to the right customer at the right time can make the difference between a lost opportunity and a sale. Traditional recommendation engines often struggled with providing delayed insights or rigid rules that failed to capture rapidly changing customer preferences. Using RHEL AI, a retail organization built real-time recommendation models that analyze shopper behavior as it happens—browsing history, location, and past purchases all feed into the system. Hosted securely on RHEL AI, these models generate personalized suggestions instantly, whether on an ecommerce site or through a mobile shopping app.

The impact was twofold. Shoppers enjoyed tailored product recommendations that felt relevant, driving higher conversion rates and boosting average order value. Meanwhile, the retailer gained tools for dynamic pricing and smarter inventory optimization, ensuring popular items were in stock without overcommitting resources. With RHEL AI's enterprise security and compliance features, the system also upheld strict data governance and GDPR compliance, protecting customer trust.

The result: more engaging customer experiences, stronger brand loyalty, and a measurable lift in revenue—powered by AI embedded directly into the shopping journey.

Example Stack: RHEL AI + Kubernetes + Python microservices

Use Case: Product recommendation engines

Example: *Alibaba* and *Walmart*[12] rely on Linux-based infrastructure, including RHEL and OpenShift, for scalable AI systems that deliver personalized shopping experiences through AI/ML pipelines.

Technology Stack: RHEL AI, Kubernetes, Python ML APIs, Kafka

---

[12] https://corporate.walmart.com/news/2024/10/09/walmart-reveals-plan-for-scaling-artificial-intelligence-generative-ai-augmented-reality-and-immersive-commerce-experiences

CHAPTER 1   INTRODUCTION TO RHEL AI

Enterprise value:

- Increased sales conversion and customer engagement
- Scalable AI microservices across cloud and edge
- Compliance-ready architecture for global markets (e.g., GDPR)

Telecommunications

Telecom providers face enormous pressure to deliver fast, reliable customer service while keeping costs under control. With thousands of support requests arriving every hour—ranging from billing questions to troubleshooting network issues—human agents alone couldn't keep up without long wait times and rising costs. By deploying LLMs and chatbot models on RHEL AI, providers introduced AI-powered virtual assistants capable of handling Tier 1 inquiries at scale. Customers could interact through mobile apps, web chat, or interactive voice response (IVR) systems, receiving instant answers to routine questions. More complex cases were automatically escalated to human agents, ensuring that support staff focused their time where it mattered most. These assistants didn't remain static. Using continuous feedback loops, the models improved over time—learning from new issues, user interactions, and updated knowledge bases. The results were clear: support costs dropped, customers experienced faster resolutions and higher satisfaction, and the system scaled seamlessly across multiple channels. By blending automation with human expertise, RHEL AI helped telecom providers deliver customer support that was not only more efficient but also more responsive and engaging.

Example Stack: RHEL AI + Hugging Face Transformers + OpenShift Service Mesh
Use Case: Chatbot automation and LLM-based support
Example: *Vodafone* and *Orange*[13] have deployed AI customer support solutions on Red Hat OpenShift with RHEL under the hood, using LLMs and NLP models to reduce human intervention in Tier 1 support, while Turkish Airlines[14] leverages Red Hat OpenShift AI to power dynamic pricing, fraud prevention, and intelligent workload deployment across its global operations.

---

[13] https://www.redhat.com/en/about/press-releases/red-hat-and-orange-collaborate-accelerate-telco-cloud-transformation-and-services-softwarization
[14] https://www.redhat.com/en/about/press-releases/turkish-airlines-pioneers-ai-led-innovation-aviation-red-hat-openshift-ai

Technology Stack: Hugging Face Transformers, Red Hat OpenShift AI, OpenShift Service Mesh, RHEL AI

Enterprise value:

- 40% reduction in customer support response time
- Multichannel scalability (chat, voice, email)
- AI-driven dynamic pricing and fraud detection
- Scalable, on-premise model deployment and autoscaling across aviation operations

Government and Defense

Government agencies deal with overwhelming volumes of unstructured information every day—emails, reports, intelligence briefs, and field notes. Sorting through this flood of data manually not only slowed operations but also created risks of delayed or missed insights. With RHEL AI, agencies deployed NLP-powered classification models to automatically process documents in real time. These models categorized content by topic and flagged sensitivity levels, ensuring the right information reached the right teams faster. Security was paramount. With role-based access control (RBAC) and SELinux enforcement built into the platform, sensitive insights were tightly protected—only authorized personnel could view classified material. Compliance with FedRAMP and ISO security standards provided further assurance that the system could operate safely within highly regulated environments. The outcome was a dramatic improvement in operational decision-making. Analysts gained faster access to relevant intelligence, leaders could act on critical information sooner, and agencies reduced the time from data collection to actionable insight—without compromising security.

Example Stack: RHEL AI + Custom LLM (trained with YAML skills) + OpenSCAP compliance

Use Case: NLP for unstructured data triage

Example: The *U.S. Department of Defense* and *NATO* partners have evaluated RHEL AI and OpenShift for secure, classified AI model training and inference, while the Government of Castilla-La Mancha (JCCM) uses Red Hat OpenShift AI to streamline environmental impact assessments via generative AI assistants, significantly reducing document processing time.

Technology Stack: Custom LLMs on RHEL AI, OpenShift, Ansible Automation Platform

Enterprise value:

- Accelerated intelligence analysis
- Zero-trust architecture with STIG, SELinux, and NIST-800 compliance
- Reduced EIA processing times by up to two months, improving citizen services and operational efficiency

From hospitals and factories to banks and data centers, RHEL AI proves its versatility in real-world environments. Its flexibility across hardware, security-hardened OS base, and ecosystem integration make it an ideal foundation for AI at enterprise scale.

Conclusion

RHEL AI represents more than merely a toolkit; it is a comprehensive platform that aligns with the requirements of enterprises for scalability, security, and reliability. By integrating the strengths of Red Hat Enterprise Linux with advanced AI functionalities, RHEL AI enables organizations to operationalize machine learning and artificial intelligence confidently.

In the next chapter, you will learn how to install, configure, and prepare your RHEL AI environment for development and production use.

CHAPTER 2

Setting Up RHEL AI

Artificial intelligence is quickly moving from research labs to the center of enterprise IT strategies. As organizations aim to expand and operationalize AI workloads, the need for a stable, secure, and reproducible platform becomes essential. RHEL AI addresses this requirement by providing a purpose-built environment designed for developing, training, and deploying AI models at scale.

This chapter sets the foundation for effectively using RHEL AI. Whether you are a data scientist creating models, a DevOps engineer setting up infrastructure, or a system administrator overseeing compliance and performance, correctly configuring RHEL AI is your first step. We will cover system requirements, installation steps, environment setup, and GPU acceleration configuration.

By the end of this chapter, you will have a fully functional RHEL AI environment ready for both development and production. This foundation will support advanced workflows and enterprise integrations discussed in later chapters.

RHEL AI Version

As we already learned in Chapter 1, RHEL AI is a specialized runtime and development toolkit that extends the capabilities of standard RHEL to support modern AI workloads, particularly fine-tuning and serving large language models (LLMs). It provides

- A secure, reproducible AI development environment built on RHEL 9

- Integrated CLI tools (`ilab`) for model lifecycle management

- Prebuilt and validated AI/ML/DL libraries, including TensorFlow and PyTorch

- A YAML-based taxonomy system for skills and knowledge extension

CHAPTER 2   SETTING UP RHEL AI

- Facilities for synthetic data generation (SDG), multiphase training, benchmark evaluation, and deployment of custom LLMs

- GPU acceleration, with support for NVIDIA H200, NVIDIA GH200 (Tech Preview), and AMD MI300X accelerators

- Inference serving with vLLM for high-throughput workloads

- DeepSpeed and FSDP for distributed, hardware-optimized training

Integration with the Ansible Automation Platform for automating RHEL AI deployments and workloads

Rather than requiring teams to assemble an AI stack from scratch, RHEL AI provides a ready-to-use enterprise platform that accelerates experimentation, ensures compliance, and standardizes AI workflows across environments.

The latest RHEL AI 1.5 image at the time of writing the book includes

- RHEL 9 base system

- InstructLab container with Python 3.11, SDG, training, evaluation, and serving

- Granite 3.1 models (version 2), with continued support for Red Hat and IBM-produced open-source LLMs

- New teacher model support: `llama-3.3-70B-Instruct` (Tech Preview) for higher-quality synthetic data generation

- Enhanced multiphase training with LAB-aligned fine-tuning techniques

- Expanded benchmark evaluation options (MMLU_BRANCH, MT_BENCH_BRANCH) for model validation

- Cross-product automation: Ansible content collections (`infra.ai`, `redhat.ai`) to provision and manage RHEL AI environments across clouds

Core Features

RHEL AI provides a comprehensive set of capabilities specifically designed to support enterprise-scale AI workloads. These features encompass runtime environments, tooling, deployment strategies, and integration with hybrid cloud infrastructure. In this section, we examine the key components that form a robust foundation for RHEL AI, enabling modern AI development and operations.

At its core, RHEL AI provides a preconfigured runtime optimized for AI workloads. It includes libraries for

- **Data Processing**: Pandas, NumPy, Dask, Apache Arrow
- **Model Training**: TensorFlow, PyTorch, scikit-learn, LightGBM
- **Natural Language Processing**: Hugging Face Transformers, spaCy
- **Visualization**: Matplotlib, seaborn, Plotly

Command-Line Tool

RHEL AI introduces a powerful companion: the Integrated Command-Line Tool, commonly referred to as `ilab`. Designed to streamline AI model development, data generation, system management, and taxonomy manipulation, `ilab` centralizes operations into a single, cohesive interface.

Whether we are a developer training models, an admin provisioning resources, or a data scientist organizing datasets, `ilab` becomes our gateway to managing InstructLab and related components within RHEL AI.

`ilab` is the CLI utility in InstructLab within RHEL AI, offering commands to manage the AI environment, including generating training data, configuring the system, managing LLMs, serving models, training skills, and navigating taxonomies.

Once RHEL AI is installed, verify that `ilab` is available by running

```
$ ilab
```

Sample Output:

```
Usage: ilab [OPTIONS] COMMAND [ARGS]...

CLI for interacting with InstructLab.
```

CHAPTER 2   SETTING UP RHEL AI

If this is your first time running ilab, it's best to start with `ilab config init` to create the environment.

```
Options:
  --config PATH    Path to a configuration file [default: ~/.config/
                   instructlab/config.yaml]
  -v, --verbose    Enable debug logging (repeat for more verbosity)
  --version        Show the version and exit.
  --help           Show this message and exit.
Commands:
  config     Manage configuration for InstructLab.
  data       Generate and manage synthetic data.
  model      Train, serve, and interact with models.
  system     Run system-level checks and diagnostics.
  taxonomy   Manage skill and knowledge taxonomies.
Aliases:
  chat       → model chat
  generate   → data generate
  serve      → model serve
  train      → model train
```

RHEL AI's `ilab` CLI tool delivers enterprise-grade efficiency in AI development, cutting through complexity with modular commands. Whether we are creating synthetic datasets or deploying LLMs on production-grade infrastructure, `ilab` streamlines our workflow while providing us complete control over the hood.

GPU Acceleration Support

Modern AI models, particularly LLMs, are computationally intensive. GPUs offer thousands of cores optimized for parallel operations—perfect for the matrix-heavy computations of training and inference.

Benefits of GPU acceleration in RHEL AI:

- Faster training times
- Higher throughput for inference

- Efficient multi-GPU scaling
- Support for advanced architectures (NVIDIA A100 and H100 at the moment of writing this book)

RHEL AI has been meticulously engineered to ensure out-of-the-box compatibility with Graphics Processing Units (GPUs), incorporating the following features:

- **vLLM (Fast Inference Engine):** This feature is optimized for high-throughput large language model (LLM) inference and is designed to operate seamlessly with GPU-backed instances.
- **DeepSpeed Integration:** This represents Microsoft's library for deep learning optimization, facilitating model parallelism, memory optimizations, and expedited training processes.
- **FSDP (Fully Sharded Data Parallel):** This capability is particularly well-suited for the training of extensive models across multiple GPUs, effectively sharing memory across devices to maximize efficiency.
- **CUDA-Compatible Base:** This component supports NVIDIA GPU drivers and CUDA libraries, ensuring compatibility with Red Hat's certified GPU-enabled hardware.

For reference, the full spectrum includes CPU, GPU, NPU, and TPU accelerators, enabling organizations to deploy AI workloads flexibly across diverse hardware architectures.

System Requirements

Getting started with RHEL AI begins with preparing our system environment and installing the necessary software components. This section walks us through the full installation process—from verifying hardware requirements to setting up a Python virtual environment. Whether we are deploying on a workstation, server, or in the cloud, these steps ensure a consistent and reproducible AI setup tailored for enterprise needs.

RHEL AI works natively with Podman/Docker, Red Hat OpenShift, and cloud platforms AWS, Azure, and GCP. This ensures AI workloads are portable, cloud-ready, and aligned with DevSecOps.

CHAPTER 2   SETTING UP RHEL AI

These are the principal requirements:

- **CPU**: x86_64 multicore processor
- **RAM**: 8 GB minimum (16+ GB recommended)
- **Storage**: 60+ GB disk space
- **GPU**: NVIDIA (CUDA) or AMD (ROCm)
- **OS**: RHEL 8.6+, RHEL 9.x

We install RHEL AI on bare metal machines using either the Graphical Installer (GUI) or Kickstart with embedded or custom container images. Kickstart enables automated, preconfigured installations. The image supports hardware acceleration, but it requires at least 1TB in /home and 120GB on / for smooth operations. RHEL AI images are built for specific hardware accelerators. Supported GPUs include NVIDIA A100, H100, V100, other CUDA-capable cards via NVIDIA driver, and multi-GPU systems for distributed training (DeepSpeed, FSDP).

When our environment is ready, we can install RHEL AI. Most of the time, on bare metal or virtual machines, our first step is to acquire the installation media by accessing the Red Hat Customer Portal and downloading the correct installation media. This section guides us through the preparation steps and illustrates what to expect during the download and trial activation process.

Download

To get started, we need access to the official Red Hat Customer Portal. Once logged in with a Red Hat account, follow these steps to download the latest RHEL AI release.

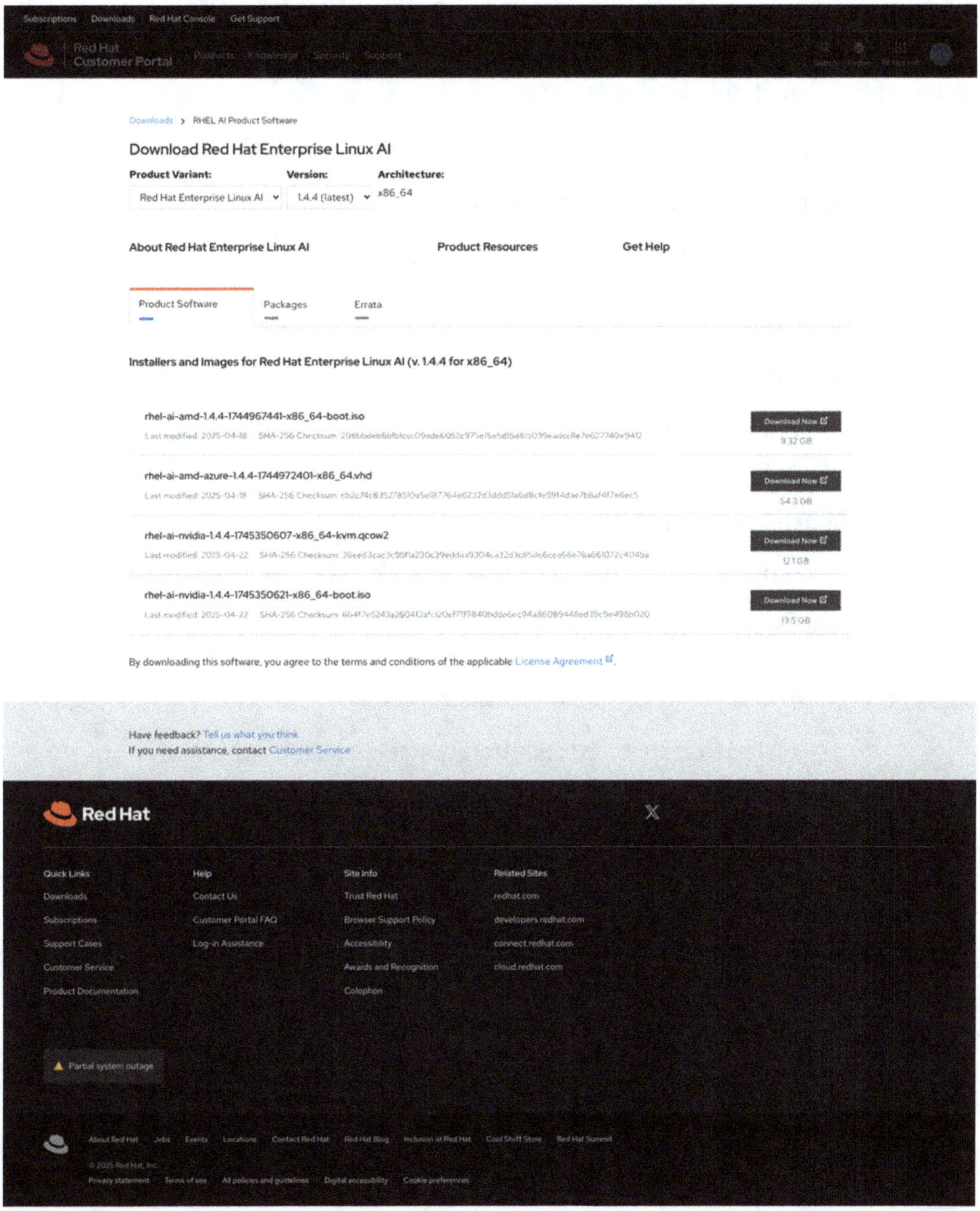

Figure 2-1. *RHEL AI download*

Figure 2-1 illustrates the download page on the Customer Portal, where various installation images are available depending on our infrastructure needs (e.g., bare metal, Azure, or NVIDIA-enabled systems).

Steps to download RHEL AI:

1. **Log in to the Red Hat Customer Portal**

    - Navigate to `https://access.redhat.com`.
    - Use our Red Hat account credentials.

2. **Access the RHEL AI Product Page**

    - Under **Downloads**, select **RHEL AI** from the list of available products.

3. **Choose Version and Architecture**

    - Set the version to the latest (e.g., `1.4.4`) and architecture to `x86_64`.

4. **Download the Appropriate Image**

    - We find several installation image options:
        - `rhel-ai-boot.iso`: For traditional installation workflows
        - `rhel-ai-azure.vhd`: For deploying on Microsoft Azure
        - `rhel-ai-nvidia-kvm.qcow2`: Optimized for GPU-accelerated environments
    - Click **Download Now** for the image that fits our platform.

License

RHEL AI is available via a Red Hat Developer subscription or a 60-day trial. The trial is intended for development and testing only. A full subscription is required for production use and enterprise support. Red Hat offers a trial period that allows users to explore the features of RHEL AI, including InstructLab and model deployment.

CHAPTER 2   SETTING UP RHEL AI

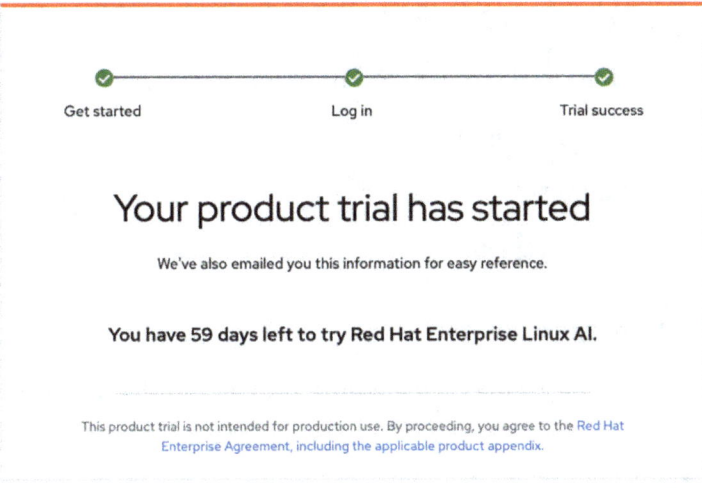

Figure 2-2. *RHEL AI trial*

Figure 2-2 shows the trial activation confirmation page. After registering, we have full access to the RHEL AI platform for a limited time (e.g., 60 days).

Trial Activation

After clicking to start our trial, we receive the following information:

1. **Trial Confirmation**
   - The system will confirm successful activation and show the number of days remaining.

2. **Guided Steps**

    - Red Hat provides a simple three-step onboarding:

        1. **Install the ISO image**

            - Follow the download links and deploy on

                - Bare metal
                - AWS
                - IBM Cloud

        2. **Configure our accounts**

            - Set up a Red Hat account and link to Red Hat Insights.

Repositories

The following repositories listed in our output correspond to various components of RHEL AI for the latest version 1.5 available at the moment of writing this book. The `subscription-manager` command enables software repositories required for RHEL AI to function on systems running RHEL 9. Here's a breakdown:

```
$ sudo subscription-manager repos --enable <repo_id>
```

This command enables a specific Red Hat content repository, allowing the system to install and update packages from it using `dnf`.

Here's what each repo is for and what it contains:

1. **rhelai-1.5-for-rhel-9-x86_64-rpms**: The central RPM repository for RHEL AI 1.5 on RHEL 9.

    Contains the core packages required for running RHEL AI, including the ilab CLI tool, foundational LLMs, and supporting libraries for model serving and orchestration.

2. **rhelai-1.5-gaudi-for-rhel-9-x86_64-rpms**: Runtime support for Intel Habana Gaudi accelerators.

    Contains the optimized libraries, drivers, and possibly tuned AI frameworks for running models on Gaudi hardware.

3. **rhelai-1.5-cuda-for-rhel-9-x86_64-rpms**: Runtime support for NVIDIA CUDA-based accelerators (e.g., H100, A100, etc.).

   It contains CUDA libraries, kernel modules, and ML frameworks (like PyTorch, TensorFlow) built with GPU acceleration support for LLM workloads.

4. **Debug RPM Repos (for all variants)**: Contain debug symbol RPMs.

   Example IDs: rhelai-1.5-for-rhel-9-x86_64-debug-rpms, rhelai-1.5-cuda-for-rhel-9-x86_64-debug-rpms, etc.

   Useful for debugging runtime issues in RHEL AI binaries or libraries.

5. **Source RPM Repos (for all variants)**: Contain source packages corresponding to the binary RPMs.

   Example IDs: rhelai-1.5-cuda-for-rhel-9-x86_64-source-rpms, rhelai-1.5-gaudi-for-rhel-9-x86_64-source-rpms, etc.

   Contents are used for rebuilding packages, code audits, or customization under open-source compliance.

RHEL AI supports heterogeneous compute environments. Enabling multiple repos ensures that the system can

- Install generic AI components (from `rhelai` repo)
- Deploy on NVIDIA, AMD, or Intel accelerator stacks depending on available hardware
- Maintain flexibility for different AI workloads or hybrid deployment environments

Each of these repos serves a distinct function depending on the target accelerator (CPU, CUDA GPU, Gaudi) and the type of RPM (binary, debug, source). For production environments, we typically enable only the relevant binary repository (and optionally the debug repository during troubleshooting). If our system only uses NVIDIA CUDA GPUs (e.g., H100, A100) or Intel Gaudi2 (but not both), for example, we may choose to enable only the relevant accelerator repository. Example:

```
$ sudo subscription-manager repos --enable rhelai-1.5-for-rhel-9-
x86_64-rpms
Repository 'rhelai-1.5-for-rhel-9-x86_64-rpms' is enabled for this system.
$ sudo subscription-manager repos --enable rhelai-1.5-cuda-for-rhel-9-
x86_64-rpms
Repository 'rhelai-1.5-cuda-for-rhel-9-x86_64-rpms' is enabled for
this system.
$ sudo subscription-manager repos --enable rhelai-1.5-gaudi-for-rhel-9-
x86_64-rpms
Repository 'rhelai-1.5-gaudi-for-rhel-9-x86_64-rpms' is enabled for
this system.
```

Make sure RHEL is able to fetch the updated repositories, including RHEL AI:

```
$ sudo dnf makecache
Red Hat Enterprise Linux AI (1.5) for RHEL 9 x86_64 - Gaudi (RPMs)
 13 kB/s | 3.0 kB     00:00
Red Hat Enterprise Linux AI (1.5) for RHEL 9 x86_64 (RPMs)
 302 kB/s | 65 kB     00:00
Red Hat Enterprise Linux AI (1.5) for RHEL 9 x86_64 - Cuda (RPMs)
 924 B/s | 512 B      00:00
Metadata cache created.
$
```

Bare Metal

RHEL AI can be deployed directly onto physical systems for maximum performance and hardware control. This section outlines two standard installation methods: the Graphical Installer, which provides an interactive interface for manual setup, and Kickstart Installation, which automates the process using a predefined configuration file—ideal for repeatable or large-scale deployments.

Please choose the method that best fits our environment and operational requirements.

GUI Installation

1. **Download the RHEL AI ISO image**.

2. **Create a bootable USB drive** using tools such as dd, Etcher, or Rufus, if needed.

3. **Boot our system** from the USB drive or CD-ROM.

4. Launch the **Graphical Installer** and follow the prompts:

    - Choose language.

    - Set up disk partitioning (ensure required space).

    - Create user accounts and set the root password.

5. Once installed, the system will reboot into RHEL AI.

Automated Kickstart Installation

A Kickstart file is designed for the following use cases:

- **Headless installs** (fully unattended)

- **Bootable container images** (OSTree + bootc)

- **GPU-ready environments** (nvidia image)

- **Security-conscious deployment** with SSH keys and locked root

- **Fast provisioning** for testing, cloud, or production pipelines

These are the steps that we need to follow to proceed with RHEL AI using Kickstart:

1. **Create a Kickstart file** (rhelai-bootc.ks) with our configuration preferences:

    - Container source

    - Disk partitioning

    - Networking

    - User setup

CHAPTER 2   SETTING UP RHEL AI

Here's a breakdown of an example Kickstart file used for automating a RHEL AI bootc-based installation. This file is well-structured for deploying RHEL AI in environments that use containers as their base image (e.g., bootable containers), particularly with GPU support (NVIDIA), and `cloud-init` disabled.

```
# use the embedded container image
ostreecontainer --url=/run/install/repo/container
--transport=oci
--no-signature-verification
```

- Purpose: Uses a container-based OSTree image as the system root.
- `--url=/run/install/repo/container`: The install image is embedded in the ISO and mounted at install time.
- `--transport=oci`: Uses the Open Container Initiative (OCI) transport format.
- `--no-signature-verification`: Skips cryptographic signature checks (standard in internal/testing scenarios).

```
# switch bootc to point to Red Hat container image for upgrades
%post
bootc switch --mutate-in-place --transport registry registry.redhat.io/rhelai1/bootc-nvidia-rhel9:1.1
touch /etc/cloud/cloud-init.disabled
%end
```

- `bootc switch`: Tells the system to switch to a specific container image (`bootc-nvidia-rhel9:1.1`) for updates and future mutations.
- `--mutate-in-place`: Updates the OSTree image in-place without a full re-deploy.
- `touch /etc/cloud/cloud-init.disabled`: Disables `cloud-init` (often used in cloud environments) for static or non-cloud systems.

```
## user customizations follow

# customize this for our target system network environment
network --bootproto=dhcp --device=link –activate
```

CHAPTER 2   SETTING UP RHEL AI

- Enables DHCP on the first network interface found (`--device=link`).
- `--activate`: Automatically brings the interface up at install time.

  ```
  # customize this for our target system desired disk partitioning
  clearpart --all --initlabel --disklabel=gpt
  reqpart --add-boot
  part / --grow --fstype xfs
  ```

- `clearpart --all`: Wipes all partitions on all disks (destructive).
- `--initlabel`: Reinitializes the partition table.
- `--disklabel=gpt`: Uses GPT instead of MBR—recommended for modern systems.
- `reqpart --add-boot`: Automatically adds EFI/boot partitions.
- `part / --grow --fstype xfs`: Sets up a root (/) partition that grows to fill remaining space, using XFS.

  ```
  # services can also be customized via Kickstart
  firewall --disabled
  services --enabled=sshd
  ```

- Disables the firewall (suitable for trusted internal networks or development).
- Enables SSH server (`sshd`) for remote access.

  ```
  # optionally add a user
  user --name=cloud-user --groups=wheel --plaintext --password <password>
  sshkey --username cloud-user "ssh-ed25519 AAAAC3Nza....."
  ```

- Adds a user `cloud-user` to the `wheel` group (grants sudo privileges).
- Sets the password in plaintext (replace `<password>` with actual string or hashed value).
- Injects an SSH public key for passwordless login.

  ```
  # if desired, inject an SSH key for root
  rootpw --iscrypted locked
  sshkey --username root "ssh-ed25519 AAAAC3Nza..."
  reboot
  ```

39

CHAPTER 2   SETTING UP RHEL AI

- Locks the root password login (recommended for security).
- Still allows SSH access to root via public key authentication.

2. **Embed the Kickstart file into the ISO** using `mkksiso`:

   ```
   $ mkksiso rhelai-bootc.ks rhel-ai.iso rhelai-bootc-ks.iso
   ```

3. **Boot from the custom ISO**: Installation starts automatically.

Warning   Kickstart installation may wipe existing data without prompt. Use carefully.

Cloud Providers

Each cloud platform requires converting the RHEL AI image into its native format.

Amazon Web Services

Deploying RHEL AI on Amazon Web Services (AWS) offers a flexible and scalable approach to running enterprise-ready AI workloads in the cloud. With AWS, organizations can choose from GPU-accelerated instance families, such as p3, p4, and g5, to optimize training and inference performance while taking advantage of the security, elasticity, and integration that AWS offers.

Many people asked me if it's possible to run RHEL AI on Free Tier. CPU-only deployment is supported (GPUs are not strictly required unless performing heavy training). The current limitations for AWS Free Tier provide a t2.micro or t3.micro instance with 1 vCPU and 1 GiB RAM. This is not enough to run RHEL AI—even in minimal configurations. RHEL AI requires at least 2 vCPUs and 8–16 GiB RAM to function reliably. The minimum hardware requirements for CPU-only execution include 2 vCPUs, 8–16 GiB RAM, and 50+ GiB disk (for model storage and runtime). These specifications can be met by at least AWS `t3.large` (2 vCPUs, 8 GiB RAM) instances, enabling the use of small Granite models to stay within CPU-only bounds.

RHEL AI on AWS can be provisioned in two primary ways:

- **AWS Marketplace purchase** for a streamlined, click-to-deploy experience as shown in Figure 2-3.

CHAPTER 2 SETTING UP RHEL AI

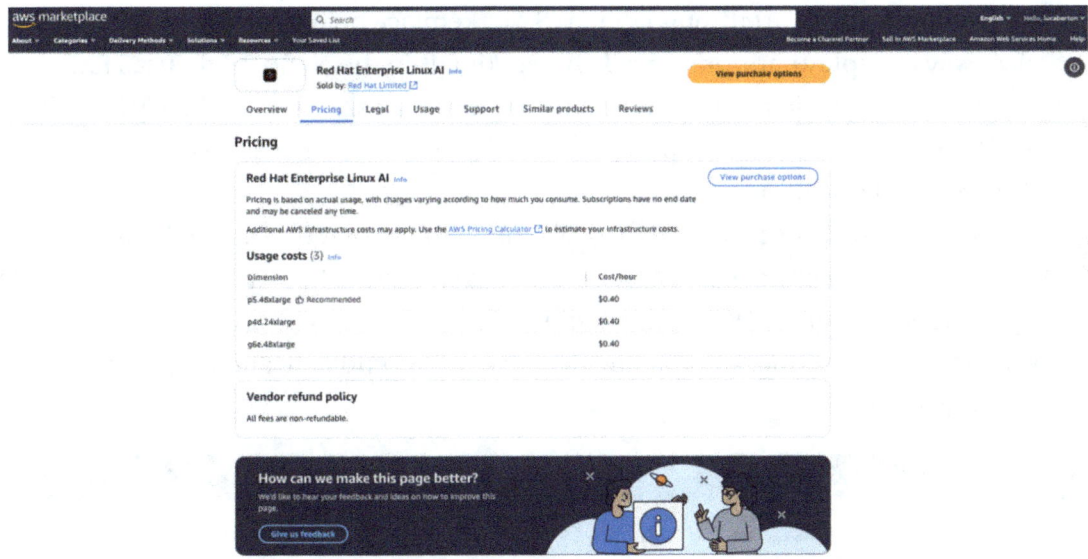

Figure 2-3. *RHEL AI in the AWS Marketplace*

- **Manual AMI conversion**, which enables advanced users to upload the bootable RHEL AI container image, import it into AWS as a snapshot, and register a custom AMI for EC2 deployment. Follow the instructions of the Red Hat documentation for "Installing RHEL AI on AWS[1]" that covers specifically how to download, convert, and deploy the RHEL AI images to AWS.

In both cases, the system defaults to the `cloud-user` account with passwordless `sudo` access, ensuring ease of management post-deployment. Before launching, ensure our AWS CLI is configured with valid credentials and IAM permissions for EC2, S3, and IAM operations and that the `.raw` RHEL AI image has been retrieved from the Red Hat Customer Portal.

---

[1] https://docs.redhat.com/en/documentation/red_hat_enterprise_linux_ai/latest/html/installing/installing_on_aws

Subscribing to RHEL AI through the AWS Marketplace offers the fastest and most seamless way to deploy enterprise-grade AI workloads in the cloud. With just a few clicks, we can review pricing, accept the subscription terms, and immediately launch our RHEL AI environment on supported AWS GPU instances such as p5.48xlarge, p4d.24xlarge, and g6e.48xlarge.

The subscription process creates an AWS Marketplace agreement and links the RHEL AI software directly to our AWS account, enabling us to launch, manage, and scale deployments with familiar AWS tools, as shown in Figure 2-4. Billing is handled through our AWS account on a usage-based model, with no fixed end date and the flexibility to cancel at any time.

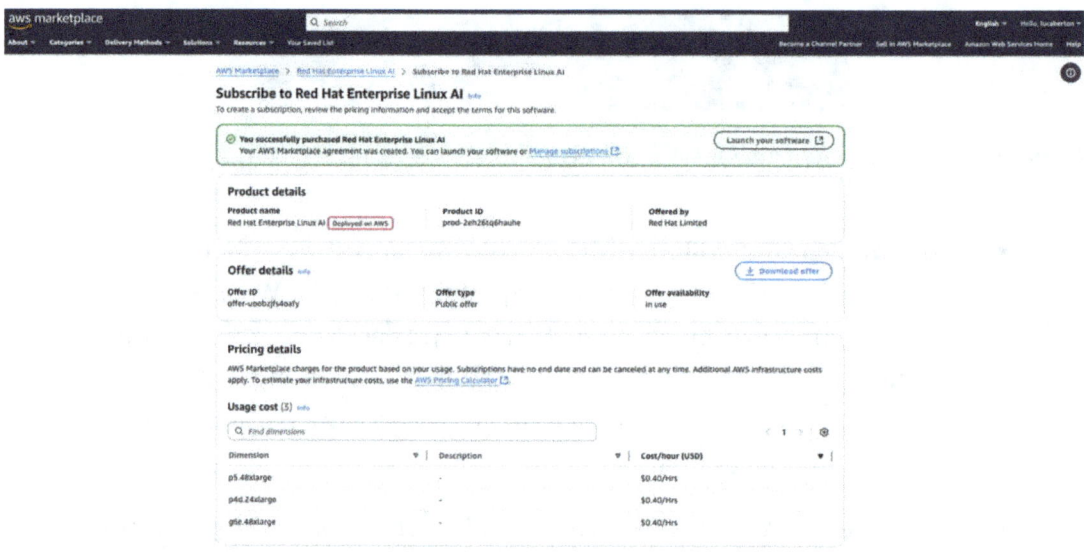

Figure 2-4. *AWS RHEL AI subscription*

By choosing the Marketplace option, organizations can accelerate time-to-value, avoid manual AMI conversions, and ensure their AI platform is supported by Red Hat support and lifecycle policies. Once subscribed, we can immediately launch RHEL AI, manage updates, and integrate with AWS-native services to power advanced machine learning and generative AI workloads.

Figure 2-5 shows the AWS Marketplace launch page for RHEL AI, where we can select the version (e.g., RHEL AI 1.5—latest, stable) and launch it on Amazon EC2. It provides launch methods, vendor instructions, and region-specific AMI IDs to deploy

RHEL AI instances with full control. Consulting Red Hat KCS "Installing RHEL AI with AWS Marketplace[2]" provides us with practical advice on the current installation process and supported instance types.

Table 2-1 lists the possible GPU-accelerated virtual machine sizes available and their prices at the time of writing this book.

Table 2-1. AWS virtual machine sizes

Name	GPUs	vCPU	Memory	Storage	Cost (USD/hr)
`p4d.24xlarge`	8×NVIDIA A100 40GB	96	1.1 TiB	8×NVMe SSD	~$32.77
`p5.48xlarge`	8×NVIDIA H100 80GB	192	1.9 TiB	EBS-Only	~$98.32 (on-demand)
`p3.16xlarge`	8×NVIDIA V100 16GB	64	488 GiB	1.8 TB NVMe SSD	~$24.48
`g5.12xlarge`	4×NVIDIA A10G	48	192 GiB	EBS-Only	~$6.18
`g4dn.12xlarge`	4×NVIDIA T4	48	192 GiB	900 GB NVMe SSD	~$4.35
`g4dn.xlarge`	1×NVIDIA T4	4	16 GiB	125 GB NVMe SSD	~$0.76
`inf2.48xlarge` *(Inferentia2)*	12×AWS Inferentia2	192	768 GiB	EBS-Only	~$34.00 (optimized for inference)

- Prices are **on-demand** in the **us-east-1** region and may vary.

- Some instances require **placement groups** or **quota approvals**.

- **T4-based instances (G4dn)** are cost-efficient for development/testing.

- **H100/A100 instances (P5/P4)** are suitable for training large models with InstructLab and SDG.

- AWS Inferentia[3] (Inf2) offers high-throughput, low-latency inference at scale but is **not compatible** with CUDA-dependent workflows.

---

[2] https://access.redhat.com/articles/7099652
[3] https://aws.amazon.com/ai/machine-learning/inferentia/

CHAPTER 2 SETTING UP RHEL AI

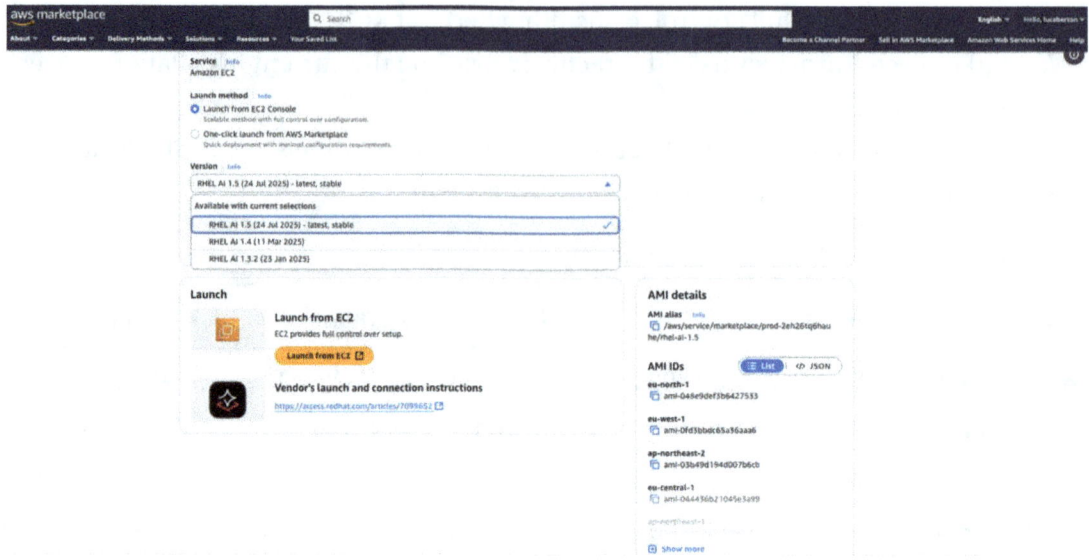

Figure 2-5. *AWS Launch RHEL AI*

Figure 2-6 shows the EC2 launch instance page using the RHEL AI 1.5 AMI from AWS Marketplace, published by Red Hat with AMI ID `ami-079b9963514fc3b8e` in the us-east-1 N. Virginia region. It highlights instance details such as username (`ec2-user`) and recommended type (p5.48xlarge with 192 vCPUs and 2048 GiB memory) and provides a summary panel to configure firewall, storage, and launch the instance.

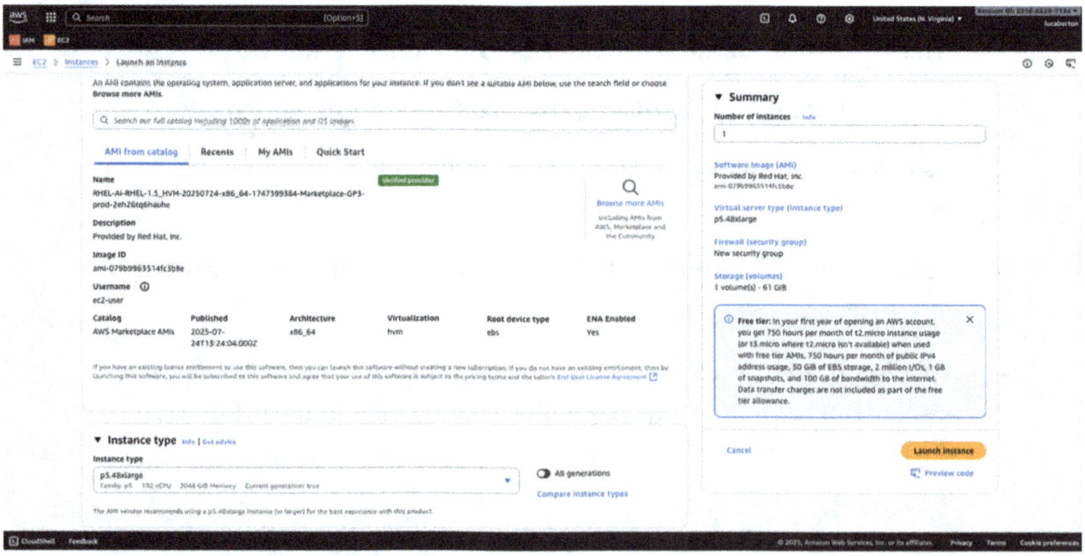

Figure 2-6. *Launch AWS Instance*

Figure 2-7 shows a failed EC2 launch attempt for a RHEL AI instance due to insufficient capacity in the selected region. As this type of instance is in high demand, we may need to either retry the launch, choose a different instance type, or switch to another AWS region with available GPU capacity.

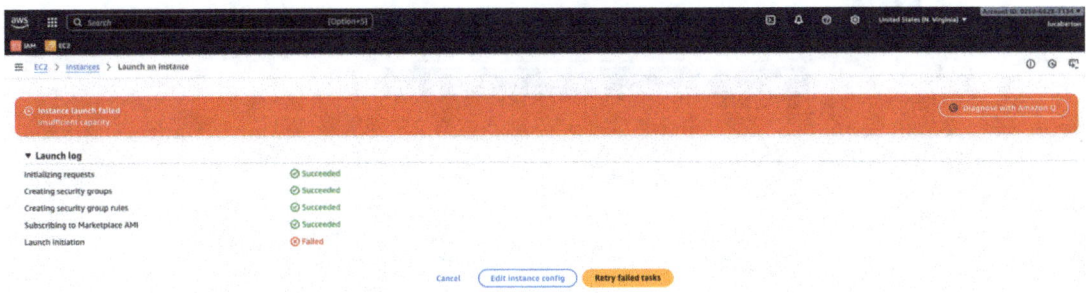

Figure 2-7. *Failed launch*

As a result of this step-by-step process, we now possess a fully operational instance in our region, prepared to execute our AI workload. By leveraging AWS, enterprises can accelerate their AI adoption with RHEL AI while maintaining the same consistency, security, and support lifecycle they rely on across Red Hat platforms.

Microsoft Azure

Deploying RHEL AI on Microsoft Azure allows organizations to scale AI workloads on the Microsoft enterprise infrastructure, utilizing powerful VM sizes and integrated cloud services. There are two main ways to install and deploy RHEL AI on Azure: purchase RHEL AI from the Azure Marketplace, as shown in Figure 2-8, or download the RHEL AI VHD image from the Red Hat Portal and convert it into an Azure-compatible image for deployment.

CPU-only installations are supported on Azure. According to the RHEL AI documentation, a GPU is not required for general usage, SDG, or serving small models, but it is recommended. The installation process uses a bootable container image compatible with any RHEL 9-based host, including Azure VMs. Azure Free Tier is limited to providing B1S or B1LS instances with 1 vCPU and 1 GiB RAM (B1S) or 512 MiB RAM (B1LS). These are insufficient for RHEL AI, which requires a minimum of 2 vCPUs, 8–16 GiB RAM, and ~50 GiB disk. The lowest-cost option for CPU-only workloads uses the following Azure VM types for RHEL AI: D2as_v5 2 with 2 vCPUs and 8 GiB RAM, which is reliable and affordable, or B2ms with 2 vCPUs and 8 GiB RAM, suitable for labs.

CHAPTER 2   SETTING UP RHEL AI

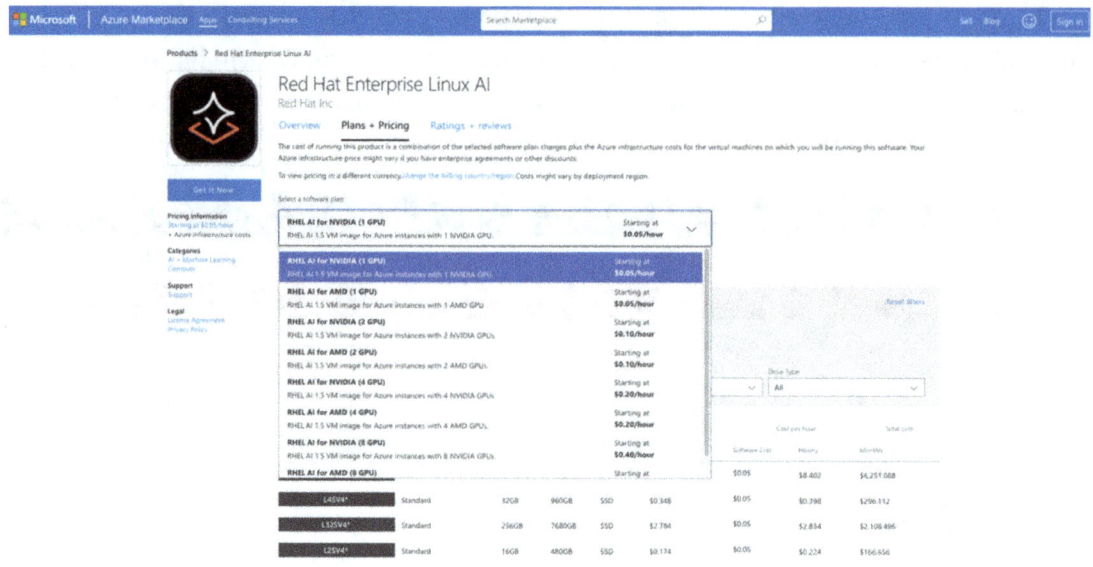

Figure 2-8. *Azure Marketplace*

In this section, we focus on the guided approach. The process of converting the RHEL AI VHD into an Azure image and launching an instance via the Azure CLI is described in the Red Hat documentation "Installing RHEL AI on Azure.[4]" This process involves configuring our Azure environment, uploading the VHD file to a storage container, creating an Azure-managed image, and deploying a VM with GPU acceleration.

For example, administrators can configure the Azure CLI and AzCopy tools, create a resource group and storage account, upload the `.vhd` image, and register it as an Azure image. From there, a VM can be launched using GPU-enabled sizes such as `ND96isr_H100_v5` for flagship NVIDIA H100 performance or cost-efficient alternatives like `NCasT4_v3` with Tesla T4 GPUs.

Table 2-2 lists the available GPU-accelerated VM sizes for RHEL AI on Azure at the time of writing this book. Based on our subscription details, we may experience a "Size not available" notification attributable to the combination of instance size, region, and market availability. It is advisable to contact the Azure support center pertinent to our circumstances. The complete message displayed on the screen is as follows:

---

[4] https://docs.redhat.com/en/documentation/red_hat_enterprise_linux_ai/latest/html/installing/installing_azure

CHAPTER 2   SETTING UP RHEL AI

This size is currently unavailable in eastus for this subscription: NotAvailableForSubscription.

> **Tip** Use ND96isr_H100_v5 for the best flagship GPU experience.

Table 2-2. *Azure VM sizes*

Name	GPUs	vCPU	Memory	Storage	Cost (USD/hr)
Standard_ND96isr_H100_v5	12 NVIDIA H100	96	1900 GiB	Local NVMe + Premium SSD supported	>$30 (varies)
Standard_ND40rs_v2	8 NVIDIA Tesla V100	40	672 GiB	Local NVMe + Premium SSD supported	$10–$15
Standard_NC24s_v3	4 NVIDIA Tesla V100	24	448 GiB	Premium SSD supported	$8–$12
Standard_NCasT4_v3	4 NVIDIA Tesla T4	Up to 64	Up to 440 GiB	Premium SSD supported	$2–$6
Standard_NV12s_v3	1 NVIDIA Tesla M60	12	112 GiB	Premium SSD supported	$1.5–$3

By leveraging Azure's GPU-enabled VM families, organizations can tune performance for training, fine-tuning, and inference tasks with RHEL AI. **ND-series (H100/V100)** VMs are best suited for large-scale training and synthetic data generation, while **NC- and NV-series** VMs provide cost-effective options for development and testing.

Figure 2-9 shows an example Azure deployment using a custom RHEL AI image, specifying GPU size, admin user, and SSH key for secure access. Once launched, the VM provides the same **enterprise-ready AI platform** as on-premises RHEL AI, with seamless integration into Azure-native monitoring, networking, and identity management.

CHAPTER 2   SETTING UP RHEL AI

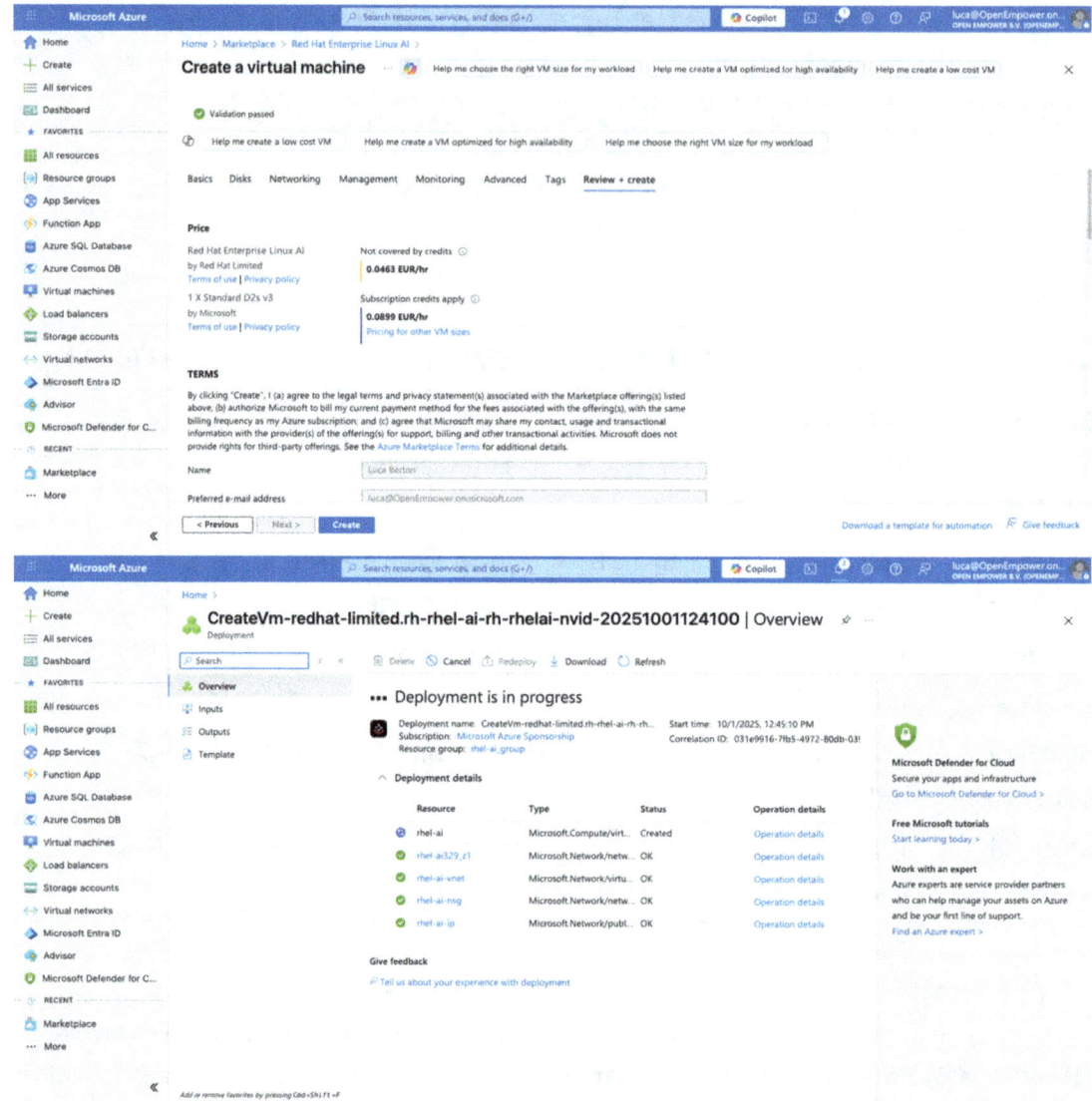

Figure 2-9. *Launch RHEL AI instance on Azure*

Figure 2-10 shows the Azure deployment in progress view, where the RHEL AI virtual machine and its associated networking resources (VNet, NIC, NSG, and public IP) are being created successfully.

CHAPTER 2   SETTING UP RHEL AI

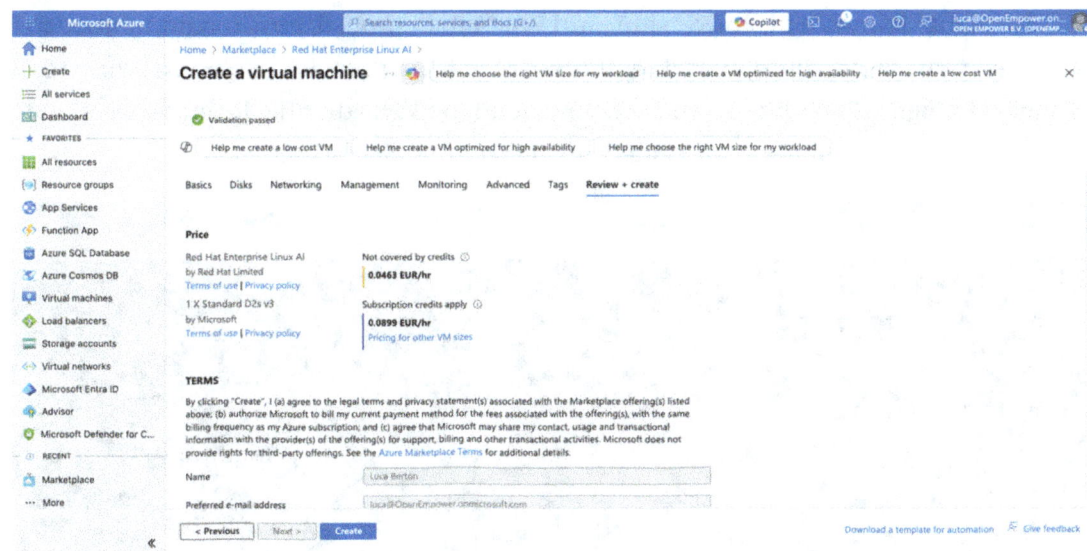

Figure 2-10. RHEL AI virtual machine on Azure

Figure 2-11 shows the Azure portal overview page for a running RHEL AI virtual machine in the *East US (Zone 1)* region, including details such as resource group, VM size, public IP, and networking configuration.

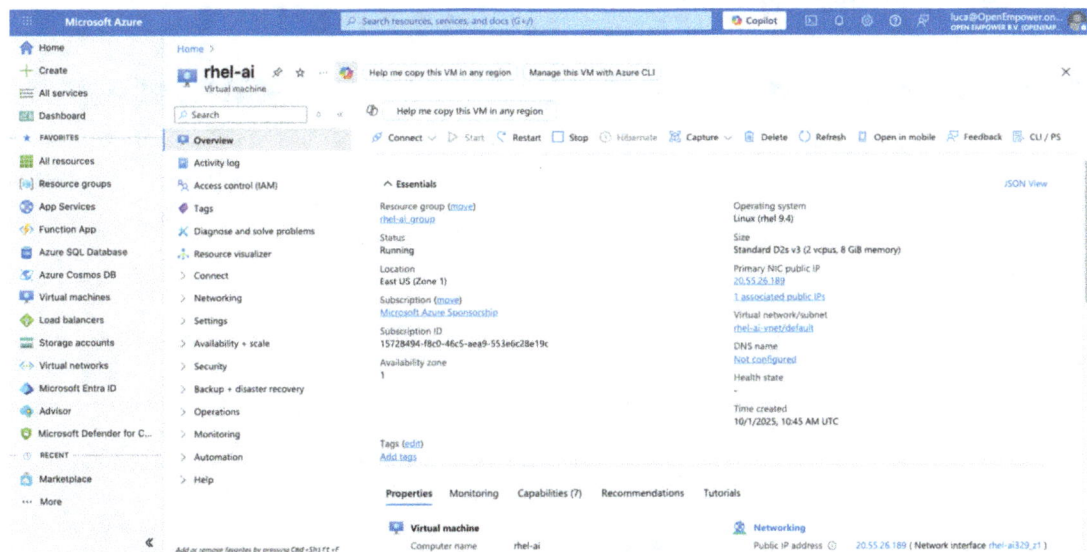

Figure 2-11. RHEL AI virtual machine on Azure

49

CHAPTER 2   SETTING UP RHEL AI

The manual download, conversion, and VM launch procedure is recommended to advanced users as it's complex and requires a lot of CLI interaction between Azure tools, as shown in Figure 2-12. Ensure that we download the VHD disk file format if we plan to launch the virtual machine immediately, instead of the ISO format.

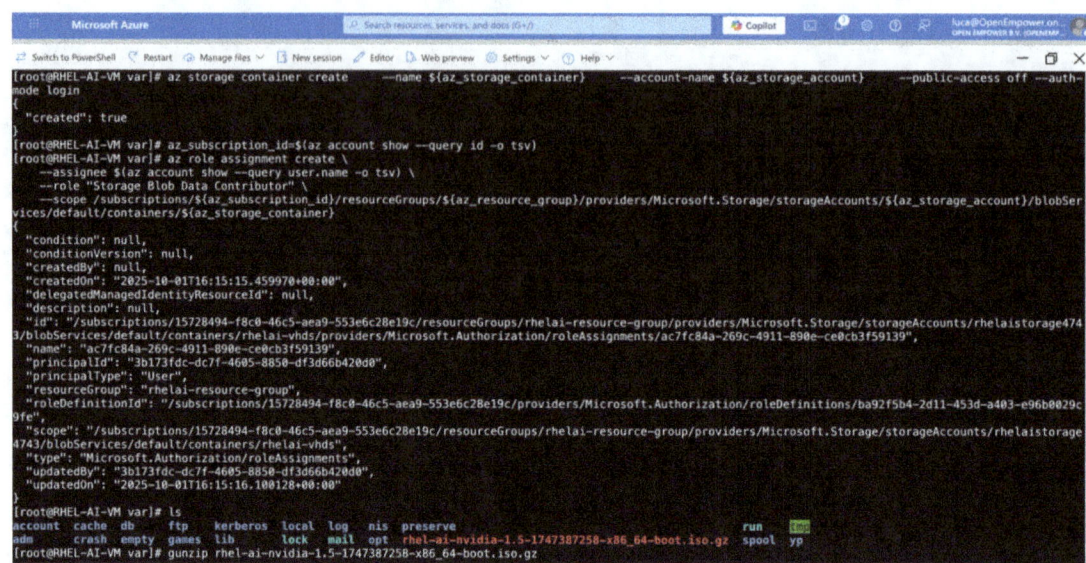

Figure 2-12. *Manual conversion process*

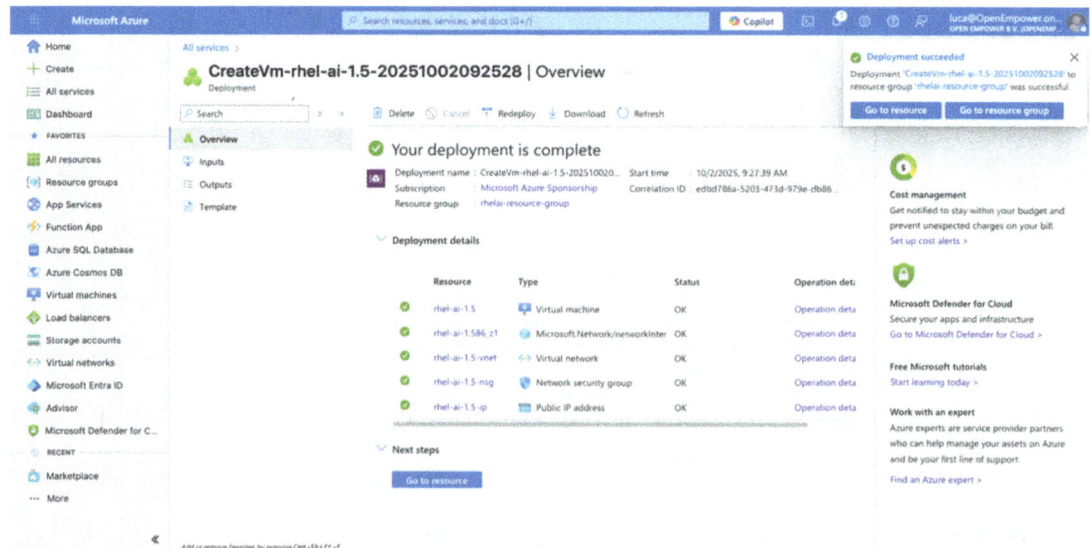

Figure 2-13. *RHEL AI deployment in Azure Azure*

As a result of all these steps, organizations gain the flexibility to deploy RHEL AI on their infrastructure, ensuring consistency, security, and Red Hat support across various cloud environments, including Azure cloud computing. This facilitates the implementation of hybrid or multicloud environments for our organization.

Google Cloud Platform

RHEL AI can be deployed on Google Cloud Platform (GCP) to take advantage of high-performance compute instances, GPU acceleration, and flexible scalability across regions. Like AWS and Azure, RHEL AI is available via the Google Cloud Marketplace (Figure 2-14) or as a custom image created by importing the Red Hat–provided `.tar.gz` image into Google Compute Engine (GCE). More details about converting the RHEL AI image into a GCP image can be found on the Red Hat Documentation—section "Installing RHEL AI on Google Cloud Platform (GCP).⁵"

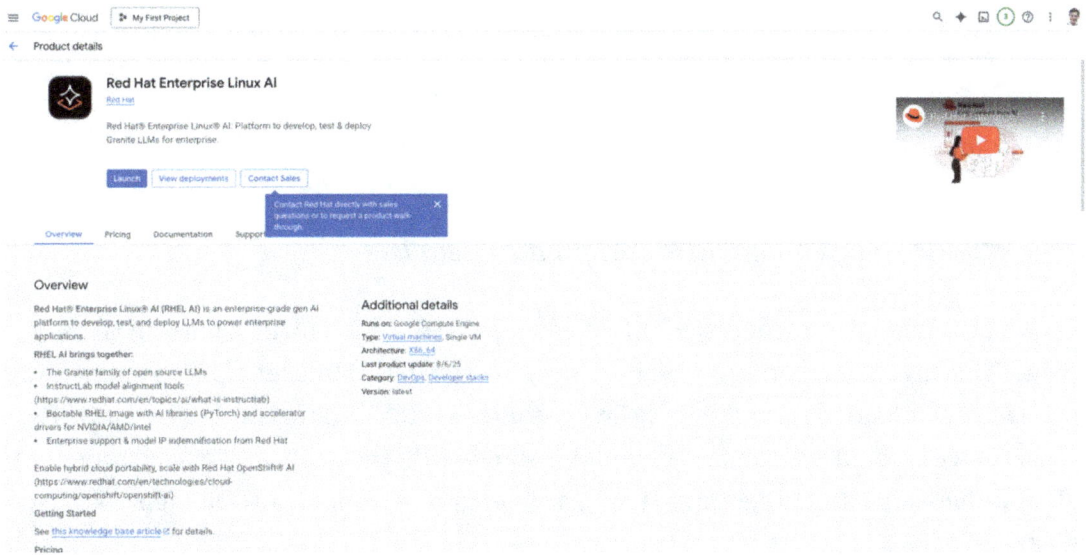

Figure 2-14. *RHEL AI in Google Cloud Marketplace*

The GCP Marketplace option provides a streamlined subscription process, allowing us to review pricing, accept the terms, and launch RHEL AI on GPU-optimized instances. Costs include both the license fee for RHEL AI and the underlying infrastructure fee, as

---

⁵ https://docs.redhat.com/en/documentation/red_hat_enterprise_linux_ai/latest/html/installing/installing_gcp

CHAPTER 2 SETTING UP RHEL AI

shown in Figure 2-12, which provides an example of pricing for a virtual machine with two NVIDIA A100 GPUs at the time of writing this book. Launching the virtual machine requires that the Compute Engine API and Infrastructure Manager API be enabled on the GCP profile. A typical deployment for "a2-highgpu-2g" includes the 2× NVIDIA A100 40GB GPUs, consisting of a virtual machine profile with 24 vCPUs, 170 GB of RAM, and 120 GiB of Balanced Persistent Disk, as shown in Figure 2-15.

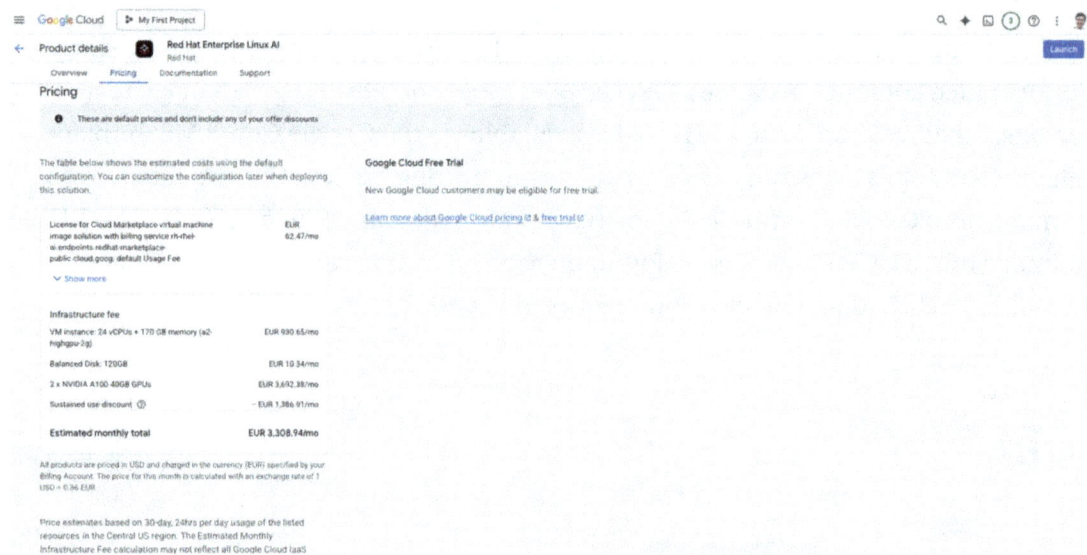

Figure 2-15. *Google Cloud RHEL AI product details*

For advanced deployments, RHEL AI can also be installed using a custom GCP image. This involves creating a Google Cloud Storage (GCS) bucket, uploading the .tar. gz image downloaded from the Red Hat Customer Portal, and registering it as a GCP image. Once created, we can launch a VM instance with the gcloud CLI, selecting from GPU families such as a3-highgpu (H100), a2-highgpu (A100), or cost-efficient T4-based instances.

Beyond manual and Marketplace-based launches, **Terraform and the gcloud CLI** can also be used to automate deployments of RHEL AI instances on GCP, integrating easily into DevOps workflows and multicloud automation pipelines.

CHAPTER 2 SETTING UP RHEL AI

Caution Quota considerations:

When deploying GPU-enabled VMs, GCP enforces both **regional and global quotas,** as shown in Figure 2-16. Common issues include

CPU Quota Exceeded: For example, *"You've gone over A2_CPUS CPU quota by 24 CPUs in us-central1."*

GPU Regional Quota Exceeded: For example, *"You've gone over GPU quota by 2 GPUs of type NVIDIA A100 40GB in region us-central1."*

GPU Global Quota Exceeded: For example, *"You've gone over GPU global quota by 2 GPUs."*

If we encounter these errors, we must either

1. Select a different region or lower CPU/GPU machine type
2. Request a quota increase via the GCP Quotas page in the Google Cloud Console

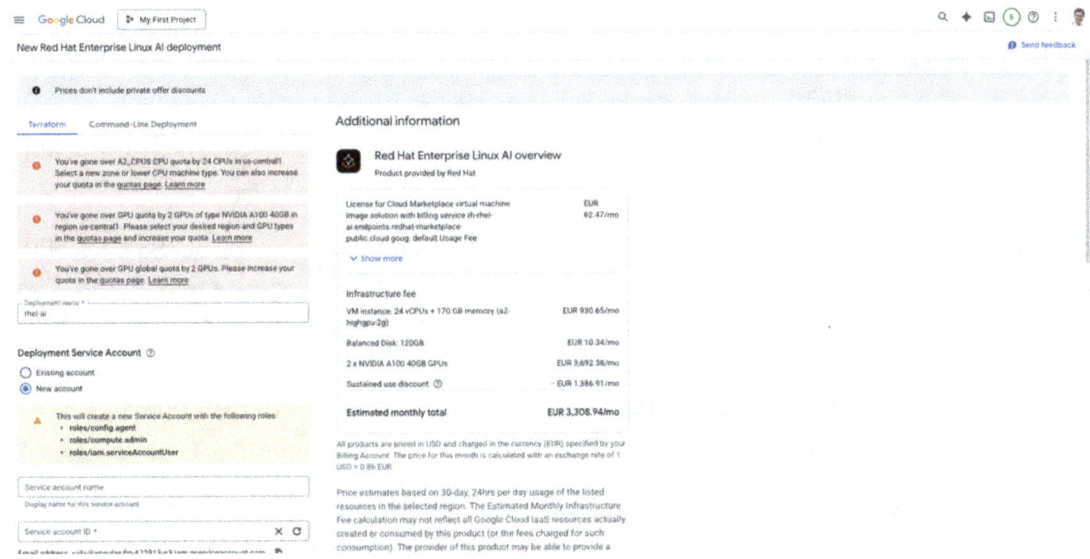

Figure 2-16. Google Cloud Launch RHEL AI

> **Tip** Use the `a3-highgpu` instance type for NVIDIA H100 or A100 GPU support.

Table 2-3 shows us the possible alternative GCP VM sizes available at the time of writing this book.

Table 2-3. *GCP VM sizes*

Name	GPUs	vCPU	Memory	Storage	Cost (USD/hr)
`a2-highgpu-2g`	2×NVIDIA A100 40GB	24	170 GiB	Local SSD	~$5–~$7
`a3-highgpu-8g`	8×NVIDIA H100 80GB	96	768 GiB	Local SSD	~$32–$35
`a2-highgpu-8g`	8×NVIDIA A100 40GB	96	680 GiB	Local SSD	~$29–$32
`a2-megagpu-16g`	16×NVIDIA A100 40GB	96	1.3 TiB	Local SSD	~$40–$50+
`a2-highgpu-4g`	4×NVIDIA A100 40GB	48	340 GiB	Local SSD	~$15–$17
`a2-highgpu-1g`	1×NVIDIA A100 40GB	12	85 GiB	Local SSD	~$4.75–$5.50
`n1-standard-8 + T4`	1×NVIDIA T4	8	30 GiB	Premium SSD	~$0.80–$1.00 + GPU fee
`n1-standard-16 + V100`	1×NVIDIA V100	16	60 GiB	Premium SSD	~$2.50–$3.50 + GPU fee

- Pricing varies by region, commitment (on-demand vs. committed), and sustained use.

- Use the Google Cloud Pricing Calculator for current costs in our region.

- Local SSDs offer high IOPS but are ephemeral (deleted when the VM stops).

- For general-purpose, training workloads with lower cost, T4-based machines may be suitable.

By deploying RHEL AI on GCP, enterprises gain the ability to run training, fine-tuning, and inference workloads on world-class NVIDIA GPU instances while maintaining consistency, lifecycle support, and integration with Red Hat OpenShift AI for hybrid deployments.

IBM Cloud

RHEL AI can be deployed on IBM Cloud to support inference serving capabilities in enterprise environments. At the moment of writing this book, the current support is limited to inference workloads; IBM Cloud provides an effective platform for container-based, GPU-enabled AI model hosting.

To deploy RHEL AI into the IBM Cloud, we first convert the downloaded image into an IBM Cloud-compatible format. This involves configuring IBM Cloud CLI, provisioning a Cloud Object Storage (COS) bucket, and registering the uploaded QCOW2 image as a custom machine image. We assume IBM Cloud CLI is installed, we have an active IBM Cloud account with appropriate IAM access, and a RHEL AI `.qcow2` image is available from the Red Hat Customer Portal.

Procedure for converting the RHEL AI Image into an IBM Cloud Image:

1. **Login and Target Configuration**

    ```
    ibmcloud login
    ibmcloud target -g Default
    ibmcloud target -r us-east
    ```

2. **Install Required Plug-ins**

    ```
    ibmcloud plugin install cloud-object-storage
    infrastructure-service
    ```

3. **Select a COS Deployment Plan**

    ```
    cos_deploy_plan=premium-global-deployment
    ```

4. **Create a COS Service Instance**

    ```
    cos_si_name=rhelai-storage
    ibmcloud resource service-instance-create ${cos_si_name}
    cloud-object-storage standard global -d ${cos_deploy_plan}
    ```

CHAPTER 2 SETTING UP RHEL AI

5. **Configure the COS CRN and Bucket**

    ```
    cos_crn=$(ibmcloud resource service-instance ${cos_si_name}
    --output json | jq -r '.[] | select(.crn | contains("cloud-object-
    storage")) | .crn')
    ibmcloud cos config crn --crn ${cos_crn} --force
    bucket_name=rhelai-bucket
    ibmcloud cos bucket-create --bucket ${bucket_name}
    ```

6. **Set Authorization for Infrastructure Service**

    ```
    cos_si_guid=$(ibmcloud resource service-instance ${cos_
    si_name} --output json | jq -r '.[] | select(.crn |
    contains("cloud-object-storage")) | .guid')
    ibmcloud iam authorization-policy-create is cloud-object-
    storage Reader --source-resource-type image --target-service-
    instance-id ${cos_si_guid}
    ```

7. **Upload and Register the QCOW2 Image**

    ```
    curl -Lo disk.qcow2 "<link-to-qcow2-image>"
    image_name=rhel-ai-20240703v0
    ibmcloud cos upload --bucket ${bucket_name} --key ${image_
    name}.qcow2 --file disk.qcow2 --region us-east
    ibmcloud is image-create ${image_name} --file cos://us-
    east/${bucket_name}/${image_name}.qcow2 --os-name red-ai-9-
    amd64-nvidia-byol
    ```

8. **Track and Confirm Image Creation**

    ```
    image_id=$(ibmcloud is images --visibility private --output
    json | jq -r '.[] | select(.name=="'$image_name'") | .id')
    while ibmcloud is image --output json ${image_id} | jq -r
    .status | grep -xq pending; do sleep 1; done
    ibmcloud is image ${image_id}
    ```

CHAPTER 2   SETTING UP RHEL AI

We are ready to launch our custom RHEL AI instance from either the IBM Cloud web console or the CLI. The following procedure uses the CLI for automated deployment. We assume that we created a custom RHEL AI image using the previous procedure, and we have our IBM Cloud VPC, subnet, SSH key, and public IP ready to go.

Procedure for deploying our instance on IBM Cloud using the CLI:

1. **Login and Install Infrastructure Plug-in**

   ```
   ibmcloud login -c <ACCOUNT_ID> -r us-east -g Default
   ibmcloud plugin install infrastructure-service
   ```

2. **Create SSH Key**

   ```
   ssh-keygen -f ibmcloud -t ed25519
   ibmcloud is key-create my-ssh-key @ibmcloud.pub --key-type ed25519
   ```

3. **Reserve Floating IP**

   ```
   ibmcloud is floating-ip-reserve my-public-ip --zone us-east-1
   ```

4. **List and Select Instance Profile**

   ```
   ibmcloud is instance-profiles
   ```

5. **Set Environment Variables**

   ```
   name=rhelai-instance
   vpc=vpc-in-us-east
   zone=us-east-1
   subnet=subnet-in-us-east-1
   instance_profile=gx3-64x320x4l4
   image=rhel-ai-20240703v0
   sshkey=my-ssh-key
   floating_ip=my-public-ip
   disk_size=250
   ```

CHAPTER 2 SETTING UP RHEL AI

6. **Launch the Instance**

```
ibmcloud is instance-create \
    $name \
    $vpc \
    $zone \
    $instance_profile \
    $subnet \
    --image $image \
    --keys $sshkey \
    --boot-volume '{"name": "'${name}'-boot", "volume": {"name": "'${name}'-boot", "capacity": '${disk_size}', "profile": {"name": "general-purpose"}}}' \
    --allow-ip-spoofing false
```

7. **Attach Floating IP**

```
ibmcloud is floating-ip-update $floating_ip --nic primary --in $name
```

The default user account in the RHEL AI image is

- **Username**: cloud-user
- **Privileges**: Full sudo access without a password

CHAPTER 2　SETTING UP RHEL AI

Table 2-4. *IBM Cloud suggested instance size for RHEL AI*

Instance Profile	GPUs	vCPU/Cores	Memory (GiB)	Storage (GB)	Bandwidth (Gbps)	Estimated Cost (USD/hr)
gx3-16x80x1l4	1×NVIDIA L4	16/8	80	32	32	~$2.00–$2.50
gx3-32x160x2l4	2×NVIDIA L4	32/16	160	64	32	~$4.00–$5.00
gx3-64x320x4l4	4×NVIDIA L4	64/32	320	128	32	~$7.50–$9.00
gx3-24x120x1l40s	1×NVIDIA L40S	24/12	120	50	50	~$5.00–$6.50
gx3-48x240x2l40s	2×NVIDIA L40S	48/24	240	100	50	~$10.00–$13.00
gx3d-160x1792x8h100	8×NVIDIA H100 80GB	160/80	1792	8×7680 (Local NVMe)	200	~$65.00–$80.00
gx3d-160x1792x8h200	8×NVIDIA H200 141GB	160/80	1792	8×7680 (Local NVMe)	200	~$80.00–$95.00
gx3d-160x1792x8gaudi3	8×Gaudi-3 AI Accelerators	160/80	1792	8×3200 (Local NVMe)	200	~$40.00–$50.00 (estimate)

- All profiles are based on **IBM Cloud VPC Gen 3** with high-performance local storage.

- Bandwidth caps are approximate and can depend on region and VM-to-network design.

- Cost values are **estimates** and may vary based on region, subscription plans, and usage models (on-demand vs. reserved).

- **H100/H200 profiles** are optimal for model training and high-throughput inference.

- **Gaudi-3** is optimized for cost-efficient large-scale transformer inference/training, especially with native support for BF16/FP8 workloads.

CHAPTER 2   SETTING UP RHEL AI

Verifying RHEL AI

Once RHEL AI is installed and the system has booted:

1. **Log in** using our credentials.

2. **Verify installation**: To ensure our setup is working correctly, use the ilab command-line interface:

   ```
   $ ilab
   ```

3. Initialize the InstructLab configuration:

   ```
   $ ilab config init
   ```

This sets up the AI environment and enables us to generate data, train models, and build skills. We learn how to use it in the following chapters.

This tool allows users to

- Configure environments (`ilab config`)
- Generate synthetic data (`ilab data generate`)
- Train and serve models (`ilab model train`, `ilab model serve`)
- Interact with taxonomies and system-level settings

In the subsequent chapters, we employ all these features.

GPU Support

GPU acceleration in RHEL AI empowers organizations to train and deploy cutting-edge AI models at an enterprise scale—whether on bare metal in their data centers or on robust cloud infrastructure. By closely integrating with NVIDIA GPUs and utilizing modern AI tools, Red Hat facilitates the development of AI applications that are fast, scalable, and ready for production.

Bare Metal

When installing on physical servers:

- Use the appropriate **bootc container image** for our GPU (e.g., `bootc-nvidia-rhel9:1.4`).

- Ensure NVIDIA drivers are installed and configured.
- Confirm GPU visibility with `nvidia-smi`. This is an example of the expected output:

```
+-----------------------------------------------------------------------+
| NVIDIA-SMI 535.86.10    Driver Version: 535.86.10    CUDA Version: 12.2 |
|-------------------------------+----------------------+------------------+
| GPU  Name                     Persistence-M| Bus-Id        Disp.A | Volatile
|                                                                    Uncorr. ECC |
| Fan  Temp  Perf               Pwr:Usage/Cap|                Memory-Usage |
|                                                              GPU-Util Compute M.|
|===============================+======================+==================|
|   0  NVIDIA A100-PCIE...  On  | 00000000:00:1E.0 Off |                0 |
| 30%  45C    P0    39W / 250W  |     0MiB / 40960MiB  |     0%   Default |
+-------------------------------+----------------------+------------------+
```

Cloud Platforms

Each major cloud provider supports GPU-backed VMs compatible with RHEL AI:

- **AWS**: p3, p4, g5 instance families
- **Azure**: ND96isr_H100_v5 and similar
- **GCP**: a3-highgpu with H100 or A100
- **IBM Cloud**: GPU-enabled VSI profiles

Each deployment guide in RHEL AI documentation walks through selecting and attaching GPU-accelerated instances.

Verifying GPU Acceleration

After deployment, use standard CLI tools to verify GPU presence:

```
$ nvidia-smi
```

And confirm that RHEL AI tools are utilizing GPU resources during training or inference via

```
$ ilab model train --gpu
$ ilab model serve --accelerator=gpu
```

When the system struggles to access the GPU, we receive the following message on the screen:

```
$ ilab
Error: setting up CDI devices: unresolvable CDI devices nvidia.com/gpu=all
```

The solution usually requires a thorough analysis of the machine and the GPU connection. In an NVIDIA-based installation, passing through the systemd unit files:

```
[systemd]
Failed Units: 2
  nvidia-persistenced.service
  nvidia-toolkit-firstboot.service
```

I suggest starting the analysis from the current status of the NVIDIA Persistence Daemon, which is responsible for keeping the NVIDIA driver loaded even when no processes are using the GPU (helps reduce startup latency and driver reloads). This is a common error when the GPU is not detected by the system or is not present at all:

```
$ nvidia-smi
NVIDIA-SMI has failed because it couldn't communicate with the NVIDIA
driver. Make sure that the latest NVIDIA driver is installed and running.
```

Additional Storage

By default, RHEL AI stores its data and configuration in the $HOME directory. This section explains how to relocate that storage to a separate disk-mounted path using the ILAB_HOME environment variable. Let's suppose we have an additional storage disk attached and mounted to the /mnt directory and we have administrative privileges or appropriate permissions on the instance.

Follow these steps to configure RHEL AI to use the additional storage:

1. **Set the ILAB_HOME Environment Variable**

    To permanently set the new path for InstructLab data, add the environment variable to our shell profile:

    ```
    echo 'export ILAB_HOME=/mnt' >> $HOME/.bash_profile
    ```

CHAPTER 2   SETTING UP RHEL AI

2. **Apply the New Configuration**

   Reload our shell profile to make the change effective immediately:

   source $HOME/.bash_profile

3. **Create a Container Configuration Directory**

   Container tools (like Podman or Buildah) require configuration under the .config/containers path. Create this directory on our new storage path:

   mkdir -p /mnt/.config/containers

4. **Copy the Default Storage Configuration**

   Copy the default container storage configuration to the new directory:

   cp /etc/skel/.config/containers/storage.conf /mnt/.config/containers/

Tip   The storage.conf file controls where images and container layers are stored. Relocating it helps manage disk utilization on high-throughput AI environments.

We verify the configuration by checking that RHEL AI tools reference the new ILAB_HOME path:

echo $ILAB_HOME
ls $ILAB_HOME/.config/containers

The expected output should show /mnt as the home path and storage.conf present within. Configuring an external storage path for our RHEL AI workflows enables better disk management and flexibility. Whether we are managing large AI datasets or isolating container storage, this setup helps maintain performance and organization as our projects grow.

CHAPTER 2   SETTING UP RHEL AI

Governance Framework

Security and compliance are at the heart of any enterprise-grade AI platform, and RHEL AI is designed with these principles at its core. As AI workloads become increasingly complex and are deployed in more production environments, organizations must ensure that their models and infrastructure meet stringent regulatory and operational standards. RHEL AI addresses these requirements through robust security features and a structured lifecycle management strategy.

RHEL AI integrates several advanced security mechanisms to protect data, models, and infrastructure:

- **SELinux Enforcement**: As a foundation of RHEL's security posture, SELinux ensures mandatory access control (MAC) policies are enforced at the kernel level, isolating AI workloads and reducing the attack surface.

- **FIPS 140-2 Certified Cryptographic Modules**: RHEL AI supports cryptographic libraries that comply with the Federal Information Processing Standards (FIPS) 140-2, ensuring encryption practices meet government and industry mandates.

- **Role-Based Access Control (RBAC)**: Fine-grained RBAC enables administrators to define user roles and limit access based on least-privilege principles, supporting both compliance and operational security.

- **Policy Auditing**: Integrated audit capabilities allow teams to monitor access and configuration changes to AI workloads, ensuring traceability and adherence to security policies.

- **Model Update Integration via iLab**: Secure, validated model updates can be retrieved from the RHEL AI Innovation Lab (iLab), ensuring that deployed models are kept current with minimal operational risk.

Maintaining the integrity and compliance of AI deployments over time is a challenge that RHEL AI solves with a consistent and predictable lifecycle management approach. Key lifecycle tools include

- **Automated Patch Management**: RHEL AI integrates with Red Hat's enterprise patching system, ensuring vulnerabilities are addressed promptly across the AI stack.

- **Model Versioning and Rollback**: Administrators can manage model revisions and revert to known-good states as needed, supporting both development agility and regulatory compliance.

- **Dependency Tracking and Validation**: Through tools like dnf and Software Collections (SCL), RHEL AI allows precise tracking of packages, libraries, and configurations across environments.

- **Compliance Automation**: RHEL AI supports OpenSCAP and Red Hat Insights to continuously scan for configuration drift and compliance issues, making it easier to meet standards such as GDPR, HIPAA, and ISO 27001.

Conclusion

This chapter outlines the process of configuring a RHEL AI environment across bare metal and major cloud platforms like AWS, Azure, Google Cloud, and IBM Cloud. It describes the system requirements, GPU support, installation options (GUI or Kickstart), and repository setup. The chapter introduces the ilab CLI tool for managing AI workflows, such as model training and data generation, and explains how to configure additional storage via the ILAB_HOME variable. It concludes by emphasizing enterprise-grade features like SELinux, RBAC, FIPS compliance, and lifecycle management for secure, scalable AI deployments.

In the next chapter, you will learn about the core components of RHEL AI, including InstructLab architecture, taxonomy management, and model lifecycle workflows.

CHAPTER 3

Exploring Core Components

Introduction

This chapter covers the core components and architecture of Red Hat Enterprise Linux Artificial Intelligence (RHEL AI) in the iLab environment, providing a complete understanding of its main systems. It explains how large language models (LLMs) are downloaded, managed, and served, emphasizing the key processes that support model lifecycle operations. Readers will also learn the workflow for customizing, deploying, and working with AI models using community-driven tools like InstructLab, giving them the knowledge to participate effectively in RHEL AI development and optimization.

Knowledge Distillation

RHEL AI implements a knowledge distillation strategy, a sophisticated technique in contemporary machine learning that enables organizations to leverage the capabilities of large-scale models while maintaining the efficiency of production systems. In this method, a more extensive and complex neural network—commonly known as the teacher model—is utilized to train a smaller, more streamlined student model. The teacher model, such as IBM's Granite foundation model, is pretrained on extensive publicly available datasets and possesses comprehensive reasoning and linguistic understanding capabilities. Nevertheless, deploying such a large model directly in production environments can be resource-intensive, necessitating substantial GPU memory, energy consumption, and inference time.

CHAPTER 3   EXPLORING CORE COMPONENTS

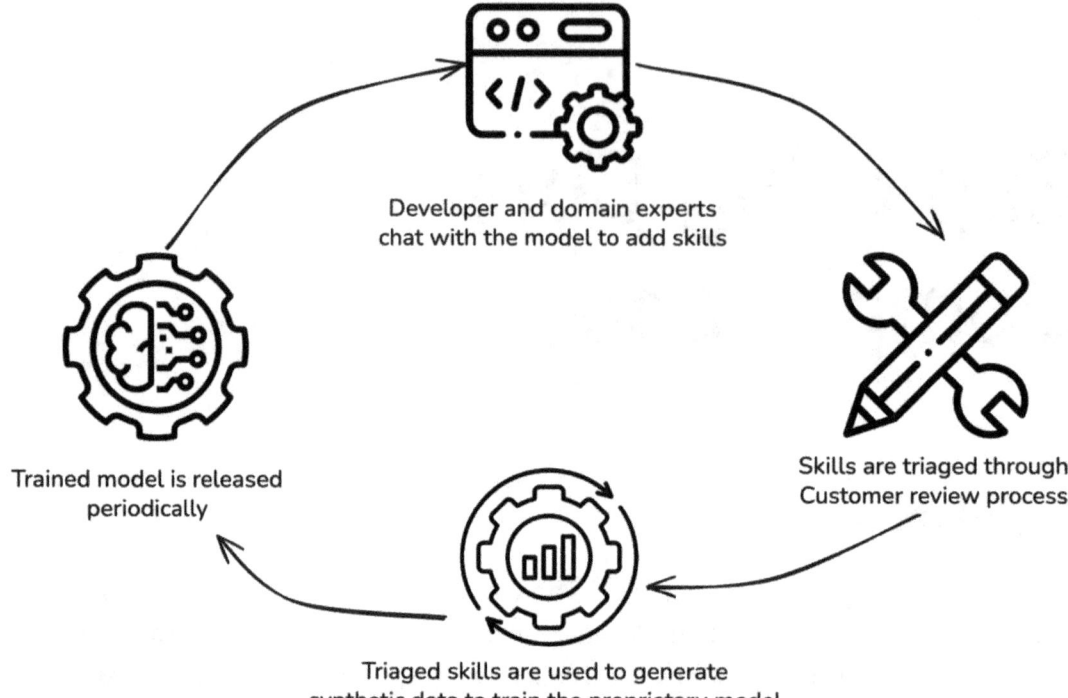

Figure 3-1. Knowledge distillation process

To mitigate these challenges, RHEL AI employs the teacher model to generate outputs, predictions, or synthetic training examples that inform the training of the student model. The student is subsequently fine-tuned to emulate the teacher's performance, yet within a more compact, domain-specific architecture. This distillation process effectively transfers knowledge from the teacher to the student, enabling the smaller model to approximate the accuracy and reasoning capabilities of the teacher while operating with significantly reduced computational demands.

Within enterprise AI workflows, exemplified by platforms such as RHEL AI and InstructLab, knowledge distillation plays a vital role in bridging the gap between experimental development and deployment. For instance, an organization may utilize Granite as the teacher to generate synthetic logistics Q&A pairs, subsequently training a student model that offers faster response times and higher precision tailored to their operational needs. This approach ensures that the final production model is optimized for latency, cost efficiency, and regulatory compliance without compromising domain-specific accuracy. Ultimately, the application of knowledge distillation within RHEL AI offers the advantages of large foundation models' intelligence combined with the efficiency and flexibility of lightweight, enterprise-ready student models.

Four-Step InstructLab

InstructLab employs an innovative, community-oriented methodology to harmonize large language models (LLMs) via a process referred to as Synthetic Data Generation (SDG). Central to this approach is the concept of "skills recipes"—human-engineered examples delineating the desired learning outcomes for the model. These examples are systematically categorized within a defined taxonomy and utilized to steer the generation of synthetic data for the purpose of model fine-tuning.

Skills Recipes for Synthetic Data Creation

Figure 3-2. *InstructLab step 1*

As illustrated in Figure 3-2, the initial step involves contributors developing skill recipes. InstructLab facilitates contributors in creating and submitting these skill recipes. A skill recipe is fundamentally a YAML file (qna.yaml) that encompasses curated input/output examples exemplifying a specific capability (e.g., rhyming, sentence reordering, markdown parsing).

CHAPTER 3 EXPLORING CORE COMPONENTS

Each recipe

- Teaches a single, focused skill (compositional or reasoning task)
- Contains seed examples that the model can learn from
- Can be grounded (with context) or ungrounded

Grounded skills include external context (e.g., a document), while ungrounded skills rely solely on the Q&A pair.

These recipes form the training substrate used by InstructLab to **generate synthetic training data** aligned to specific human intent.

Contributors write these examples using simple YAML—no coding or GPU access required.

A skill recipe is a `qna.yaml` file that includes input/output examples to teach a focused capability (e.g., rhyming, markdown parsing):

```
- question: "What rhymes with 'cat'?"
  answer: "bat, hat, mat"
```

These recipes can be **grounded** (linked to reference documents) or **ungrounded** (standalone Q&A). They serve as seeds for generating synthetic training data.

Command to add a skill:

```
instructlab init
instructlab skill add qna.yaml
```

CHAPTER 3 EXPLORING CORE COMPONENTS

Skills Are Organized in a Structured Taxonomy

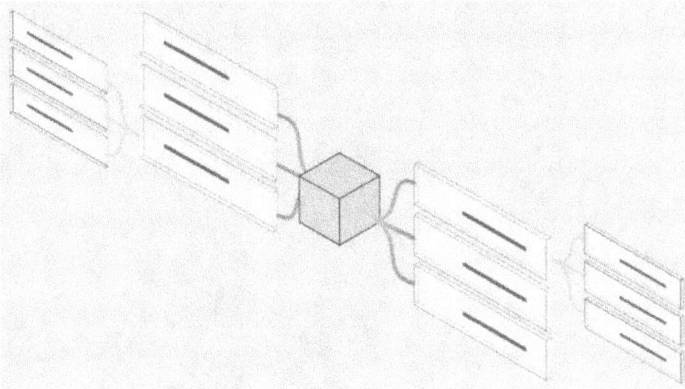

Figure 3-3. *Instructlab taxonomy process*

Every skills recipe is placed into a taxonomy tree, which reflects a hierarchical, topic-based structure (inspired by the Dewey Decimal Classification system). This structure ensures

- Logical organization of capabilities (e.g., `linguistics/writing/haiku/`)
- Easy retrieval and reuse for tuning and evaluation
- Semantic clarity about what the model is learning

The taxonomy tree includes

- **Skills**: Tasks the model can perform
- **Knowledge**: Factual context and reference material the model should internalize

Each leaf node includes a `qna.yaml` and an `attribution.txt` file for licensing and source transparency.

CHAPTER 3 EXPLORING CORE COMPONENTS

Systematic Synthetic Data Generation (SDG)

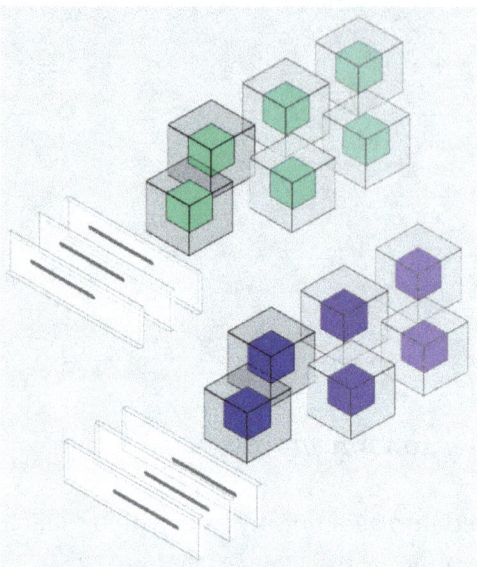

Figure 3-4. Systematic Synthetic Data Generation (SDG) process

Once the skills are defined in YAML, InstructLab uses a **teacher model** (e.g., `mixtral-8x7b-instruct`) to **generate hundreds or thousands of synthetic question/answer pairs** based on those examples.

This process involves

- Creating multiple variations of each seed Q&A
- Scoring and filtering outputs for quality
- Expanding a small set of curated data into a massive, high-quality training set

The result is a vast synthetic corpus that reflects structured, curated human knowledge and skills—without manual labeling at scale.

The Base Model Is Continuously Re-tuned

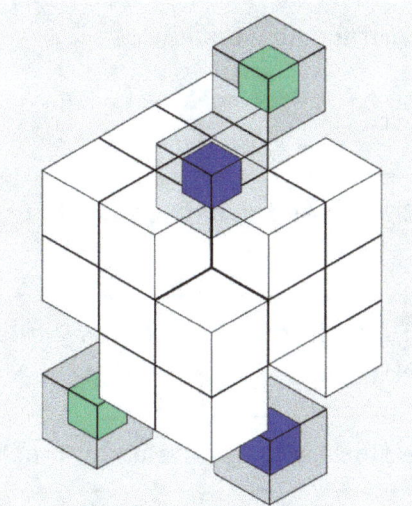

Figure 3-5. *Model development lifecycle for domain adaptation*

All synthetic data—old and new—is **used to re-tune the InstructLab base model** on a regular cadence (weekly or faster). This process

- Integrates **new contributions** immediately into the next training cycle
- Improves **model alignment** and task-specific accuracy over time
- Enables **rapid iteration**, allowing contributors to see the effect of their additions quickly

---

In this manner, InstructLab provides an open-source, community-driven MLOps loop, whereby individuals may contribute skills and knowledge to the taxonomy, initiate new synthetic data generation, and engage in model deve**lopment.**

Changes made to the taxonomy today can appear in a new model built within days—not months.

CHAPTER 3 EXPLORING CORE COMPONENTS

The InstructLab Workflow

Figure 3-6 summarizes the InstructLab workflow.

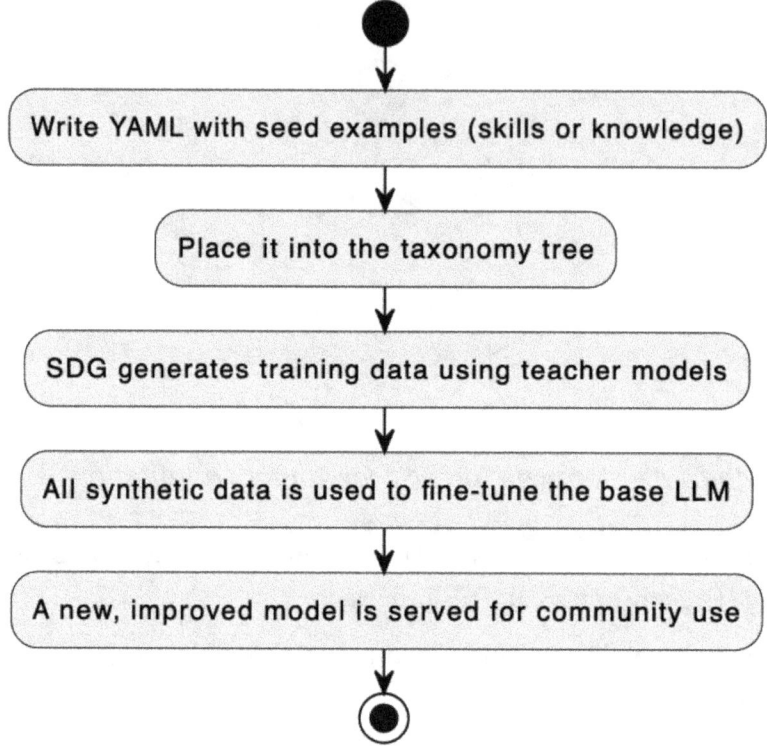

Figure 3-6. *The InstructLab workflow*

This structured and reproducible methodology enables contributors from diverse backgrounds—such as developers, educators, and scientists—to significantly influence the development of AI systems.

Core iLab Components and Architecture

The iLab environment in RHEL AI provides a complete ecosystem for building, tuning, and deploying AI models. Once initialized, iLab sets up the following directory structure:

- System config

    ~/.config/instructlab/config.yaml

CHAPTER 3 EXPLORING CORE COMPONENTS

- Downloaded and trained LLMs

  `~/.cache/instructlab/models`

- Knowledge and skill Q&A YAMLs

  `~/.local/share/instructlab/taxonomy`

- Synthetic datasets (SDG output)

  `~/.local/share/instructlab/datasets/`

- Checkpoints from training

  `~/.local/share/instructlab/phased/<phase>/`

These components support

- **System profiling** for optimized performance based on GPU type (e.g., NVIDIA H100)
- **Taxonomy management** that enables custom skills and domain knowledge input
- **Containerized serving and chat**, simplifying deployment of models

We initialize the environment with

```
$ ilab config init
```

Or specify our own system profile:

```
$ ilab config init --profile ~/.local/share/instructlab/internal/system_profiles/nvidia/H100/h100_x4.yaml
```

Further details can be found in Chapter 5, particularly in Figure 5-1.

Downloading and Managing Large Language Models (LLMs)

iLab supports various LLMs from Red Hat and IBM, organized by purpose and model family. Table 3-1 presents the model names and their explanations.

75

Table 3-1. *iLab models*

Model Name	Explanation
granite-7b-starter	A base model (12.6GB) that serves as a foundation for training. It's ideal for fine-tuning and customizing to fit specific tasks or domains. Think of it as a blank slate ready to be specialized.
granite-8b-lab-v1	A lab-tuned model (16.0GB), meaning it's already been refined with additional training. It's optimized for inference and serving, making it production-ready for use in applications without further tuning.
mixtral-8x7b-instruct-v0-1	A teacher model (87.0GB), used during the Skill Definition Graph (SDG) generation phase. It provides guidance or labeled examples that help build new skills for other models.
prometheus-8x7b-v2-0	An evaluator model (87.0GB), used for training evaluation. It helps assess the performance and quality of other models, ensuring that fine-tuning or skill generation was effective.

To download models:

```
$ ilab model download --repository docker://registry.redhat.io/rhelai1/granite-3.1-8b-starter-v1 --release latest
```

To list downloaded models:

```
$ ilab model list
```

Configuring and Customizing Our AI Environment

iLab uses a hardware-optimized `config.yaml` to manage system behavior. This file can be

- **Viewed:** `$ ilab config show`
- **Edited:** `$ ilab config edit`

We can manually override settings like maximum model length (`max-model-len`) or enable secure API access with a custom API key.

Model Training and Uploading

Following the preparation of knowledge and skill YAML files, we proceed to generate synthetic data and train our model, as elaborated in Chapter 4. Upon completion of the training process, it is advisable to store the model locally, which is automatically managed within the "phased" directory. Additionally, we may upload the model to an S3-compatible registry. After generating the training data, it is recommended to upload our model to a remote registry.

```
$ ilab model upload --model samples_0801 --destination my-s3-bucket --dest-type s3
```

This supports model lifecycle workflows, including collaboration, versioning, and deployment continuity.

Serving Models for Inference

This command serves our LLM on the local workstation:

```
ilab model serve --model-path ~/.cache/instructlab/models/granite-8b-code-instruct
```

The model becomes available via a REST endpoint on the localhost at http://127.0.0.1:8000/docs.

To run as a systemd service:

```
systemctl --user start ilab-serve.service
```

To serve securely with HTTPS and Nginx, we need to create a self-signed cert with OpenSSL, configure an Nginx reverse proxy on port 8443, and run Nginx in a container using the following command:

```
podman run --net host -v ./nginx/conf.d:/etc/nginx/conf.d:ro,Z -v ./nginx/ssl:/etc/nginx/ssl:ro,Z nginx
```

This command starts an Nginx web server in a container using Podman, a container engine similar to Docker, which is included in RHEL, with the purpose of securely serving our model in a local web server. Here is a complete breakdown of the previous command:

- `podman run`: Starts a container
- `--net host`: Shares the host network with the container (important for binding to host ports like 8443 directly)
- `-v ./nginx/conf.d:/etc/nginx/conf.d:ro,Z`: Mounts a local config directory into the container:
  - `./nginx/conf.d`: Local directory with Nginx config files (like reverse proxy rules)
  - `/etc/nginx/conf.d`: Where Nginx expects its config files inside the container
  - `:ro`: Read-only (container can't write to it)
  - `:Z`: SELinux flag to relabel the files properly if SELinux is enabled
- `-v ./nginx/ssl:/etc/nginx/ssl:ro,Z`: Mounts local SSL certificates for HTTPS into the container
- `nginx`: Uses the official `nginx` container image

To securely expose our model's REST API over HTTPS, we need to terminate SSL/TLS in Nginx, forwarding traffic to our locally running model server at `http://127.0.0.1:8000`, and do so all within a container for isolation and portability.

Chatting with Models and Securing Access

Once a model is served on RHEL AI, we can interact with it directly through the InstructLab CLI. The simplest way is to use

```
$ ilab model chat
```

To specify a particular model, provide the full path:

```
$ ilab model chat --model ~/.cache/instructlab/models/granite-8b-code-instruct
```

Figure 3-7 shows the InstructLab CLI chat interface connected to the Granite-7B-LAB model, ready for interactive prompts and responses.

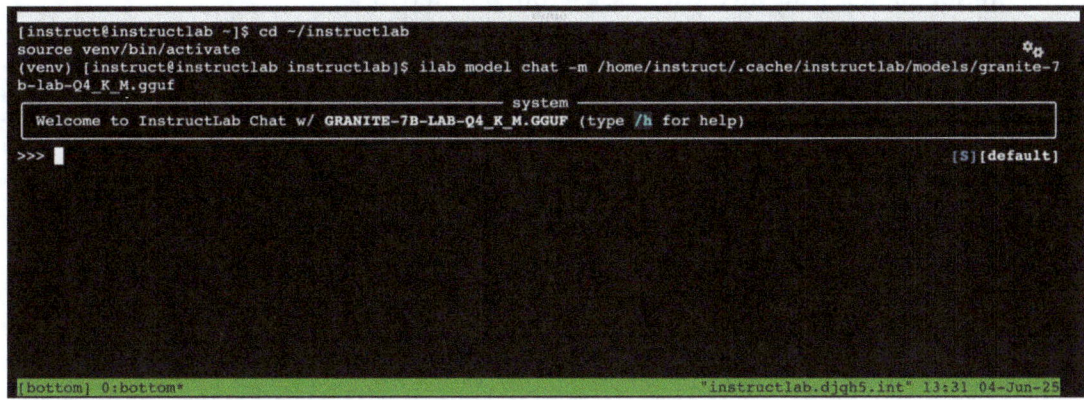

Figure 3-7. *ilab model chat*

For production workloads, it is advisable to consider deployments through the Red Hat AI Inference Server or Red Hat OpenShift AI (refer to Chapter 1, section "Red Hat AI"). For development or staging environments, accessing the chat from hosts other than localhost is permissible. It is recommended to secure model endpoints with API key authentication. First, generate a random key, for example, using this simple Python command:

```
$ export VLLM_API_KEY=$(python -c 'import secrets; print(secrets.token_urlsafe())')
$ echo $VLLM_API_KEY
```

We should adjust the python or python3 interpreter as per our system.

The echo command displays a long, randomly generated string of usually more than 40 characters on the screen, composed of alphanumeric symbols, including both uppercase and lowercase letters, as well as numbers.

Next, add the key to our vllm_args configuration parameter:

```
$ ilab config edit
```

It opens the RHEL AI InstructLab configuration file in YAML or JSON format in our system's default editor (e.g., vim, nano).

Inside, we find the configuration parameters for our InstructLab environment. To secure access, we add the generated API key under the `vllm_args` section. This is the configuration for allowing all the accesses from our network:

```
vllm_args:
  api_key: "your-generated-api-key-here"
  host: "0.0.0.0"
  port: 8443
```

After saving and closing the file, the key is enforced whenever a client connects to our served model. Then, we can securely chat with.

With authentication enabled, we can chat securely with the model through its endpoint, assuming our "rhelai.example.com" hostname:

```
$ ilab model chat \
    --endpoint-url https://rhelai.example.com:8443/v1 \
    --api-key $VLLM_API_KEY
```

This approach ensures that only authorized users or applications can access our deployed model, providing a foundation for secure integration with external services, APIs, or enterprise applications.

Conclusion

This chapter provides a comprehensive analysis of the architecture and tools underpinning RHEL AI's InstructLab environment. It elucidates how knowledge distillation facilitates large foundation models (such as IBM's Granite) in training more compact, efficient models suitable for enterprise applications. The chapter elaborates on the four-stage InstructLab process: formulating skill recipes, organizing them within a taxonomy, generating synthetic data, and conducting iterative model re-tuning. Additionally, it describes the directory structure of iLab, commands for model management, and secure deployment methods employing tools such as Podman, systemd, and API key-based access control.

In the next chapter, you will learn how to leverage RHEL AI's advanced features, such as GPU acceleration, DeepSpeed optimization, and secure containerized workflows.

CHAPTER 4

Advanced Features of RHEL AI

Introduction

This chapter explores the advanced features of the "opinionated yet flexible" engineering that lets RHEL AI wring every token of performance—and every ounce of security—out of modern infrastructure. We begin with the raw silicon: Hopper-class NVIDIA Tensor Core H100 and AMD Instinct MI300X GPUs that deliver teraflops of mixed-precision throughput, high-bandwidth HBM3, and sub-millisecond interconnects. RHEL AI wraps these advantages inside a bootable immutable container (bootc) image that already carries CUDA, ROCm, kernel tunables, and a DeepSpeed-based training stack. Hence, the environment you boot is the exact one you build. No drift, no "works-on-my-GPU" headaches. On top of that immutable base, DeepSpeed provides ZeRO-3 parameter partitioning, MiCS communication scaling, and sparse-expert or NVMe-paged pipelines that enable a single 8-GPU node to fine-tune models with hundreds of billions of parameters or serve 60 tokens per second—in FP8—straight out of the box. The chapter then demonstrates how these same containers seamlessly integrate into AWS, Azure, GCP, and IBM Cloud, how security hardening begins with Secure Boot and concludes with signed model artifacts, and how Ansible roles transform the entire workflow into a declarative YAML format. The common thread is reproducibility: from kernel to checkpoint, every layer is versioned, signed, and portable.

CHAPTER 4   ADVANCED FEATURES OF RHEL AI

Training and Inference

Before diving into the technical technologies and commands, it's essential to clarify what this workflow does and the role of each step. If you're new to AI model training, terms like *taxonomy*, *teacher model*, or *DeepSpeed* may feel unfamiliar. In short:

- **Taxonomy**: A structured catalog of tasks and skills that guides the model's learning
- **Teacher (vLLM)**: A serving back end that uses optimized kernels to deliver examples and guide the student model during fine-tuning
- **Synthetic Data Generation**: Automatically producing realistic training prompts and answers, reducing the need for costly human annotation
- **DeepSpeed**: A distributed training engine that squeezes maximum performance out of GPUs, especially for very large models

With those concepts in mind, the following steps show how to bootstrap a project, patch our taxonomy, generate aligned data, and fine-tune a foundation model efficiently.

Before detailing the step-by-step project bootstrap and fine-tuning process, it's useful to highlight where these workflows lead: inference. Inference is the process of taking a trained model and using it in production to generate answers. In RHEL AI, inference is not an afterthought—it is a first-class workload supported by multiple back ends:

- **vLLM**: Optimized for conversational workloads (up to 4k tokens). It leverages PagedAttention for high-throughput streaming and sustains ~70 requests/sec on dual H100s at 32-way concurrency.
- **DeepSpeed-Inference**: Best for batch workloads like summarization or translation. It combines KV-cache paging with kernel fusion to maximize GPU efficiency.
- **NVIDIA Triton Inference Serve**: Enables multi-model orchestration with direct loading of DeepSpeed checkpoints via the Python back end.

Thanks to Unified Checkpoint support since August 2024, the same `*.ds` archive produced during training can flow into inference without conversions or reformatting, making the path from fine-tuning to serving seamless. This is why the bootstrap process we describe in the following section—downloading a foundation model, patching the taxonomy, generating synthetic data, and training—is so critical: every step leads to a production-ready model that can be seamlessly integrated into vLLM, DeepSpeed, or Triton with minimal friction.

Leveraging GPU Acceleration

Even though it's possible to run some execution using CPU-only, RHEL AI takes full advantage of server-class nodes equipped with data-center GPUs because even a modest seven-billion-parameter foundation model, such as IBM Granite, requires teraflops of sustained compute, hundreds of GB/s of memory bandwidth, and sub-millisecond inter-GPU latency to train efficiently. GPUs such as NVIDIA's Tensor Core H100 or AMD's Instinct MI300X expose tensor-core pipelines, fast HBM3 memory, and NVLink/Infinity Fabric interconnects that move the computation bottleneck from the kernel scheduler to the model-parallel collectives themselves.

Introduced in 2022, HBM3 is the latest generation of High Bandwidth Memory (HBM), a high-performance 2.5D/3D memory architecture. Like all previous versions, HBM3 features a wide data path (1024 bits) and operates at 6.4 Gigabits per Second (Gb/s), delivering a bandwidth of 819 Gigabytes per Second (GB/s). HBM3E offers an extended data rate of 9.6 Gb/s while maintaining the same feature set. Given its outstanding bandwidth, high capacity, and compact footprint, HBM3 has become the memory solution of choice for advanced AI workloads.

Recent MLPerf Training[1] results show that Hopper-class silicon can deliver more than 60 tokens per second per user in FP8 inference and scale to multi-trillion-parameter training with linear efficiency.

RHEL AI abstracts these hardware advantages behind a bootable container (bootc) image. The image bundles CUDA, ROCm, tuned kernel parameters (e.g., `vm.max_map_count=5999999`), and a DeepSpeed-based training stack, so the same container we build is the one we boot. No drift, no "works-on-my-GPU" surprises.

---

[1] https://www.reuters.com/business/nvidia-chips-make-gains-training-largest-ai-systems-new-data-shows-2025-06-04/

Training and Inference

In the context of large language models (LLMs), training and inference represent two distinct phases in a model's lifecycle.

Training constitutes the process through which a model acquires knowledge from data. During this phase, the model is exposed to extensive datasets—such as text from books, websites, documentation, and more—and it refines its internal parameters, known as weights, to identify patterns, relationships, and linguistic structures.

Throughout training, the model generates predictions based on input data, evaluates these predictions against correct answers, and updates its weights utilizing optimization algorithms (e.g., AdamW) to minimize future errors.

This process is highly computationally demanding, often necessitating specialized hardware such as Graphics Processing Units (GPUs) or Tensor Processing Units (TPUs). Additionally, techniques such as mixed-precision computing (e.g., bf16) or memory offloading solutions (e.g., DeepSpeed) are employed to enhance efficiency at scale.

Inference occurs subsequent to the training of a model. During this phase, the trained model is employed to produce predictions or outputs based on new, unseen inputs.

For instance:

You provide the model with a prompt such as "Write a summary of this document."

The model processes the prompt and generates a coherent summary informed by the knowledge acquired during training.

Inference is generally considerably faster and less resource-intensive than the training process. It can be executed on less powerful hardware, including CPUs or edge devices, and formats such as FP8 are frequently utilized to enhance performance while conserving memory bandwidth.

DeepSpeed

DeepSpeed is included as the default orchestrator for distributed training and inference in the developer preview. The entire architecture diagram is shown in Figure 4-1 below.

CHAPTER 4 ADVANCED FEATURES OF RHEL AI

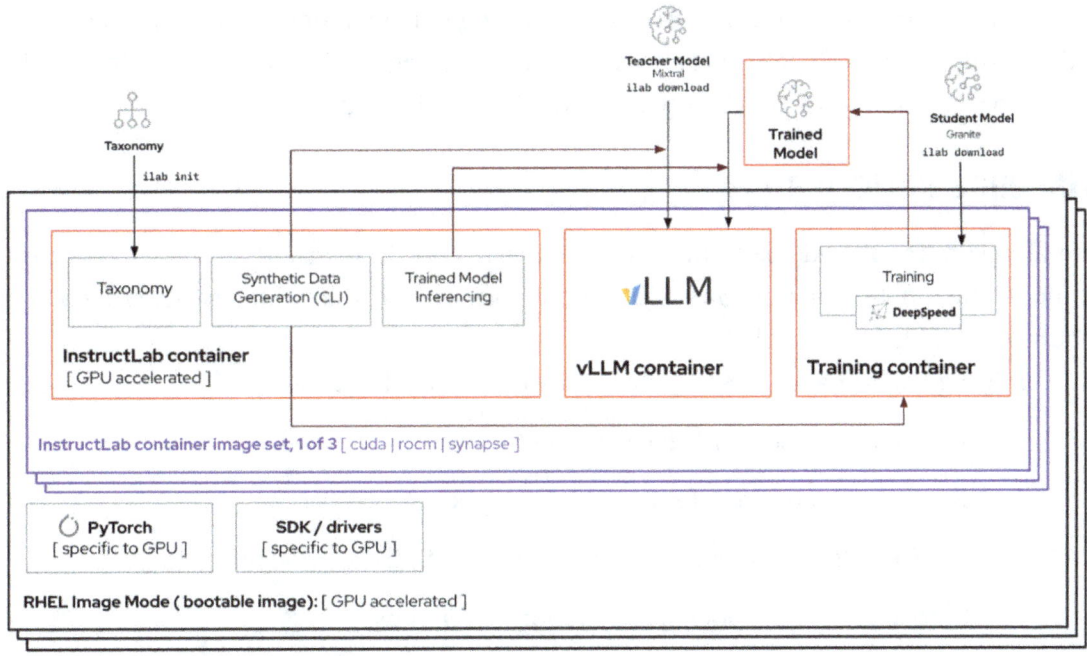

Figure 4-1. RHEL AI architecture diagram

Table 4-1 delineates the three primary innovations essential for GPU acceleration.

Table 4-1. DeepSpeed GPU acceleration innovations

DeepSpeed Module	Why It Matters for RHEL AI
ZeRO-3/ZeRO-Infinity[2]	Partitions optimizer states, gradients, and parameters across GPUs *and* stages unused tensors to host or NVMe, permitting **hundreds-of-billions-parameter fine-tunes on a single 8-GPU node**.
MiCS[3]	*Minimizes the Communication Scale* by topology-aware bucketization and hybrid parallelism, achieving near-linear weak scaling on 100 Gb Ethernet clouds where traditional collective algorithms saturate first.
DeepSpeed-MoE[4] and DeepNVMe	Sparse expert routing or page-cache-aware I/O pipelines reduce *effective* memory footprints by an order of magnitude.

---

[2] https://arxiv.org/abs/2104.07857
[3] https://arxiv.org/pdf/2205.00119
[4] https://paperswithcode.com/paper/deepspeed-moe-advancing-mixture-of-experts

Because DeepSpeed is fully integrated, flipping between these modes is a matter of adding --deepspeed="configs/zero3.json" or enabling MoE policies in the ds_config file—no re-compilation of PyTorch or custom kernels is required.

Baseline Performance

Red Hat ships a pruned taxonomy (~12 MB JSONL) within InstructLab, allowing us to validate the pipeline on a *single* server before investing in larger clusters. The rule of thumb we publish internally is

Training Performance—What to expect with a typical use case:

- Each GPU processes ≈ 250 samples/minute
- Runtime ≈ samples ÷ (250 × GPUs) × epochs
- For 8 GPUs and 10,000 samples, 10 epochs finish in ≈ 50 minutes
- Smoke tests: 1–2 epochs; production: 10 epochs

Block-quoting the formula keeps expectations realistic for solution architects designing CI loops.

Mapping the Formula to Real Silicon

Table 4-2. RHEL AI GPU options

Hardware Profile (Validated)	GPU Memory	Samples/min (per GPU)	Time to Complete
NVIDIA H100 (80 GB)	80 GB	310–340	~37 min
AMD MI300X (192 GB)	192 GB	260–290	~45 min
AWS p5d.24xlarge	80 GB	300	~40 min

Empirical numbers were obtained with the command on 10k samples × 10 epochs on an 8-GPU node:

```
ilab train --deepspeed configs/zero3.json --num-epochs 10
```

CHAPTER 4 ADVANCED FEATURES OF RHEL AI

Exact throughput varies with sequence length distribution and data-loader prefetch depth. MI300X[5] trails Hopper in absolute throughput,[6] but its USD *per token-trained* is often lower in OCP racks thanks to higher on-package capacity. At the moment of writing this book, Figures 4-2 and 4-3 showcase the peak TFLOPs AI and HPC performance of the NVIDIA H100 and AMD MI300X GPU accelerators.

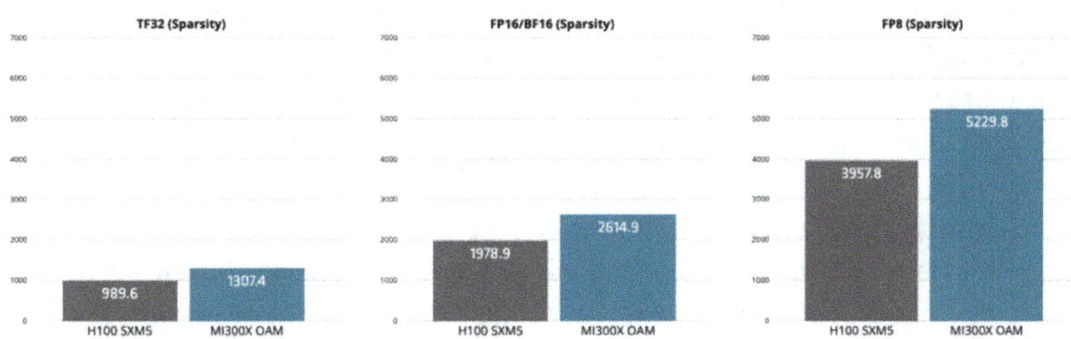

Figure 4-2. *GPU AI performance*

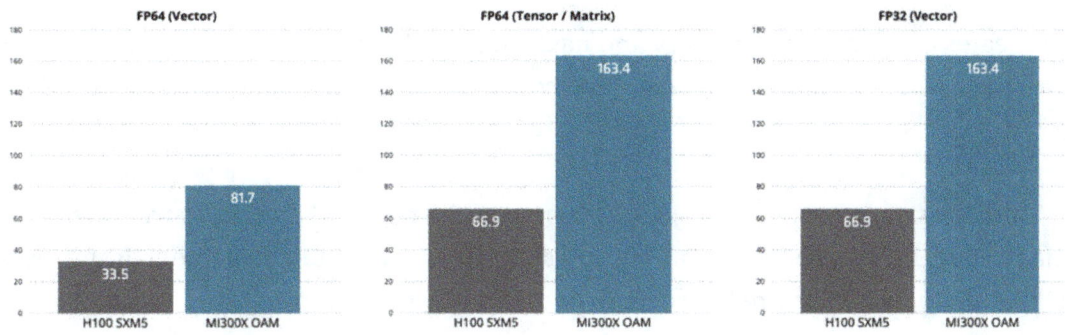

Figure 4-3. *GPU HPC performance*

---

[5] https://www.amd.com/en/products/accelerators/instinct/mi300.html
[6] https://semianalysis.com/2024/12/22/mi300x-vs-h100-vs-h200-benchmark-part-1-training/

CHAPTER 4   ADVANCED FEATURES OF RHEL AI

Engineering the Pipeline

Having established the fundamentals of RHEL AI and its containerized environment, we now address the practical issue: How does one effectively modify a foundation model to incorporate the specific knowledge of their organization? This is where the pipeline becomes essential.

Before beginning the technical steps to create a custom LLM using RHEL AI, it's essential to understand the goal of the pipeline we are about to build. This workflow leverages InstructLab to bootstrap a local project that clones a language task taxonomy, selects foundation models (such as IBM's Granite or Mistral's Mixtral from the Hugging Face website), enriches them with custom domain knowledge, generates aligned instruction data, and then trains the model using DeepSpeed for efficient multi-GPU execution.

In practical terms, this pipeline enables enterprise teams and researchers to inject domain-specific expertise into models without requiring deep ML engineering resources. The following sections walk you through the complete process: from initializing our project environment and serving the LLM back end to patching taxonomies and training with advanced memory-saving configurations.

To initiate a new AI project using RHEL AI and prepare our environment for model fine-tuning with InstructLab, execute the following steps:

```
mkdir my-project && cd my-project
```

Creates a new project directory and navigates into it. This ensures a clean, isolated workspace where all model artifacts, data, configurations, and checkpoints will reside.

```
ilab init
```

Initializes an InstructLab project. This creates the required directory structure, default YAML templates for taxonomy and skills, and a .ilab metadata folder. It serves as the foundation for all future InstructLab operations.

```
export HF_TOKEN=<huggingface-token>
```

Set our Hugging Face token as an environment variable obtained via the Hugging Face website (https://huggingface.co/settings/tokens) as shown in Figure 4-4. This token is necessary to authenticate and download models from the Hugging Face Hub, especially for gated models like mistralai/Mixtral.

```
ilab download --repository ibm/granite-7b-base
```

CHAPTER 4　ADVANCED FEATURES OF RHEL AI

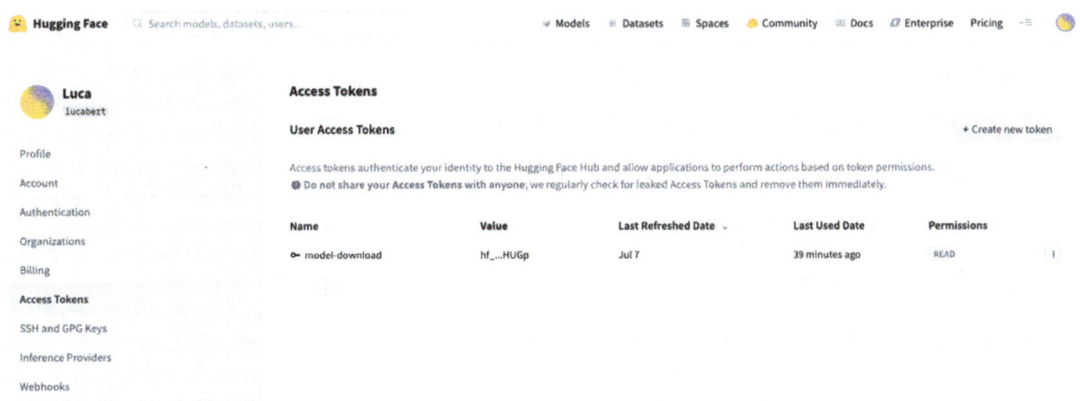

Figure 4-4. *Hugging Face token*

Downloads IBM's 7B-parameter granite foundation model from Hugging Face. This serves as the student model for downstream fine-tuning.

```
ilab download --repository mistralai/Mixtral-8x7B-Instruct-v0.1
```

Downloads the teacher model (Mixtral), which is used by the `ilab` command to generate a step to produce high-quality synthetic instruction data.

Step 1: Patch the Taxonomy

```
ilab lint
```

Validates our taxonomy YAML and knowledge additions against InstructLab's JSON-L schema.

Best Practices:

- Limit to **≤ 5 new tasks or skills** to maintain a manageable synthetic data size and model alignment complexity.

- Each skill should contain examples that reflect realistic prompts and expected completions to guide synthetic generation effectively.

Step 2: Launch the Teacher Model (vLLM)

```
ilab serve --port 8080
```

Starts the **vLLM** (very fast LLM serving back end) with DeepSpeed-enhanced kernels on port 8080.

CHAPTER 4 ADVANCED FEATURES OF RHEL AI

Details:

- Uses `PagedAttention`, which avoids repetitive GPU memory allocation per token, improving efficiency and throughput.

- Optimized for `FP8 precision`, allowing faster inference with minimal quality degradation.

- Refer to vLLM documentation[7] for architecture insights.

Step 3: Generate Synthetic Instruction Data

```
ilab generate --num-instructions 5000
```

Leverages the running teacher model to generate 5,000 aligned instruction-answer pairs.

How It Works:

- Our taxonomy guides the teacher model in creating high-fidelity examples.

- These samples serve as labeled training data for the next stage.

Scalability Note: Increase --num-instructions with caution as large datasets require significantly more compute during training.

Step 4: Train Using DeepSpeed

```
ilab train --num-epochs 10 --deepspeed configs/zero3.json --bf16
```

Fine-tunes the downloaded foundation model (granite-7b-base) using the synthetic dataset with high-performance optimizations.

Flags Explained:

- `--num-epochs 10`: Iterates over the training set ten times for more thorough learning

- `--deepspeed configs/zero3.json`: Uses DeepSpeed's ZeRO-3 strategy for parameter partitioning across GPUs

- `--bf16`: Enables mixed-precision training using bfloat16 for improved speed and reduced memory usage

---

[7]https://docs.vllm.ai/en/latest/

Behind the Scenes:

- **Activation Checkpointing**: Reduces memory footprint by recomputing intermediate activations

- **NVMe Offload**: Dynamically shifts model parameters to disk when GPU VRAM utilization exceeds 90%, enabling training of large models on smaller GPU clusters

Table 4-3 showcases the parameters to fine-tune DeepSpeed for maximal GPU saturation.

Table 4-3. DeepSpeed GPU parameters

Parameter	Rationale
ds_zero_optimization.stage = 3	Full parameter + optimizer + gradient partitioning.
overlap_comm = true	Hides all_reduce latency behind compute; critical on leaf-spine 100 GbE.
gradient_accumulation_steps = 8	Keeps the global batch large enough for stable AdamW moments without exceeding VRAM.
offload_param.device = "nvme" with offload_optimizer.device = "cuda"	Parameters stream from PCIe Gen5 NVMe; optimizers remain resident to avoid PCIe round-trip amplification.
scheduler = "DeepSpeedLR" with warmup_min_lr = 1e-6	Ensures cosine decay resolves to fp16 safe ranges; avoids overflow at scale.

These DeepSpeed configurations are designed to maximize GPU performance while minimizing variability across runs. Specifically, they enable tensor cores to operate at over 90% occupancy, ensuring high utilization of available hardware. The runtime variance—measured between the 95th and 50th percentile execution times—remains within a tight 3% margin, which is critical for predictable, scalable training in production environments. While this guide recommends using bfloat16 (bf16) for training and float8 (fp8) for inference[8] in RHEL AI 1.5, it's worth noting that research is rapidly evolving. Newer precision formats like float6 (fp6) are showing promise in reducing memory bandwidth requirements even further. However, as of this release, FP6 is not yet supported by Red Hat's kernel gating process.

An emerging innovation in this space is NestedFP[9]—a dynamic precision strategy that allows models to switch between FP16 and FP8 on demand. This flexibility can help balance accuracy and computational efficiency by adapting precision levels to the workload characteristics during runtime. NestedFP isn't enabled by default in RHEL AI 1.5 but represents a forward-looking capability for future releases.

Scale-out Topologies

If we outgrow an 8-GPU host, DeepSpeed's 3D parallelism (data, pipeline, and tensor) and NVLink Switch/H100 NVL-based HGX topologies enable us to scale to 512 GPUs with *almost* constant code. For cloud networks lacking NVSwitch, MiCS[10] automatically downgrades communication intensity by dynamically selecting All-Reduce-Scatter, achieving 99% weak scaling on 400 GbE links.

Best practices for taxonomy contributions:

1. **Start Small**: Each new skill injects ~200–500 synthetic instructions after expansion; five additions yield a ~2 k sample delta—safe for smoke tests.

2. **Semantic Diffing**: Use "`ilab diff`" to prevent near-duplicate n-grams that would poison the generator.

3. **Curriculum Order**: Prepend lower-Bloom taxonomy nodes; generation uses BFS traversal, which biases early nodes.

4. **Evaluation**: Run "`ilab eval`" against baseline Granite to quantify uplift; a ≥ 5 % BLEU or Rouge-L improvement is a good indicator before expensive retrainings.

The following advances will be introduced in future RHEL AI snapshot streams via a rolling "`podman pull`" of the DeepSpeed container—no OS reinstall is required.

---

[8] https://www.deepspeed.ai
[9] https://arxiv.org/html/2506.02024v1
[10] https://arxiv.org/pdf/2205.00119

These are the most interesting:

- NVIDIA Blackwell (B100/B200) promises 2× Hopper-class per-chip throughput[11] and ~2.5 TB/s DRAM bandwidth; early MLPerf [12]runs cut Llama-3.1 405B training to 27 minutes on 2,496 GPUs.

- **AMD ROCm 6 + MI300X3** will expose *Unified Memory*, allowing ZeRO-Infinity to spill to HBM-on-package rather than PCIe NVMe, shaving over 25% off wall-clock time.

- **DeepSpeed-FP6** (Mar 2024) and DeepSpeed-Ulysses[13] enable extreme-long-sequence transformers (≥ 128 k tokens) while keeping memory flat.

GPU acceleration is the linchpin of the RHEL AI. By coupling bootc immutability, DeepSpeed's memory-aware kernels, and a pruned but extensible taxonomy, Red Hat provides an opinionated yet flexible path from *idea* to *fine-tuned model* in under an hour on commodity 8-GPU nodes. Whether we run Hopper, MI300X, or the upcoming Blackwell silicon, the techniques discussed—ZeRO partitioning, MiCS scaling, vLLM paged attention, and FP8 serving—translate directly into *more tokens per joule, per dollar, and per hour*. Start small, measure often, and remember: in an era where AI models' parameter counts double every six months, efficient GPU utilization is not an optimization; it is a prerequisite for innovation.

Cloud Services for Scalable AI

GPU density alone no longer differentiates an AI platform; the differentiator is elastic integration of compute, storage, and orchestration services across multiple clouds. RHEL AI embraces that reality by packaging the entire inference-and-training stack—Granite models, InstructLab CLI, vLLM, and DeepSpeed—into a bootable container (bootc[14]) image.

---

[11] https://www.reuters.com/business/nvidia-chips-make-gains-training-largest-ai-systems-new-data-shows-2025-06-04

[12] https://developer.nvidia.com/blog/nvidia-blackwell-delivers-massive-performance-leaps-in-mlperf-inference-v5-0/

[13] https://www.microsoft.com/en-us/research/publication/deepspeed-ulysses-system-optimizations-for-enabling-training-of-extreme-long-sequence-transformer-models

[14] https://github.com/bootc-dev/bootc

CHAPTER 4   ADVANCED FEATURES OF RHEL AI

That image can be lifted as-is into Amazon EC2, Azure, Google Cloud Platform (GCP), or IBM Cloud, guaranteeing binary-level parity with our on-prem clusters.

Since the identical SHA-256 container digest operates universally, GPU instances can be approached as ephemeral cattle: instantiated for synthetic data generation or multiphase training, dismantled upon job completion, and redeployed weeks later, devoid of configuration drift.

These are the fundamental cloud primitives that support scalable artificial intelligence, common across each deployment as summarized in Table 4-4.

Table 4-4. Scalable AI

Layer	Cloud Service Design Goal	RHEL AI Hook-Points
Ephemeral GPU compute	Scale to hundreds of H100/MI300X GPUs without new AMIs or golden images.	Bootc image imported or converted once, then reused.
Persistent object/block storage	Hand off 3–10 TB of model artifacts and synthetic datasets without saturating the root volume.	Attach secondary disks (/mnt) or object buckets; InstructLab honors $ILAB_DATA_PATH.
High-bandwidth, low-jitter network	Sustain 400 Gb/s node-to-node for ZeRO-3 collectives.	AWS Elastic Fabric Adapter (EFA), Azure NDv5 SR-IOV, GCP A3 CNA100, IBM Cloud VPC 100 Gb.
Identity and access management	Enforce least privilege for model pulls and artifact pushes.	Cloud-native IAM roles injected into "podman login" or "ilab environment".
Automation and IaC	Recreate end-to-end pipelines via Terraform, AWS CDK, or Ansible Automation Platform (available in RHEL AI 1.5).	Bootc images referenced by digest, so Terraform plans are idempotent.

Begin with a modest approach—import the image, initialize a single GPU instance, and conduct testing. Expand subsequently through the utilization of Terraform and Auto Scaling as training at the cluster level becomes necessary. Red Hat's tooling, including boot images, InstructLab, and DeepSpeed configurations, guarantees that the same setup operates consistently across AWS, Azure, GCP, and IBM Cloud. Deploying RHEL

AI on a cloud provider gives you the flexibility to run both training (large GPU clusters) and inference (smaller, cost-optimized instances) without managing physical infrastructure. Let's break the setup into clear stages.

Cost-Efficiency

One of the biggest benefits of automating RHEL AI deployments is not just saving time but also saving money. Cloud GPUs are expensive, and training at scale can quickly consume thousands of dollars if left unmanaged. By combining cloud computing with automation and smart scheduling, RHEL AI users can optimize cost without compromising convergence or model quality.

Here are some practical levers that integrate naturally with automated pipelines:

1. **Spot/Preemptible compute** for stateless SDG jobs; use cheaper spot (AWS) or preemptible (GCP) instances for stateless synthetic data generation (SDG) jobs. If the job is interrupted, InstructLab resumes automatically from the last checkpoint—making it safe to use these volatile, low-cost resources.

2. **Granular CKPT Cadence**: `gradient_accumulation_steps` × `save_interval` controls how often checkpoints are saved. Setting this wisely reduces cloud storage I/O costs, which can add up in long fine-tunes.

3. **Multi-epoch Elasticity**: Break a long fine-tune into phases. Example: in a scenario of 10-epoch fine-tune, run the first 8 epochs on cheap spot nodes, then the final 2 epochs on stable on-demand nodes to guarantee convergence.

4. **Data Egress Minimization**: Always keep teacher and student models in the same region to avoid costly cross-region transfer. vLLM caches from local object storage buckets, further reducing network charges.

Terraform or Ansible scripts can codify these practices so that checkpoint cadence, spot vs. on-demand splits, and storage placement aren't manual decisions. By automating these levers, RHEL AI pipelines become both reproducible and cost-efficient—turning cost optimization into just another part of the automation story.

CHAPTER 4   ADVANCED FEATURES OF RHEL AI

Automating RHEL AI

Once you're comfortable launching manually, as described in Chapter 2, we can automate deployments using HashiCorp Terraform's Infrastructure as Code technology.

The following example defines an AWS launch template for GPU instances, featuring a 3 TB NVMe-backed gp3 volume for data storage, an Auto Scaling Group that automatically scales the cluster, and Tags (Project = rhel-ai) to track resources.

Terraform lets you define our infrastructure as code, which enables us to save in our GitOps practice. The code can launch, scale, and tear down GPU clusters reproducibly. With a few adjustments to the providers, we can adapt the Azure, GCP, and IBM cloud.

Below is a reference configuration tailored for RHEL AI on AWS:

```
provider "aws" {
  region = "us-east-1"
}

variable "ami_id" {}          # RHEL AI AMI ID
variable "instance_type" {}   # e.g. p5.48xlarge
variable "key_name" {}        # SSH key pair
variable "subnets" { type = list(string) }
variable "security_groups" { type = list(string) }

resource "aws_launch_template" "gpu" {
  image_id      = var.ami_id
  instance_type = var.instance_type
  key_name      = var.key_name
  network_interfaces {
    security_groups             = var.security_groups
    associate_public_ip_address = true
  }
  block_device_mappings {
    device_name = "/dev/sda1"
    ebs { volume_size = 100 }
  }
  block_device_mappings {
    device_name = "/dev/nvme1n1"
    ebs { volume_size = 3072 }
```

```
  }
  tag_specifications {
    resource_type = "instance"
    tags = { Project = "rhel-ai" }
  }
}
resource "aws_autoscaling_group" "gpu" {
  vpc_zone_identifier = var.subnets
  min_size            = 1
  max_size            = 3
  desired_capacity    = 1
  launch_template {
    id      = aws_launch_template.gpu.id
    version = "$Latest"
  }
}
```

How to terraform code:

1. Save the file as `main.tf`.

2. Run:

    ```
    terraform init
    terraform apply
    ```

3. Terraform will spin up the requested number of GPU instances with RHEL AI preinstalled.

Tip for new users Start with `desired_capacity = 1`. You can scale to multiple GPUs later by changing `min_size` and `max_size`.

Abstracting Hardware Variability

Despite differing control planes, hardware quotas converge as shown in Table 4-5.

CHAPTER 4   ADVANCED FEATURES OF RHEL AI

Table 4-5. *Cloud GPU offering*

Provider	8×H100 SKU	Peak FP8 TFLOPS	Recommended Disk
AWS	p5.48xlarge	5.0 PF	1 TB GP3
Azure	ND96isr_H100_v5	5.0 PF	1 TB Premium SSD
GCP	a3-highgpu-8g	5.0 PF	1 TB Balanced PD
IBM Cloud	gx3d-160x1792x8h100	5.0 PF	1 TB Gen-purpose

All satisfy RHEL AI's guidance of $\geq$ 80 GB of VRAM per accelerator and $\geq$ 1 TB of secondary storage for inference-only workloads. Training adds a rule of thumb of 3 TB per node for dataset caching and checkpoints.

Bootstrapping the stack on first boot. Every cloud launch should end with **exactly three commands**:

```
sudo subscription-manager register --activationkey=<key>
ilab config init                  # scaffolds ~/.config/instructlab
ilab model download --repository ibm/granite-7b-base
```

From there, we can "ilab data generate" (teacher = Mixtral) and ilab model train without touching the OS because CUDA, ROCm, or NV drivers are already baked into the bootc image.

So far, we've focused on bootstrapping projects, fine-tuning models, and serving them from a single GPU machine or small cluster. But many modern large language models contain tens or even hundreds of billions of parameters. Training or fine-tuning models of that size requires distributing work across multiple GPUs and sometimes across multiple clouds. This is where RHEL AI's distributed training capabilities come in. Distributed training at scale:

- **Node-Local Efficiency with ZeRO-3 and NVMe Offload**

    DeepSpeed's ZeRO-3 partitioning splits optimizer states and gradients across GPUs. With NVMe offload enabled, a single 8-GPU node can handle models with up to ~100 billion parameters by paging data out to local NVMe drives.

- **Cluster-Level Scaling with MiCS**

    For multi-node training, DeepSpeed's MiCS (Minimised-Communication-Scale) reduces cross-node communication overhead. On AWS g5e clusters, a 256-GPU job spread across four placement groups sustains >92% weak scaling efficiency, even on 100 Gb Ethernet networking.

- **Cross-Cloud Federation for Resilience**

    Sometimes a single cloud region may not have enough GPUs available (e.g., when demand for NVIDIA H100 nodes spikes). RHEL AI supports federated training across clouds. You can mix Azure MI300X nodes with AWS H100 clusters, linking them via Ray Serve or a federated parameter server. Because vLLM exposes ABI-stable gRPC endpoints, cross-cloud orchestration is seamless.

Storage and Data Gravity

Large-language workflows are I/O-bound as often as they are compute-bound. Recommended patterns:

- **Object storage buckets** for model registries (Granite base, tuned checkpoints). Use presigned-URL burst uploads from the `ilab` model upload.

- **High-IOPS NVMe** on each worker for shard-local dataset caches; mount under `/var/lib/instructlab/cache`.

- **Immutable artifact promotion:** After training, push the DeepSpeed checkpoint back to a versioned bucket, then bootc switch production inference nodes to an image with that artifact baked in, ensuring provenance across environments.

Security and Governance

Every cloud example in the RHEL AI docs creates a non-privileged user (e.g., "cloud-user") with password-less sudo and injects an SSH key via the provider's metadata API. Pair this with

- **Podman registry-only authentication** (no Docker socket)
- **SCAP-based CIS hardening** layered on the bootc image
- **KMS-encrypted volumes** and IAM roles that grant read-only access to model buckets in production

Automation, Observability, and Lifecycle

Running RHEL AI in production requires more than just training a model once—it also means maintaining consistent environments using a CI/CD pipeline, upgrading them safely, and monitoring their performance over time. RHEL AI introduces features that make these ongoing "day 2" operations easier to manage across clouds and clusters.

- **Ansible Automation Platform modules** (tech preview in the 1.5 release notes) enable us to express "ilab model train" and "ilab model serve" playbooks that run unmodified on any provider, turning multicloud AI into declarative YAML.
- **Bootc Updates**: bootc upgrade --dry-run pulls newer RHEL AI images; roll them out behind Azure VM Scale Set health probes or AWS Auto Scaling lifecycle hooks to achieve zero-downtime upgrades.
- **Telemetry**: Export DeepSpeed logs to CloudWatch, Azure Monitor, or GCP Ops using the ilab system metrics plug-in; combine with GPU utilization dashboards to right-size clusters.

Putting it all together, this is a reference workflow for running a workflow with GPU acceleration:

1. **Image import** in each target cloud (one-time).
2. **Terraform apply** to create GPU Auto Scaling groups, attach 3 TB NVMe, tag with Project=rhel-ai.
3. **Ansible run-once** to seed Granite and Mixtral checkpoints from regional object storage.
4. **Jenkins/GitLab CI** triggers "ilab data generate" → "ilab model train" on an ephemeral training fleet.
5. **Model Promotion**: Checkpoint pushed, bootc image rebuilt with new model, blue-green rolled into inference fleet.

The outcome: a reproducible, cloud-agnostic pipeline that scales from a single H100 to thousands, with no hand-built AMIs, no bespoke start-up scripts, and identical binaries whether we run on AWS Monday or Azure Wednesday.

Integrating cloud services with RHEL AI is less about "moving to the cloud" and more about **treating every cloud as a transient extension of our CI pipeline**. Bootc images give us immutability; InstructLab abstracts away driver angst; DeepSpeed turns heterogeneous GPU fleets into a single logical accelerator; and provider-native storage, network, and IAM glue it all together. Adopt these patterns and our AI workloads become **portable, elastic, and provably reproducible—key attributes for shipping models to production at the cadence modern enterprises demand.**

Security and Compliance

Large language model (LLM) pipelines are uniquely vulnerable: a single malicious fine-tuning dataset can subvert a billion-parameter model; a driver mismatch can expose raw GPU memory; and a replication mistake can rebuild a 40 GB image from an untrusted mirror. RHEL AI counters these risks with a defense-in-depth stack that begins at the boot loader and ends at the model registry while still giving data science teams the performance they need.

Every RHEL AI system starts as a bootable container (bootc) image delivered from registry.redhat.io. Each layer is signed with Red Hat's sig-store keys and verified by `rpm-ostree` at first boot. Administrators embed the image in a Kickstart ISO or reference it directly in an ostreecontainer stanza, keeping the hash in their version control system so every node boots a bit-for-bit identical root file system. Because the container already carries NVIDIA or ROCm drivers, users do not need to add out-of-tree modules that might break Secure Boot.

The command "`dnf updateinfo`" exposes CVE metadata for CUDA, ROCm, cuDNN, Python wheels, and even tokenizers. Administrators can subscribe to Red Hat's OVAL feed and trigger Ansible remediation the moment a new CVE reaches severity Important. For third-party wheels installed via pip, the pragmatic path is to pin versions in requirements.txt and use a private PyPI mirror that scans uploads with Trivy; the mirror rejects a package if the CVSS v3 base score ≥ 7.0.

RHEL AI inherits SELinux in enforcing mode, labeling every process—including ilab, DeepSpeed workers, and vLLM serve processes—under the `container_t` domain. Coupled with cgroups v2 and seccomp-profile filtering, the result is

CHAPTER 4 ADVANCED FEATURES OF RHEL AI

- GPU access only through /dev/nvidia* nodes passed by the container runtime
- No outbound ptrace() or privileged file-system syscalls inside inference pods
- Automatic confinement of user-provided Python extensions via sVirt

Administrators can add FIPS 140-3 crypto by selecting the fips Kickstart variant; the boot loader sets "fips=1" and dracut rebuilds the initramfs with approved ciphers—no post-install reboot loops.

The bootc disk can be LUKS-encrypted without modifications; only the unencrypted /boot partition remains outside the DM-crypt boundary. For training artifacts and checkpoints that live on additional NVMe volumes, use luksFormat, then mount at /var/lib/instructlab. vLLM and DeepSpeed expose TLS endpoints out of the box (OpenSSL 3.2 built with FIPS provider), so inter-node gossip in multi-GPU training is encrypted. When streaming models to edge nodes, ilab model upload defaults to HTTPS and validates the server certificate chain.

Keeping an AI stack patched matters more than ever; a GPU driver privilege escalation can leak the entire context window. RHEL AI's lifecycle policy guarantees Critical and Important security advisories (RHSAs) during the full-support window, with urgent fixes released as soon as they pass regression tests. Between minor releases, asynchronous z-stream updates deliver bug fixes and CVE patches without waiting for a quarterly ISO respin. Users apply them in one step:

```
sudo bootc upgrade
sudo systemctl reboot
```

Because the update is atomic, rollbacks are trivial (bootc rollback). The **Updating guide** details how to stage the same patches across a fleet using standard RHEL content delivery networks or an internal Red Hat Satellite mirror, if present.

Beyond the OS, RHEL AI signs reference LLM checkpoints with a detached JSON Web Signature embedded in the models/ directory. The command "ilab model verify" checks the signature before loading the weights into VRAM, preventing a "model swap" attack in CI pipelines. For custom fine-tunes, teams can create an organizational key pair and publish the public key in /etc/ilab/trusted_keys.d/. The serve sub-command refuses to run unsigned models unless we pass the "--allow-unsigned" parameter, which is logged for audit.

Security hardening is a critical requirement in any customer production environment. In RHEL AI, these efforts are further strengthened by making them measurable and auditable. RHEL AI ships with SCAP Security Guide (SSG) profiles tuned for GPU hosts. Running

```
oscap xccdf eval --profile xccdf_org.ssgproject.content_profile_cis /usr/share/xml/scap/ssg/content/ssg-rhel9-ds.xml
```

produces a NIST-aligned compliance score in both HTML and ARF formats. These evaluations can be orchestrated at scale through the Ansible Automation Platform, which now includes RHEL AI modules for `ilab` operations (see the latest RHEL AI Release Notes). Noncompliant items—such as an open SSH port or an unencrypted swap partition—can be remediated in-place with the same playbook.

All container output funnels through `systemd-journald`, which in turn writes to persistent storage; audit events are tagged with the SELinux context and cgroup path, letting security operations map a rogue process back to a particular training job. The "`ilab system audit`" command (documented in the CLI reference) exports these events in JSON Lines so they can be shipped to Splunk or Elastic via Filebeat. GPU utilization metrics collected by "`nvidia-dcgm-exporter`" or "`rocm-smi`" integrates with Prometheus, closing the loop between resource misuse and security alerts.

The official installation guide prescribes provider-native import workflows that preserve signatures and minimize human error. For AWS operators:

1. Copy the raw image to an S3 bucket owned by their account.
2. Create a least-privilege IAM role (`vmimport`) whose policy allows only `s3:GetObject` and `ec2:CopySnapshot`.
3. Convert the snapshot to an AMI with a single CLI call.

Similar recipes exist for IBM Cloud, GCP, and Azure and can be automated in Terraform. The important takeaway is that the image never traverses an unencrypted channel, and import roles cannot spawn instances—a textbook separation between image provenance and runtime permissions.

CHAPTER 4   ADVANCED FEATURES OF RHEL AI

Multi-tenancy

In many enterprises, multiple data science teams share the same GPU hardware to maximize utilization. Without careful design, this can lead to "noisy neighbor" effects (one workload consuming excessive VRAM or I/O) or unintentional cross-access to models and data. When multiple data science teams share the same hardware, we need a strong separation. RHEL AI supports strong separation for multi-tenant environments through the following:

- Namespace-level cgroup delegation stops a noisy neighbor from exhausting VRAM.

- podman quadlet units run under distinct systemd slices (ai-team-alpha.slice). Quadlet is a tool for running Podman containers under systemd in an optimal way by allowing containers to run under systemd in a declarative way. Quadlet files for non-root users can be placed in the following directories: $XDG_RUNTIME_DIR/containers/systemd.

- IAM roles or OpenShift ServiceAccounts restrict S3 bucket access to one model directory.

Note   The AWS install section showed exactly how to tag the AMI, attach an **instance profile**, and lock the bucket policy to "aws:ResourceTag/Project=rhel-ai" so an EC2 node can pull only its own weights.

Upgrade

The Red Hat AI Updating Guide stresses a dual-lane strategy: update the OS image first, then update models. "ilab model update" performs an in-place replacement but keeps the previous symlink at "models/<name>-PREVIOUS/" for instant rollback. In regulated environments (HIPAA, PCI-DSS), we can require **four-eyes approval** before moving a model from "Staging" to "Prod" by integrating ilab with GitLab Protected Environments.

If things still go wrong, RHEL AI's **kdump integration** captures a compressed vmcore of GPU memory in "/var/crash"—a one-liner in the Release Notes shows how to enable it when booting over NFS. Post-mortem, security teams can

1. Verify the bootc digest in the vmcore matches production
2. Rehydrate checkpoints from object storage to reproduce the run
3. Use the command "`ilab data diff`" to inspect whether poisoned samples entered the taxonomy

Because the entire environment is declared by template—image hash, Kickstart, and Terraform state—teams can replay the incident in a quarantined VPC for root cause analysis.

Security

Security is a process, not a one-time snapshot of a product. Red Hat commits to backporting critical fixes to all supported minor versions and publishing advisory metadata in real time.

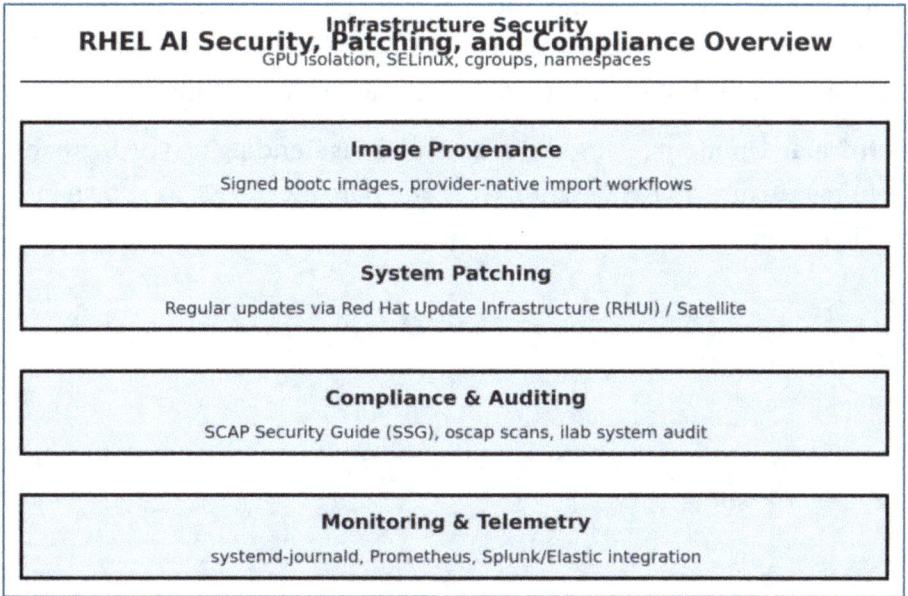

Figure 4-5. *RHEL AI security posture*

Figure 4-5 exemplifies how RHEL AI combines security posture combining

- **Automatic bootc upgrade** in CI once advisories appear.
- **SCAP re-scan** after the upgrade to verify compliance drift is zero.
- **GitOps promotion**: A signed merge triggers model rebuild, container export, and scale-set refresh.

CHAPTER 4   ADVANCED FEATURES OF RHEL AI

The outcome is a robust security pipeline where detection, remediation, and validation are automated processes. AI workloads amplify traditional security risks, as they handle sensitive prompts, incorporate unverified datasets, and necessitate the use of privileged GPU drivers. RHEL AI addresses these challenges through a layered architecture—comprising immutable boot images, SELinux confinement, signed model artifacts, auditable CLI workflows, and enterprise-grade errata. By following the best practices outlined in this article—such as trusted image import, encrypted storage, SCAP automation, z-stream hygiene, and RBAC-driven runtime isolation—organizations can deploy advanced LLMs while ensuring compliance with regulations, satisfying auditors, and maintaining internal confidence.

Ansible Automation

We can leverage Ansible automation to define an inventory and run an end-to-end playbook to provision a GPU instance, bootstrap RHEL AI, and execute the LAB workflow on-premises or in a hybrid cloud. RHEL AI ships with curated Ansible collections that simplify both infrastructure provisioning and model lifecycle operations:

- **infra.ai**: Opinionated modules and roles for standing up GPU-capable infrastructure on AWS, Azure, GCP, and bare metal PXE as shown in Figure 4-6.

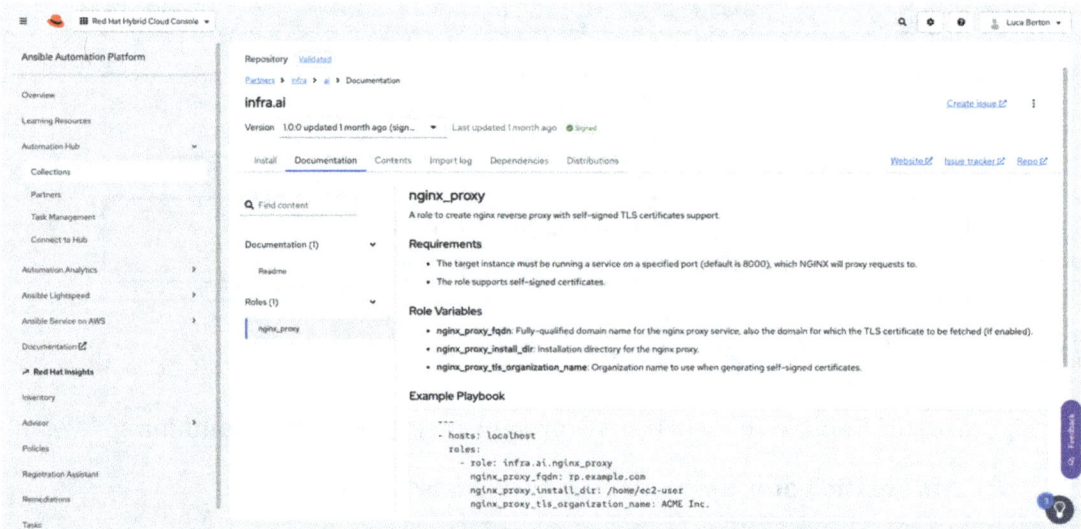

Figure 4-6. Ansible collection infra.ai

CHAPTER 4 ADVANCED FEATURES OF RHEL AI

- ***redhat.ai***: Higher-level roles that wrap the ilab CLI for project bootstrap, data generation, training, serving, and day 2 operations such as bootc upgrade and model rotation, as shown in Figure 4-7.

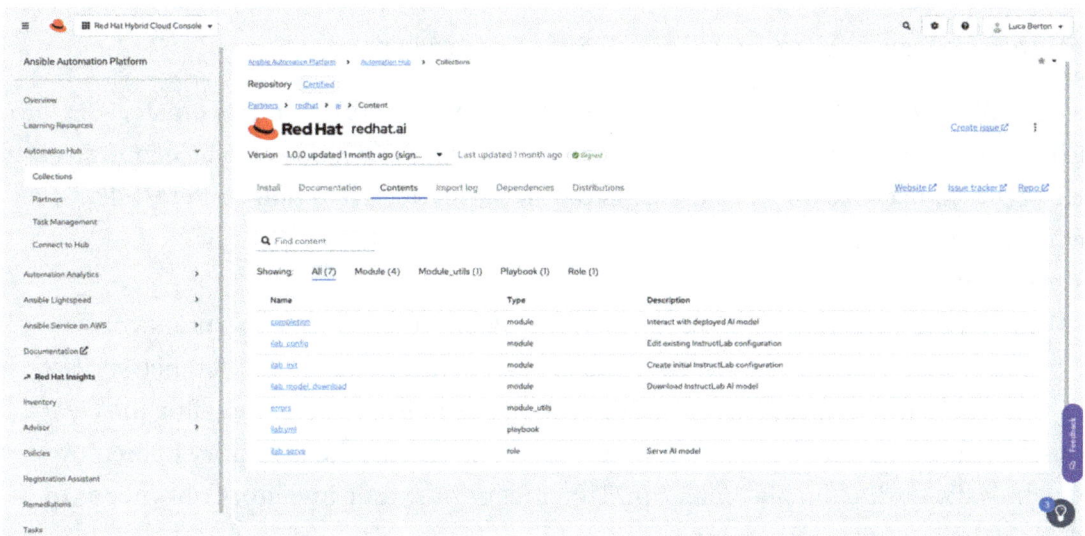

Figure 4-7. *Ansible collection redhat.ai*

The two Ansible collections that matter are listed in Table 4-6.

Table 4-6. *Ansible collections*

Collection	Purpose	Typical Outcome
`infra.ai`	Provisions RHEL AI stacks across AWS, Azure, GCP, and bare metal; attaches the optimal accelerator profile; wires storage and networking.	A fully operational InstructLab cluster (OS, Python 3.11, drivers) delivered in <30 minutes via a single `ansible-playbook bootstrap.yml`.
`redhat.ai`	Orchestrates the higher-level ML lifecycle: pulls Granite or Mixtral models, triggers SDG, kicks off multiphase training, runs MMLU/MT-Bench, and finally serves through vLLM.	One click from "new knowledge YAML committed" to "fine-tuned model exposed on /v1/chat/completions" with metrics uploaded to Grafana.

These collections are accessible through Red Hat's Automation Hub and are included with an Ansible Automation Platform subscription. Access can be gained via an Ansible control node equipped with the `ansible-core` package or through Ansible

Execution Environments (EE). To connect to Red Hat Automation Hub, authenticate using our Automation Hub token ("ansible-galaxy login") and proceed to install the RHEL AI collections. The "ansible-galaxy" command downloads both the collection via CLI:

```
ansible-galaxy collection install infra.ai redhat.ai
```

An AWS, Azure, GCP, *or* on-prem target that we have permission to create/SSH into (the example below uses AWS). A Hugging Face access token needs to be exported as HF_TOKEN, because the "redhat.ai.ilab" role will need it to pull Granite/Mixtral checkpoints, as shown in Figure 4-4.

Inventory Layout

In Ansible, an inventory is simply a list of systems that Ansible can manage. Normally, we would list all of our servers here (e.g., training nodes, inference servers).

However, when using the infra.ai collection, we don't need to predefine the GPU hosts as they are retrieved by AWS directly. Ansible creates the inventory in memory dynamically during the playbook run. That means our static inventory only needs to declare the local control machine:

```
[local]
localhost ansible_connection=local
```

Here's what happens when the playbook runs:

1. Ansible starts on our **control node** (the machine where you run ansible-playbook).

2. The infra.ai role provisions new GPU instances on AWS, Azure, GCP, or bare metal.

3. As soon as each instance is ready, it is **added dynamically** to a group called rhelai.

4. Later tasks in the playbook then target this new rhelai group to install and configure RHEL AI.

This makes automation powerful: from a single YAML file, you can go from no infrastructure at all to a fully trained and serving RHEL AI model. This is the full Ansible code:

Playbook: end-to-end RHEL AI workflow on AWS (file: deploy_rhelai.yml):

```yaml
---
- name: Provision an 8-GPU p5 instance and run the full LAB workflow
  hosts: local
  gather_facts: false
  vars:
    aws_region: us-east-1
    instance_type: p5.48xlarge        # 8×H100, 640 GB VRAM
    key_name: rhelai_key
    ami_id: ami-0123456789abcdef0     # RHEL AI 1.5 AMI we imported
    volume_size: 1024                 # GiB for /dev/sda1
    hf_token: "{{ lookup('env','HF_TOKEN') }}"
  tasks:
    - name: Launch GPU instance
      infra.ai.aws_ec2_instance:
        region: "{{ aws_region }}"
        image_id: "{{ ami_id }}"
        instance_type: "{{ instance_type }}"
        key_name: "{{ key_name }}"
        security_group: rhelai-sg
        wait: true
        volumes:
          - device_name: /dev/sda1
            size: "{{ volume_size }}"
        tags:
          Project: rhel-ai-demo
      register: ec2
    - name: Register new host in inventory
      add_host:
        name: "{{ ec2.instances[0].public_ip }}"
        groups: rhelai
        ansible_user: cloud-user
        ansible_ssh_private_key_file: ~/.ssh/rhelai_key.pem
- name: Configure RHEL AI and train the model
  hosts: rhelai
```

```yaml
  become: true
  roles:
    # Registers the node with subscription-manager, applies latest
      z-stream errata
    - redhat.ai.bootstrap
    # Optional: formats /dev/nvme1n1, labels it ilab-data and
      mounts at /mnt
    - redhat.ai.disk_setup
    # End-to-end LAB workflow (init → download → generate → train
      → serve)
    - role: redhat.ai.ilab
      vars:
        project_dir: /home/cloud-user/my-project
        hf_token:    "{{ hf_token }}"
        teacher_model: mistralai/Mixtral-8x7B-Instruct-v0.1
        student_model: ibm/granite-7b-base
        num_instructions: 5000
        epochs: 10
        serve_port: 8080
```

The playbook accomplishes four important tasks:

1. **Provision GPU Infrastructure**: In this case, an 8×H100 instance on AWS.

2. **Register the New Host Dynamically**: The instance is added to the inventory under the `rhelai` group.

3. **Bootstrap and Configure RHEL AI**: Applying patches, setting up storage, and preparing the node for model work.

4. **Run the LAB Workflow**: Using the `redhat.ai.ilab` role to initialize the project, download models, generate synthetic data, train, and serve.

In Ansible, a **role** is a reusable building block that bundles together tasks, variables, and templates to accomplish a specific goal. Instead of writing long playbooks by hand, you can simply "call" a role and let it handle the details.

CHAPTER 4 ADVANCED FEATURES OF RHEL AI

RHEL AI ships with curated Ansible collections (`infra.ai` and `redhat.ai`) that provide roles designed specifically for GPU infrastructure and the InstructLab workflow. These roles wrap best practices into simple modules, so you don't need to reinvent them.

Below are the key roles from the **redhat.ai collection** and what each one does:

Role	Key Actions
`redhat.ai.bootstrap`	• Registers the node to Red Hat Subscription-Manager • Enables FIPS (optional) • Ensures SELinux is enforcing • Performs an immediate bootc upgrade if errata are available
`redhat.ai.disk_setup`	Implements the official "label = ilab-data, mount → /mnt" recipe to give InstructLab a fast scratch location for datasets and checkpoints.
`redhat.ai.ilab`	Mirrors the CLI steps documented in the Install and CLI guides: "`ilab config init`", model downloads, synthetic data generation, DeepSpeed training, and model serve under a systemd unit.

With roles, complex tasks (like bootstrapping a GPU node, configuring storage, or running InstructLab end-to-end) collapse into a single line in a playbook. This makes our automation declarative, repeatable, and much easier to understand. The following command executes the playbook:

`ansible-playbook -i inventory deploy_rhelai.yml`

This is the typical execution time (might vary based on host and network performance):

- Provisioning + cloud-init: $\approx$ **4 minutes**
- Model downloads (Granite 7B + Mixtral 8×7B): $\approx$ **10–15 minutes,** depending on bandwidth
- SDG (5,000 instructions) + 10-epoch training on 8 × H100: $\approx$ **45–50 minutes** (the same rule-of-thumb published in the docs)

When the play completes, we can curl "`http://<public-ip>:8080/v1/chat/completions`" to interact with our trained model.

Why this matters:

- **Idempotent**: Rerunning the playbook leaves an already-trained node unchanged except for patch drift.

- **Portable**: Switch to Azure or GCP by changing the provisioning task to infra.ai.azure_vm or infra.ai.gcp_instance; everything after the "add_host" task stays the same.

- **Auditable**: Every "redhat.ai.ilab" invocation is logged by Ansible and by SELinux, satisfying the compliance guidance in the Security and Compliance docs.

- **Supported**: Both collections are covered under the same support SLA as the rest of RHEL AI, as specified in the Feature Tracker section of the release notes.

For the next steps, we can integrate the playbook into the AWX/Ansible Automation Platform Controller, allowing our organization's team members to launch it from a streamlined self-service catalog instead of searching for YAML files on GitHub. Once that on-demand workflow is in place, we can enlist Ansible Event-Driven Automation as a watchful sentry: it listens for fresh CVE advisories and, the moment a vulnerable package pops up, automatically kicks off a bootc image upgrade on every affected node—no 2 a.m. patch parties required. And to close the loop, we'll bolt on SCAP roles (ansible.posix.oscap) so that each newly provisioned system generates a compliance report the moment it comes online, providing auditors with the evidence they need without slowing down the pipeline.

By fully automating our project, we achieve the following three outcome-oriented automation patterns:

a. **GitOps for Taxonomy and Playbooks**

   Your domain knowledge (markdown + YAML) and your Ansible roles live side-by-side in a single repository. A push to the main branch immediately triggers SDG and training pipelines through the redhat.ai.model role, guaranteeing that models never drift from the source truth.

b. **Event-Driven GPU Provisioning**

   `infra.ai` playbooks can subscribe to a message bus (e.g., AMQ Streams). When a "training-requested" event arrives, they spin up the cheapest region offering the requested accelerator tier, attach spot instances where tolerated, and tear everything down when the evaluation score is posted.

c. **Declarative MLOps**

   High-level CRDs—in a typical use case, YAML snippets consumed by `redhat.ai.workflow`—declare *intent* ("fine-tune granite-3.1-8b-starter-v2 on telecom-NOC corpus, target MMLU ≥ 78%"). The collection maps that intend to take concrete steps, surface real-time progress, and fail early if benchmarks do not hit the guardrail.

Conclusion

This chapter shows how RHEL AI combines immutable bootable containers with GPU acceleration and DeepSpeed optimizations to enhance model training and inference processes. It elaborates on how RHEL AI facilitates scalable and secure AI pipelines through technologies such as ZeRO-3, MiCS, and vLLM within hybrid and multicloud environments. The chapter emphasizes the importance of cost efficiency, security measures (including SELinux, FIPS, and signed artifacts), and compliance, which can be achieved through automation tools such as Ansible, Terraform, and SCAP. Ultimately, it demonstrates how RHEL AI provides a reproducible, high-performance, and auditable platform suitable for enterprise-scale AI deployment.

In the next chapter, you will learn how to develop and deploy custom AI applications using RHEL AI's end-to-end workflow for model creation, training, evaluation, and serving.

CHAPTER 5

Developing Custom AI Applications

Introduction

This chapter outlines the complete process of developing and deploying a domain-specific AI model using RHEL AI and InstructLab. It demonstrates how to transform business intent into a production-ready large language model through a structured workflow: curate ➤ generate ➤ train ➤ evaluate ➤ serve.

Readers will learn how to curate domain knowledge using YAML-based taxonomies, expand datasets with Synthetic Data Generation (SDG), fine-tune models with multiphase training strategies, and evaluate quality through automated benchmarking. The chapter also introduces model deployment using vLLM, which provides an OpenAI-compatible API for seamless integration into enterprise applications.

By applying these steps, organizations can efficiently develop optimized, auditable, and scalable AI solutions tailored to their operational needs—all within a secure and reproducible RHEL AI environment.

Create a Custom AI Model

First, let's start with a business outcome. Every successful custom LLM starts with a crisp capability statement written in plain language ("Our underwriting team needs the model to classify commercial-property claims into five risk buckets with >90% recall"). Fill out the structured design checklist for shaping a successful custom LLM use case on Table 5-1 to create an AI Design Document Template before opening a terminal.

Table 5-1. AI Design Document Template

Pillar	Key Questions
Domain	What proprietary knowledge or skills differentiate us?
User Journey	How will end users call the model (chat, batch, API, internal tool)?
Latency and Load	Real-time (<1 s) chat? Or nightly batch?
Compliance	Does data ever leave EU borders? Any PII constraints?
Hardware Budget	On-prem NVIDIA A100s vs. cloud MI300X profiles?

Capture those answers in a concise design document for management, as we will choose the right RHEL AI tooling in this section. The following is a fully tailored AI Design Document Template, utilizing Synapse Logistics' fictional logistics insurance company, which reflects real-world enterprise AI adoption patterns.

AI Design Document

This document captures the business and technical intent of Synapse Logistics' AI initiative, before initiating any RHEL AI tooling or model development. It reflects a realistic logistics optimization journey from pilot to production.

1. **Capability Statement**

   "Our Operations Optimization team needs a model that predicts delivery delays across regional hubs with at least **92% recall**, enabling proactive rerouting, optimized resource allocation, and improved customer transparency."

2. **Business Context**

   Company: Synapse Logistics (Fictional)

   Use Case: Modernizing the Delivery Management System (DMS)—a business-critical orchestration layer spanning shipments, fleets, and warehouses.

CHAPTER 5   DEVELOPING CUSTOM AI APPLICATIONS

Business Drivers:

- Reduce average delivery delays by **30%**.
- Optimize truck and driver allocation, reducing fuel costs by **15%**.
- Enhance customer trust through real-time **ETA accuracy >95%**.
- Minimize SLA violations with predictive insights.

Proof of Concept Origin: Initially prototyped on a laptop with RHEL AI's lightweight stack and **InstructLab synthetic data generation**. Now scaling to hybrid-cloud deployment with OpenShift AI MLOps integration.

3. **Design Checklist**

Pillar	Response
Domain	Proprietary logistics history (five years shipment/delay data), IoT fleet telemetry, and third-party weather/traffic APIs.
User Journey	DMS back end invokes the model via API during order intake and dynamically updates ETA dashboards.
Latency and Load	Real-time (<1s) inference for ~25,000 shipments/day, batch predictions for nightly 1M+ records.
Compliance	Customer and location data includes PII and geolocation; must comply with GDPR and US transport regulations.
Hardware Budget	**Training on-prem**: 4× NVIDIA H200 (80GB) + 6 TB NVMe.
	Inference in cloud: AMD MI300X (h200_x2 profile) for scalable throughput.
Integration	Exposed through OpenAI-compatible APIs, orchestrated by Red Hat OpenShift AI GitOps pipelines.

4. **Success Criteria**

Accuracy Goal: ≥92% recall for "delayed vs. on-time" shipment classification.

System SLA: 97% of predictions must return within **750ms** latency.

Business KPI: Delivery delay reduction ≥30% in the first six months of production.

Go-Live Target: Production rollout in Q3 FY2026, integrated into DMS APIs and customer portals.

Operationalization:

- Managed with Red Hat OpenShift AI MLOps pipelines
- Continuous retraining on weekly synthetic + real-world telemetry data using InstructLab
- Lifecycle updates aligned with RHEL AI Full Support Phase

Provision the Right Infrastructure

Right-sizing your AI infrastructure is critical to ensure you allocate just enough resources to meet performance needs without incurring unnecessary cost. Large language models (LLMs) are compute- and memory-intensive, and the requirements vary significantly between training and inference phases. Red Hat recommends starting with a clear understanding of your use case: the size of the model, whether you're performing end-to-end fine-tuning or running inference only, and the desired latency and throughput targets.

Artificial intelligence requires costly hardware; therefore, using it effectively can yield a significant economic return. Table 5-2 showcases a typical resource allocation for the end-to-end fine-tune and inference phases.

Table 5-2. Typical AI infrastructure

Workflow Phase	Minimum Hardware
End-to-end fine-tune	2 × A100 80 GB + 3 TB NVMe
Inference only	1 × L4 **or** 1 × MI300X

Red Hat publishes GPU memory and disk targets for every workflow phase. For typical RHEL AI workflows, end-to-end fine-tuning of a Granite model requires a minimum of 2 × NVIDIA A100 80GB GPUs and 3 TB of NVMe storage. This configuration supports full checkpointing, data shuffling, and multiphase training workflows. On the other hand, inference-only deployments can be run on a single NVIDIA L4 or AMD

MI300X, with the l4_x1 or h200_x1 profile selected during RHEL AI initialization. These profiles offer sufficient compute for low-latency model serving using vLLM's OpenAI-compatible API.

When sizing an environment, consider several factors. Model size directly impacts GPU memory requirements—for example, 7B models typically need at least 40–80GB of GPU memory, while 13B+ models scale up from there. Synthetic Data Generation (SDG), a common pretraining step in RHEL AI, is CPU- and RAM-intensive. For SDG workloads, systems with 32 or more vCPUs and at least 128GB RAM are recommended to ensure efficient parallel generation. For training phases, plan on 2–4× the compute footprint of inference, especially if you plan to run multiple fine-tuning passes.

Latency-sensitive applications, such as real-time claims triage, benefit from co-locating the model-serving process and API interface on the same node. This minimizes I/O bottlenecks and improves response time. Finally, disk I/O is often overlooked—fast NVMe storage is essential not only for saving model checkpoints but also for handling large input datasets. Red Hat also supports Grace Hopper GH200 accelerators in technology preview; if you plan to use these, make sure to add `max_startup_attempts: 1200` to your `config.yaml`.

In summary, scaling RHEL AI infrastructure should align with your model's compute profile, your data pipeline complexity, and your operational goals. Matching the hardware footprint to actual workload demands ensures both performance and cost efficiency.

Bootstrap InstructLab

Before generating synthetic data, fine-tuning, or serving models, the first step is to bootstrap InstructLab. This process sets up the environment, initializes configuration files, and ensures the system correctly detects available hardware accelerators. All commands should be run as a **non-root user** to maintain best practices for security and environment isolation.

Log in as a non-root user and initialize the environment:

```
ilab config init
```

CHAPTER 5 DEVELOPING CUSTOM AI APPLICATIONS

This command detects our system and suggests the appropriate GPU profile and paths. A YAML configuration file, located at ~/.config/instructlab/config.yaml, is created, and a starter taxonomy is provided as shown in Figure 5-1.

```
(venv) [instruct@instructlab instructlab]$ ilab config init
Existing training profiles were found in /home/instruct/.local/share/instructlab/internal/train_configuration/profiles
Do you also want to restore these profiles to the default values? [y/N]:
Welcome to InstructLab CLI. This guide will help you to setup your environment.
Please provide the following values to initiate the environment [press Enter for defaults]:
Path to taxonomy repo [/home/instruct/.local/share/instructlab/taxonomy]: clear
`clear` seems to not exist or is empty. Should I clone https://github.com/instructlab/taxonomy.git for you? [Y/n]: clear
Error: invalid input
`clear` seems to not exist or is empty. Should I clone https://github.com/instructlab/taxonomy.git for you? [Y/n]: y
Cloning https://github.com/instructlab/taxonomy.git...
Path to your model [/home/instruct/.cache/instructlab/models/merlinite-7b-lab-Q4_K_M.gguf]:
Generating `/home/instruct/.config/instructlab/config.yaml`...
Detecting Hardware...
We chose Nvidia 1x L4 as your designated training profile. This is for systems with 24 GB of vRAM.
This profile is the best approximation for your system based off of the amount of vRAM. We modified it to match the number of GPUs you have.
Is this profile correct? [Y/n]: Y
Initialization completed successfully, you're ready to start using `ilab`. Enjoy!
(venv) [instruct@instructlab instructlab]$
```

Figure 5-1. *ilab config init*

We can verify the current configuration for GPU, CPU, and RAM using the command:

`ilab system info`

We can inspect effective parameters using the command:

`ilab config show`

If our accelerator mixes change later, edit the file with the following command:

`ilab config edit`

The command opens our favorite command-line editor, typically Vim. We can customize using the $EDITOR environment variable in our user profile.

Cheatsheet

```
ilab config init   → Bootstrap and create baseline config + taxonomy.
ilab system info   → Validate hardware.
ilab config show   → Inspect config.
ilab config edit   → Adjust config manually.
```

Baseline Model

The baseline model is a pretrained model developed by an organization (such as Red Hat, IBM, Meta, etc.) that we can use as a reference or baseline for our business case. Training a large language model (LLM) from scratch requires massive datasets, extensive computational resources, and considerable engineering effort. Instead, enterprises typically adopt a pretrained model and then adapt it to their domain using fine-tuning or Synthetic Data Generation (SDG). Quantization reduces compute and memory overhead by representing weights with smaller datatypes:

- **float32 → float16**: Halves memory use
- **float32 → int8**: Reduces storage further and speeds up inference

This allows Granite to run more efficiently, even in embedded or constrained environments.

> *Quantization is a technique that reduces the computational and memory costs of running inference by representing weights and activations with low-precision data types, such as 8-bit integers (int8), instead of the usual 32-bit floating-point (float32) data types.*
>
> *Reducing the number of bits means the resulting model requires less memory storage, consumes less energy, and operations like matrix multiplication can be performed much faster with integer arithmetic. It also allows running models on embedded devices, which sometimes only support integer data types.*
>
> *The two most common quantization cases are float32 -> float16 and float 32 -> int8.*

IBM Granite models are designed for this use case, as they are trained on publicly available information and are pre-quantized for optimal performance. IBM's Granite models are designed for this exact scenario, as they are pretrained on broad, publicly available datasets and pre-quantized (optimized to run efficiently on enterprise GPUs/CPUs) and provide a solid foundation for measuring performance gaps and guiding fine-tuning.

RHEL AI implements knowledge distillation, a technique where a larger, more complex neural network (often referred to as the "teacher") is used to train a smaller, more efficient network (the "student"). InstructLab applies the teacher–student paradigm concept. The teacher model refers to the large, general-purpose model (e.g., IBM Granite 7B, Llama, or Mistral). It has already been pretrained on extensive, publicly accessible data. It is utilized to generate synthetic training data or to provide "reference answers." There is no requirement for domain specialization—it serves as a knowledge-rich baseline. The student model is the smaller or fine-tuned model that you aim to adapt to your specific domain, such as logistics operations. It learns from synthetic question-and-answer pairs generated by the teacher. Ultimately, it becomes a production-ready custom large language model, optimized for your particular use case.

Download the IBM Granite 7B model starter or any other open-source model as shown in Figure 5-2 with the command:

```
ilab model download --repository instructlab/granite-7b-lab-GGUF -filename=granite-7b-lab-Q4_K_M.gguf –hf-token $HUGGINGFACE_RO_TOKEN
```

The model is stored in GGUF[1] format, a compressed and efficient file type designed for fast inference on local hardware, especially when using quantized models. The flag `--repository instructlab/granite-7b-lab-GGUF` specifies the Hugging Face model source, while `--filename` defines the local output file name. The `--hf-token` variable authenticates our Hugging Face access on the `https://huggingface.co/` website, as shown in Figure 4-4.

---

[1] https://huggingface.co/docs/hub/en/gguf

CHAPTER 5 DEVELOPING CUSTOM AI APPLICATIONS

Figure 5-2. ilab model download Granite

Granite is Red Hat/IBM's enterprise-grade open-source model, tested with RHEL AI. Once the model has been downloaded, we can serve it locally to test baseline functionality before any fine-tuning or customization. Alternatively, we can download and use the Merlinite 7B model—a fine-tuned, open-weight LLM optimized for use with RHEL AI and vLLM inference servers.

Merlinite-7B and Granite-7B are both 7-billion-parameter open-source large language models developed under the IBM and Red Hat ecosystem, but they serve slightly different purposes within the RHEL AI landscape. Merlinite-7B is derived from Mistral-7B and fine-tuned using the LAB (Large-scale Alignment for ChatBots) method, where a powerful teacher model such as Mixtral-8x7B generates synthetic instruction-response pairs to align the student model. This results in a smaller, more efficient chat-optimized model that performs exceptionally well on instruction-following tasks while maintaining low latency through formats like GGUF and INT4 quantization. Its focus is on interactive workloads—domain chat, task automation, and reasoning—while minimizing compute requirements for on-prem or edge environments.

CHAPTER 5   DEVELOPING CUSTOM AI APPLICATIONS

In contrast, Granite-7B is part of IBM's broader Granite family of enterprise-grade foundation models, designed for general-purpose and regulated environments where transparency, safety, and traceability are critical. Granite models power enterprise AI platforms such as IBM watsonx.ai and RHEL AI, offering strong integration with governance tooling, SPDX lineage, and model provenance tracking. While the base Granite-7B model provides wide language and reasoning coverage, its Granite-7B-lab variant mirrors Merlinite's LAB alignment process to achieve similar instruction-following performance. In practice, Merlinite offers a lightweight, high-speed option for experimentation and edge inference, whereas Granite provides the stable, auditable backbone for production-grade, compliant AI deployments.

In Figure 5-3, we can see the model downloading to the user's local cache directory (`~/.cache/instructlab/models`), reaching 61% completion of a 4.37 GB file.

Figure 5-3. ilab model download Merlinite

CHAPTER 5   DEVELOPING CUSTOM AI APPLICATIONS

The following command launches Granite with vLLM—the high-performance inference runtime included with RHEL AI:

```
ilab model serve --model-path ~/.cache/instructlab/models/granite-7b-lab--Q4_K_M.gguf
```

This tells the `ilab` CLI to

1. Load the Granite-7B model (a 7-billion parameter variant) from the local cache.
2. Start the vLLM inference server, a highly optimized runtime that serves LLMs using efficient memory management, dynamic batching, and fast token streaming.
3. Expose a REST API interface and an interactive shell for testing.

When you see the message:

```
Starting server process ... see http://127.0.0.1:8000/docs
```

...it means the Granite model is now successfully running and accessible at `http://127.0.0.1:8000`, where `/docs` provides a Swagger-style API page. From here, you can interact with the model using REST calls, test chat prompts, or integrate it directly into your applications via the standard OpenAI-compatible API that vLLM implements.

The system features a REST interface, along with an interactive shell, as illustrated in Figure 5-4.

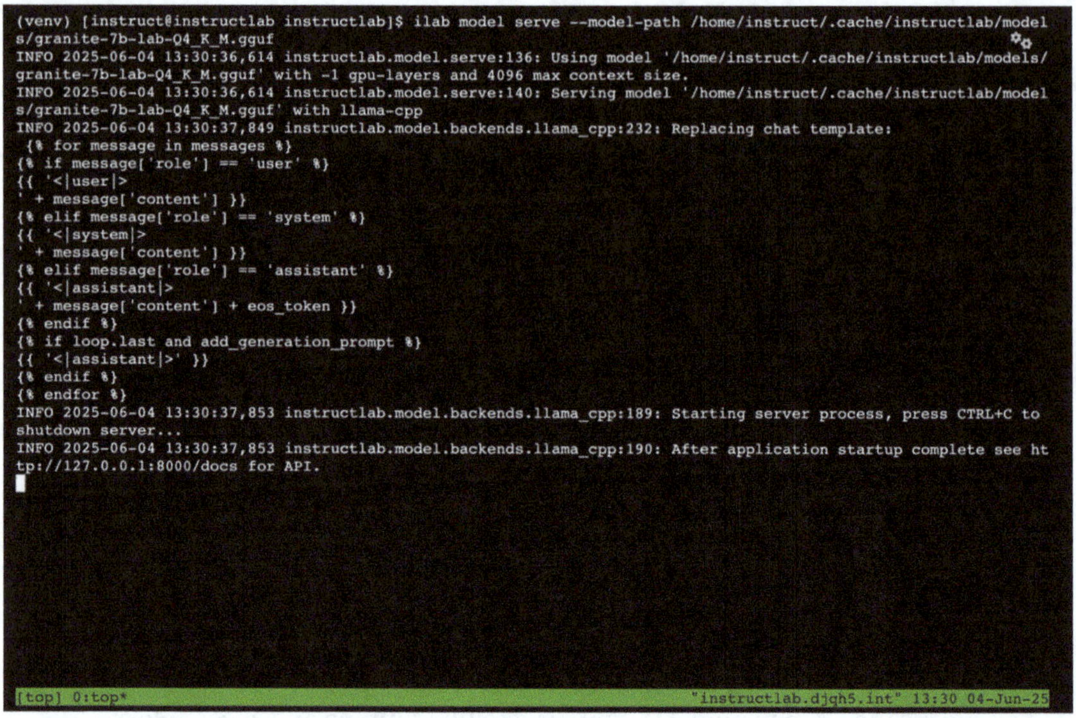

CHAPTER 5　DEVELOPING CUSTOM AI APPLICATIONS

Figure 5-4. *ilab model serve*

Now that the Granite model is running in inference mode, the next step is to interact with it directly to understand its baseline behavior. This is an important part of the RHEL AI workflow—it helps you measure how the model performs *before* you begin any fine-tuning or domain adaptation. By observing its responses now, you can later quantify the improvements that your training pipeline delivers.

Open a second terminal and run:

```
ilab model chat --model ~/.cache/instructlab/models/granite-7b-lab--Q4_K_M.gguf
```

This command connects to the Granite model you just served through vLLM and opens an interactive chat shell. We can type natural-language questions and receive real-time responses directly from the model. At this stage, you should ask a few domain-specific questions—for example, if your use case involves logistics, try questions such as

```
What is OpenShift in 20 words or less?
```

CHAPTER 5 DEVELOPING CUSTOM AI APPLICATIONS

The goal is not to expect perfect answers yet but rather to measure the gap between Granite's general-purpose knowledge and your organization's specific domain language or expertise. Take note of any hallucinations (incorrect or overly confident statements), tone mismatches, or missing context in the model's replies. These observations will serve as baseline regression tests—a reference point to compare against once you fine-tune the model with your own taxonomy or synthetic data.

Figure 5-5 illustrates an example of this interactive chat session, showing how Granite responds to a domain question and how to interpret early performance.

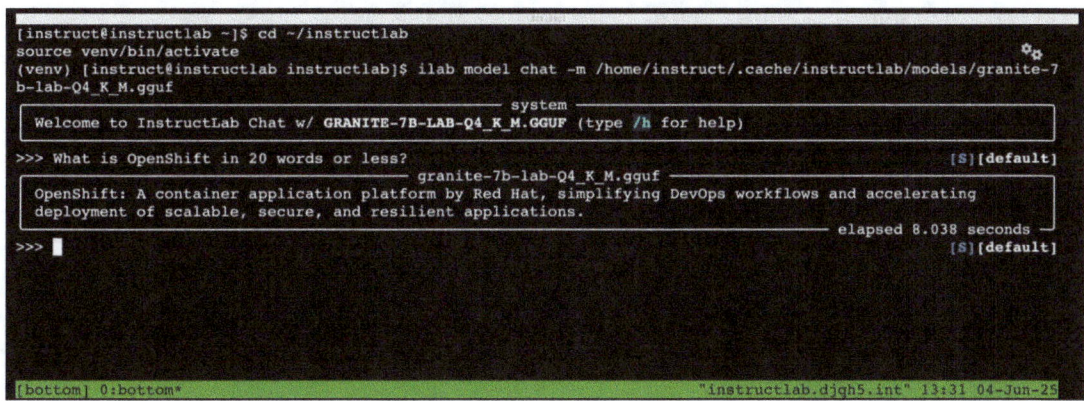

Figure 5-5. *ilab model chat granite*

Curate Domain Knowledge (Taxonomy)

Before fine-tuning a model in RHEL AI, it's essential first to understand *what* knowledge the model already knows—and *where* it falls short. By serving the baseline IBM Granite model and posing domain-specific questions (e.g., "Why would a shipment from Rotterdam to Munich be delayed in winter?"). We can quickly spot strengths, gaps, and hallucinations in our model's understanding. This initial exploration defines the road map for fine-tuning: the goal isn't to retrain everything but to surgically teach the model what it doesn't yet know about our business domain. RHEL AI organizes this knowledge curation step using a taxonomy-based structure, designed for transparency and collaboration. All new domain knowledge lives under a taxonomy folder that mirrors your organization's knowledge areas, following this path pattern:

taxonomy/<domain>/<topic>/qna.yaml

Each `qna.yaml` file is a compact, human-readable dataset that contains both context and question-answer (Q/A) pairs. This format is intentionally simple, allowing subject matter experts—not just data scientists—to contribute content safely and reproducibly. A typical file might look like this, as shown in Figure 5-6:

```
context: >
  Internal underwriting guidelines for commercial fire coverage in
  multi-tenant
  industrial buildings. These rules align with ISO fire safety
  standards and
  must be applied to all inspections.
qnas:
  - question: "When must a sprinkler inspection be recorded?"
    answer: "Within 24 hours according to section 4.3."
  - question: "What documentation must accompany a failed fire inspection?"
    answer: "The incident report and insurer notification form."
  - question: "Who authorizes the reopening of a closed property after
    inspection?"
    answer: "A licensed fire safety officer or equivalent authority."
```

The context field sets the scene—it provides background information the model should use when interpreting the Q/A pairs. Each Q/A pair then represents a distinct piece of factual or procedural knowledge that you want the model to internalize during fine-tuning. Best practices include

- Keeping each question-and-answer pair under 250 words for clarity and efficient tokenization

- Supplying at least three Q/A pairs per topic, which gives the fine-tuning process enough examples to learn consistent patterns

- Writing questions in natural language that reflect how real users might ask them

CHAPTER 5 DEVELOPING CUSTOM AI APPLICATIONS

```
(venv) [instruct@instructlab instructlab]$ mkdir -p /home/instruct/.local/share/instructlab/taxonomy/knowledge/i
nstructlab/overview
(venv) [instruct@instructlab instructlab]$ cp -av ~/files/instructlab_knowledge/qna.yaml /home/instruct/.local/s
hare/instructlab/taxonomy/knowledge/instructlab/overview
'/home/instruct/files/instructlab_knowledge/qna.yaml' -> '/home/instruct/.local/share/instructlab/taxonomy/knowl
edge/instructlab/overview/qna.yaml'
(venv) [instruct@instructlab instructlab]$ head /home/instruct/.local/share/instructlab/taxonomy/knowledge/instr
uctlab/overview/qna.yaml
---
version: 3
created_by: instructlab-team
domain: instructlab
seed_examples:
  - context: |
      InstructLab is a model-agnostic open source AI project that facilitates
      contributions to Large Language Models (LLMs).
      We are on a mission to let anyone shape generative
      AI by enabling contributed updates to existing
(venv) [instruct@instructlab instructlab]$
```

Figure 5-6. *qna.yaml*

During fine-tuning, RHEL AI's InstructLab reads all `qna.yaml` files in our taxonomy to generate synthetic instruction data, which trains a custom model for specific domains, such as logistics, insurance, or safety standards. The `qna.yaml` file bridges our expertise and the model's understanding. Maintaining these files, such as source code, allows for continuous, structured updates to our model's knowledge without requiring a complete restart. We can validate the file using the following command:

`ilab taxonomy diff`

When the file is syntactically correct, the expected output on the screen is as shown in Figure 5-7:

`Taxonomy is clear and valid :)`

Figure 5-7. *ilab taxonomy diff valid*

If any errors are present in the file, the validation fails, and we must manually correct them before proceeding to the next step.

We can organize our taxonomy as a tree, as shown in Figure 5-8.

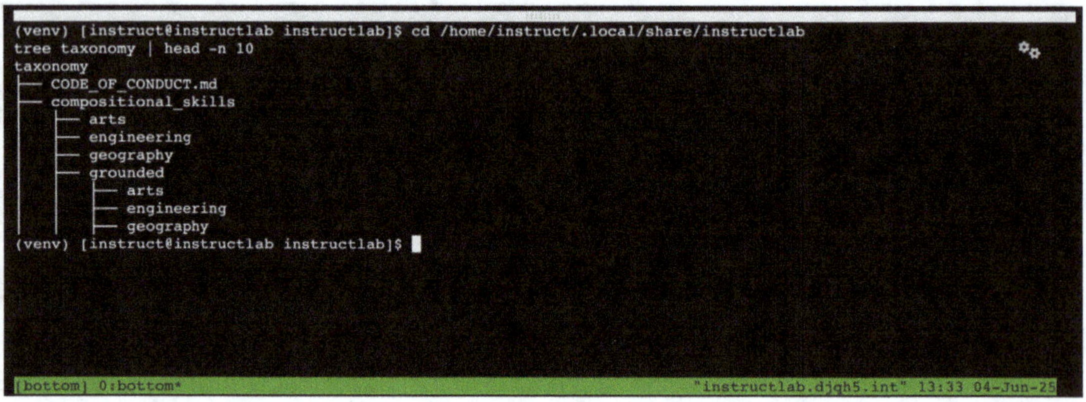

CHAPTER 5   DEVELOPING CUSTOM AI APPLICATIONS

```
(venv) [instruct@instructlab instructlab]$ cd /home/instruct/.local/share/instructlab
tree taxonomy | head -n 10
taxonomy
├── CODE_OF_CONDUCT.md
├── compositional_skills
│   ├── arts
│   ├── engineering
│   ├── geography
│   ├── grounded
│   │   ├── arts
│   │   ├── engineering
│   │   └── geography
(venv) [instruct@instructlab instructlab]$
```

Figure 5-8. Taxonomy tree

Synthetic Data Generation (SDG)

Synthetic Data Generation (SDG) is a powerful feature in RHEL AI that automatically expands our dataset by creating high-quality, AI-generated training examples. Using a teacher model like `Mixtral-8x7B`, SDG synthesizes realistic knowledge and skill entries that enhance model performance while reducing manual data engineering effort. Instead of manually writing thousands of Q&A or skill-based entries, SDG uses a teacher model—such as IBM Granite or Mixtral-8x7B—to create high-quality, realistic training data. This synthetic data is then used to train your own "student" model, improving its accuracy and reasoning without extensive human effort. For example, in a logistics domain, SDG can automatically generate realistic Q&A pairs about topics like shipping delays, customs clearance, or warehouse routing based on a few seed examples you provide in your taxonomy directory.

Step 1: Run Synthetic Data Generation

SDG multiplies our seed data via a **teacher model** (Mixtral-8×7B by default) and filters for quality. Granite is used as the teacher model to generate synthetic Q&A pairs in our logistics taxonomy (delays, routing, customs, etc.). These become the training set for our student model.

```
ilab data generate \
    --taxonomy-path ~/.local/share/instructlab/taxonomy \
    --gpus 2 \
    --sdg-scale-factor 30 \
    --enable-serving-output
```

Let's break this down line by line:

- `ilab data generate`: This is the core command that launches the Synthetic Data Generation workflow. It reads our domain Q&A seeds (from `taxonomy/<domain>/<topic>/qna.yaml`) and uses a teacher model to generate new examples.

- `--taxonomy-path ~/.local/share/instructlab/taxonomy`: Points to the folder where your taxonomy and `qna.yaml` files are stored. This is the knowledge base SDG will expand.

- `--gpus 2`: Specifies that SDG should use two GPUs for generation. You can adjust this based on available hardware.

- `--sdg-scale-factor 30`: Multiplies our dataset size by 30×. If your taxonomy had 100 Q&A examples, the generated dataset would contain around 3,000 enriched examples.

- `--enable-serving-output`: Prepares the output data in a format ready for model training and serving, storing the results in a structured directory under your user data folder.

Once the process begins, we will see vLLM spin up, perform the generation, and log progress as it creates and scores your new data. When finished, SDG produces two key output files saved to ~/.local/share/instructlab/datasets/<timestamp>/ each with a timestamp in the filename:

- **Knowledge Messages**: Factual or declarative information—`knowledge_train_msgs_<timestamp>.jsonl`

- **Skill Messages**: Instructional or procedural examples—`skills_train_msgs_<timestamp>.jsonl`

The data can be displayed on the screen as shown in Figure 5-9.

Figure 5-9. *SDG documents*

Step 2: Use a Higher-Quality Teacher Model (Optional)

For tasks that require higher accuracy, more nuanced reasoning, or advanced domain understanding, you may need to go beyond the default SDG teacher model. In these cases, using a premium-quality teacher model can make a significant difference in the quality of your generated data—and ultimately, the performance of your fine-tuned LLM. The tech-preview `llama-3.3-70B-Instruct` model is currently the state-of-the-art instruction-tuned LLM with a much larger parameter count (70B compared to Granite 7B), making it ideal for generating more contextually accurate, sophisticated, and diverse training examples.

When we need premium quality, try the tech-preview llama-3.3-70B-Instruct as teacher:

```
ilab model download --repository docker://registry.redhat.io/rhelai1/llama-3.3-70b-Instruct
ilab data generate --pipeline llama
```

The first command downloads the model into your local cache, and the second command tells ilab to use that model as the teacher for SDG instead of the default.

Step 3: Train Our Model Using the Generated Data

Once your synthetic data has been generated using SDG, the next step is to train a model using that data. The ilab CLI supports a multiphase training strategy that separates knowledge-based training from skill-based training for better model convergence.

This strategy involves

- **Phase 1—Knowledge Training**: Training the model on knowledge messages (factual or declarative content)

- **Phase 2—Skill Training**: Training the model on skill messages (procedural or instructional content)

- **Checkpoints**: Automatically saved between and during phases, with evaluation metrics captured

Each SDG run creates a timestamped directory, which you'll use to tell RHEL AI which data to train on. Start by exporting that timestamp as an environment variable:

```
export GEN_DATE=2025-11-28_101530
```

This ensures the next command can find the correct data files automatically.

Now run the fine-tuning process:

```
ilab model train --strategy lab-multiphase --phased-phase1-data ~/.local/share/instructlab/datasets/$GEN_DATE/knowledge_train_msgs_*.jsonl --phased-phase2-data ~/.local/share/instructlab/datasets/$GEN_DATE/skills_train_msgs_*.jsonl --enable-serving-output
```

Here's what each flag does:

- `--strategy lab-multiphase`: Enables InstructLab's two-stage fine-tuning method (knowledge first, skills second)

- `--phased-phase1-data`: Tells the trainer where to find the knowledge dataset

- `--phased-phase2-data`: Points to the skill dataset

- `--enable-serving-output`: Prepares the trained model for deployment once training completes

CHAPTER 5   DEVELOPING CUSTOM AI APPLICATIONS

While the console displays detailed logs, we can safely ignore most of the verbose output unless you're debugging a failed run, as shown in Figure 5-10.

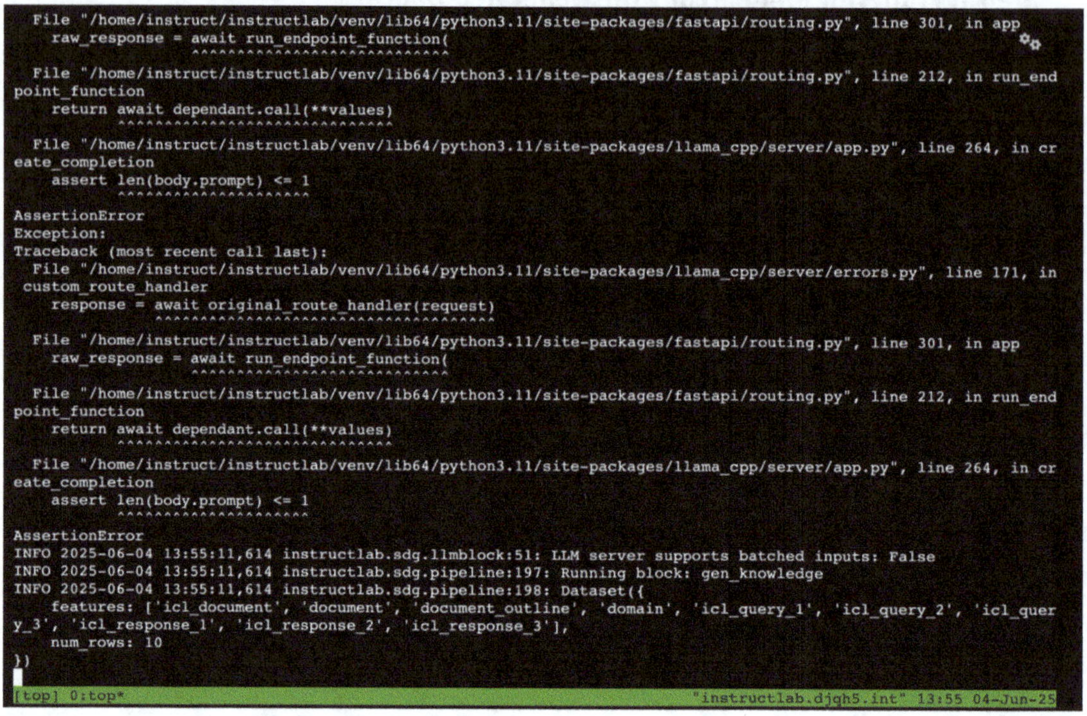

Figure 5-10.   ilab model train

During training, we will see logs streamed to your console:

- Epoch-by-epoch progress updates
- Checkpoints being saved automatically
- Evaluation metrics like loss and accuracy

When the process finishes, RHEL AI reports the best-scoring checkpoint—the model version that performed best during validation. Note its path; you'll need it for serving your model.

Note   If interrupted, we resume with --continue-from <checkpoint_dir>; detailed options are in the CLI reference under **ilab model train**.

Step 4: Completion and Next Steps

When training completes successfully, we will see a message similar to

```
Model training complete.
Best checkpoint saved to: ~/.cache/instructlab/models/granite-7b-lab-finetuned-v1
Total time elapsed: 64.27 seconds
```

Figure 5-11 shows what a completed training run looks like.

You can now serve your model using

```
ilab model serve --model-path ~/.cache/instructlab/models/granite-7b-lab-finetuned-v1
```

The SDG workflow allows us to scale our dataset exponentially while maintaining quality control and traceability. Using `ilab data generate` and `ilab model train` together, we can move from domain Q&A files to a fully fine-tuned model—all within the RHEL AI environment and without writing a single training script.

Figure 5-11. Model generation complete

CHAPTER 5   DEVELOPING CUSTOM AI APPLICATIONS

Serving, Chatting, and Integrating

Once we have trained and evaluated our fine-tuned model, the next step is to serve it so that we (and our applications) can interact with it. In RHEL AI, serving means deploying our trained model into an inference engine—powered by vLLM—that listens for input requests and returns text responses, just like ChatGPT does. RHEL AI makes this simple using the `ilab model serve` command to serve our fine-tuned asset:

```
ilab model serve --model-path ~/.local/share/instructlab/phased/phase2/checkpoints/hf_format/best/
```

What this does:

- Launches vLLM, the high-performance inference engine used in RHEL AI
- Loads your fine-tuned model from the specified --model-path directory (in this case, your best checkpoint)
- Starts a local web service—usually at http://127.0.0.1:8000—that exposes a REST API compatible with OpenAI's format

Once launched, your terminal will display logs similar to this:

```
INFO:     Started server process [12345]
INFO:     Waiting for application startup.
INFO:     Application startup complete.
INFO:     Uvicorn running on http://127.0.0.1:8000 (Press CTRL+C to quit)
```

Chat as before, or hit the REST API:

```
curl -X POST http://127.0.0.1:8000/v1/chat/completions \
    -H "Content-Type: application/json" \
    -d '{
        "model": "best",
        "messages":[{"role":"user","content":"Summarise claim
        2025-123 in 50 words"}]
    }'
```

Because vLLM speaks OpenAI-compatible JSON, we swap ChatGPT SDKs with a single endpoint change.

CHAPTER 5 DEVELOPING CUSTOM AI APPLICATIONS

Evaluating the quality of the generated model is crucial in determining how to proceed with accepting or rejecting the produced output. We run automated benchmarks to prove value:

```
ilab model evaluate --benchmark mmlu_branch    --model <checkpoint>
ilab model evaluate --benchmark mt_bench_branch --model <checkpoint>
```

For domain QA, we supply our own JSONL:

```
ilab model evaluate --benchmark dk_bench --input-questions /path/questions.jsonl --model <checkpoint>
```

The tool prints per-question scores and an average, making it ideal for gatekeeping in Continuous Integration/Continuous Deployment (CI/CD).

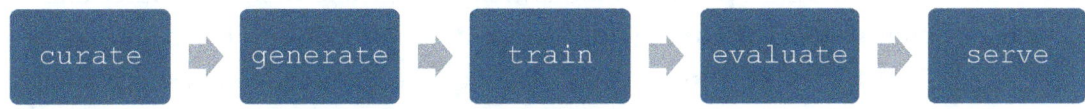

Figure 5-12. InstructLab workflow

With RHEL AI and InstructLab, we move from idea to domain-specific LLM in a single day without proprietary tooling. The workflow—curate ➤ generate ➤ train ➤ evaluate ➤ serve—is opinionated yet flexible, as shown in Figure 5-12. Every step is scripted through the ilab CLI we walked through:

Command	Area
ilab config init	Environment
ilab data generate	Synthetic data
ilab model train	Multiphase fine-tune
ilab model evaluate	Objective QA
ilab model serve	Deployment

By grounding our process in business intent, storing knowledge in plain YAML, and automating the pipeline, we deliver custom AI applications that are maintainable, auditable, and—most importantly—useful.

CHAPTER 5   DEVELOPING CUSTOM AI APPLICATIONS

Extend RHEL AI with Third-Party Libraries and Tools

RHEL AI provides a robust, enterprise-grade foundation for deploying and utilizing large language models. However, organizations frequently require the extension of their functionalities through supplementary libraries and frameworks, as outlined in Table 5-3. Such enhancements serve to address functional deficiencies, boost performance, and tailor AI workflows to specific business needs.

For instance, incorporating retrieval-augmented generation (RAG) frameworks, such as Chroma, facilitates sub-second vector searches and enhances recall. This enables models to base their responses on proprietary organizational knowledge rather than relying exclusively on pretraining data. If you're looking for alternatives to ChromaDB,[2] what you really need are other vector databases that can store and query embeddings efficiently. Some of the most popular options include Weaviate,[3] an open-source and production-ready system with strong hybrid search (vector + keyword) capabilities and a thriving ecosystem; Pinecone, a fully managed service that offers easy scalability, simple APIs, and a pay-as-you-go model; Milvus, one of the most widely adopted open-source vector databases known for high performance and supported by the Zilliz ecosystem; Qdrant, a Rust-based open-source solution built with a strong focus on speed and reliability; and Vespa, a platform originally from Yahoo that supports large-scale search by combining vector and keyword retrieval. These alternatives vary in deployment model, performance characteristics, and ecosystem maturity, so the best choice depends on whether you prioritize ease of use, scalability, or flexibility. PostgreSQL has expanded its reach to contemporary artificial intelligence and data management applications, thanks to its extensibility. The pgvector extension enables developers to store embeddings and conduct similarity searches directly within Postgres, thereby making it a preferred option for small- to medium-scale retrieval-augmented generation (RAG) systems that also require robust relational querying capabilities. Furthermore, recent initiatives such as DocumentDB[4]—an open-source, PostgreSQL-based document database now overseen by the Linux Foundation—expand Postgres's functionality with enhanced JSON/BSON support and document-oriented query capabilities while maintaining full compatibility with MongoDB drivers and tools. Consequently, teams are able to utilize Postgres not only for vector search but also as a

---

[2] https://www.trychroma.com
[3] https://weaviate.io
[4] https://documentdb.io

versatile document database, amalgamating the dependability of a relational database engine with the adaptability of NoSQL, alongside the expanding artificial intelligence ecosystem associated with Postgres. Should there be an interest in exploring alternative model families, including Llama 3 or DeepSeek, integration with these libraries ensures comprehensive coverage across various languages and reasoning capabilities, thereby providing flexibility in selecting the most suitable foundation for a given domain.

In scenarios where operational efficiency is paramount, tools such as Ollama allow for the execution of lightweight models locally using the same OpenAI-compatible interface as vLLM. For large-scale training endeavors, distributed optimization frameworks like DeepSpeed ZeRO-3 or Fully Sharded Data Parallel (FSDP) facilitate training with larger batch sizes and reduce GPU memory consumption, supporting cost-effective scaling over multiple GPUs or mixed-vendor configurations.

Beyond core AI workloads, extensions are instrumental in enhancing operational productivity. The Ansible Automation Platform enables the construction of reproducible pipelines that seamlessly transition from fine-tuning through evaluation and deployment. In cases involving multi-agent orchestration, frameworks such as crewAI offer structured solutions, including planner–writer–checker "crews," to manage complex workflows. Additionally, tools like RamaLama streamline artifact packaging and distribution, while Kickstart with custom boot configurations provides image-level control for monitoring, CUDA updates, and open-source driver management.

Lastly, for organizations adopting public cloud deployment strategies, provider CLIs for AWS, Azure, GCP, or IBM Cloud facilitate the replication of the same RHEL AI bootable container image across various environments. This approach guarantees consistency and portability, regardless of the execution environment of the workloads.

To integrate RHEL AI, n8n,[5] Ansible, LangChain,[6] and RamaLama,[7] we can consider them as complementary layers within a unified pipeline: Ansible provisions and configures the GPU-enhanced infrastructure on RHEL AI, ensuring reproducible environments for training and deployment; RamaLama packages and distributes finely tuned models as portable artifacts; RHEL AI subsequently deploys these models reliably in production; LangChain offers the orchestration logic for utilizing these models in applications, such as retrieval-augmented generation or agent workflows; and ultimately, n8n connects these AI workflows to the broader enterprise ecosystem

---

[5] https://n8n.io
[6] https://www.langchain.com
[7] https://ramalama.ai

CHAPTER 5   DEVELOPING CUSTOM AI APPLICATIONS

by automating triggers and integrations across CRMs, chat systems, and business applications. Collectively, they establish a cohesive stack where infrastructure, model lifecycle management, AI reasoning, and business process automation are seamlessly integrated.

Table 5-3. Third-party libraries and tools

Gap	Tool	Outcome
Retrieval-Augmented Generation (RAG)	ChromaDB, Weaviate, Pinecone, Milvus, Qdrant, Vespa, DocumentDB	Sub-second vector search and MMR recall
Alternative Model Families	Llama 3-70B, DeepSeek-R1-72B	Different language coverage, stronger reasoning
Feather-Weight Local Serving	Ollama	GGUF runner with the same OpenAI JSON as vLLM
Multi-GPU or Mixed-Vendor Training	DeepSpeed ZeRO-3, FSDP	bigger batch sizes, lower VRAM use
Pipeline Automation	Ansible Automation Platform, n8n, LangChain	reproducible fine-tune ➤ evaluate ➤ deploy
Multi-agent Coordination	crewAI	"planner–writer–checker" crews for complex tasks
Artifact Packaging and Shipping	RamaLama	ramalama run
Image-Level Customizations	Kickstart + bootc	custom monitoring, CUDA 12.x, OSS drivers
Public-Cloud Rollout	Provider CLIs (AWS, Azure, GCP, IBM Cloud)	same bootable image everywhere

RHEL AI runs inside a bootc immutable container image, which means the base system cannot be altered directly. This design ensures stability, consistency, and repeatability across environments—but it also means you cannot simply `pip install` new Python packages into the system image itself.

All of these extensions can be layered onto RHEL AI without modifying its immutable bootc base image. Instead, they are treated as user-level dependencies, typically installed in a virtual environment that persists across upgrades.

To extend RHEL AI with additional libraries, we treat those extra Python wheels as user data, layered on top of the immutable base. The best practice is to create a virtual environment (venv) in your user space. This keeps your custom libraries separate from the system and ensures they persist across upgrades or image switches.

Here's how to set up a dedicated `venv` for our AI applications:

```
python -m venv ~/venvs/aiapps
source ~/venvs/aiapps/bin/activate
pip install --upgrade pip wheel
pip install langchain chromadb gradio crewai fastapi uvicorn
```

Our venv survives `bootc upgrade`, `ilab model download --update`, and even a full image switch.

With this environment, you can install third-party tools like LangChain, ChromaDB, Gradio, or crewAI to extend your workflows with retrieval-augmented generation, web-based interfaces, multi-agent coordination, and more—all without touching the base image.

If you have additional storage available, such as an SDD or NVMe device mounted at /mnt, you can persist your InstructLab data and models by redirecting the home directory for InstructLab (`ILAB_HOME`) to that mount:

Mounting a spare NVMe at /mnt? Persist *everything*:

```
echo 'export ILAB_HOME=/mnt' >> ~/.bash_profile
```

This approach ensures that your models, configurations, and virtual environments remain intact—even if you

- Perform a bootc upgrade
- Run `ilab model download --update`
- Switch to a completely new RHEL AI bootc image

In summary, while the fundamental image remains unaltered to ensure consistency and security, your extensions and libraries retain their flexibility, portability, and complete control. By integrating the robustness of RHEL AI with meticulously selected third-party libraries, enterprises achieve enhanced flexibility, efficiency, and adaptability—thereby enabling them to customize AI environments to meet their specific operational requirements, all while benefiting from Red Hat's enterprise-grade support and lifecycle assurances.

CHAPTER 5 DEVELOPING CUSTOM AI APPLICATIONS

Conclusion

This chapter delineates the complete lifecycle for developing a domain-specific LLM utilizing RHEL AI and InstructLab. It systematically covers the structured workflow—curate, generate, train, evaluate, and serve—illustrating the process of translating a business objective into a deployable AI model. The chapter introduces various tools such as YAML taxonomies, Synthetic Data Generation (SDG), multiphase training, automated evaluation, and vLLM-based serving. It also presents a real-world case study (Synapse Logistics) that exemplifies how to document business goals, infrastructure requirements, and success criteria prior to commencing development.

In the next chapter, you will learn how to monitor, maintain, and optimize RHEL AI systems through observability metrics, automated recovery, and performance monitoring.

CHAPTER 6

Monitoring and Maintenance

Introduction

Let us examine the telemetry associated with an AI solution, which converts raw data into meaningful Service-Level Objectives (SLOs) and proactive rollback scripts that identify issues before they impact users. I will guide you through how RPO/RTO budgets define clear boundaries for each component—and how boot images, geo-replicated Quay registries, and GitOps automation assist in preemptive problem resolution with minimal delay. This approach aims to transition from midnight emergencies to seamless confidence.

The essential point? Metrics are reliable and continuously vigilant. Incorporate detailed telemetry across every layer, automate the fail-back procedures, and that 3 a.m. pager disturbance becomes merely background noise. When your dashboards subtly indicate necessary actions, you will already know how to address them—while your coffee remains warm and your system continues to function efficiently and consistently.

Observability

In AI systems, observability is crucial, as it ensures the reliable performance of both models and the underlying infrastructure over time. The RHEL AI evaluates the workflow and integrates multiple evaluation metrics, notably BLEU and BERTScore. While both metrics are extensively employed in natural language processing (NLP), they serve distinct functions and complement each other within production workflows.

BLEU (Bilingual Evaluation Understudy)

BLEU is one of the oldest and most widely used automatic metrics for text generation. Initially developed for machine translation, it compares the overlap of n-grams (sequences of words) between a model's output and one or more reference texts.

- **How It Works**
    - Split both candidate and reference sentences into tokens.
    - Count how many n-grams match between them (for n = 1, 2, 3, 4).
    - Apply a brevity penalty if the candidate is much shorter than the reference.

- **Why It Matters in RHEL AI**

    BLEU is fast, interpretable, and works well when the target text has rigid structures, such as compliance rules, JSON responses, or command-line outputs. For example, if fine-tuning a Granite model to produce JSON responses, BLEU can reveal whether the model consistently reproduces expected keys and structures.

- **Limitations**

    BLEU struggles with synonyms and semantic similarity. Two sentences with identical meaning but different word choices may score poorly.

BERTScore

BERTScore, introduced much later, uses contextual embeddings from transformer models (e.g., BERT, RoBERTa, or more recently, DeBERTa) to evaluate similarity between candidate and reference texts. Instead of n-gram matches, it computes cosine similarity between the embeddings of each token.

- **How It Works**
    - Encode candidate and reference sentences using a pretrained BERT-like model.

- Align tokens based on maximum similarity.
- Compute precision, recall, and F1 from these alignment scores.

- **Why It Matters in RHEL AI**

    BERTScore captures semantic equivalence. This makes it ideal for domains where wording can vary but meaning is critical—for example, summarizing fire safety procedures or answering HR policy questions.

- **Limitations**

    BERTScore requires heavier computation than BLEU and depends on the quality of the chosen embedding model.

In practice, RHEL AI workflows often utilize both metrics together: BLEU for format fidelity, which checks that generated outputs match the expected syntax (e.g., JSON, SQL, command responses), and BERTScore for semantic quality, which verifies that the generated text conveys the correct meaning, even if the word choice differs. This is the reason why forthcoming releases of RHEL AI might transition toward integrated attribution pipelines: metrics such as BLEU and BERTScore will not be appended as afterthoughts. Still, it will operate automatically within the ilab model evaluation phase. For example:

```
ilab model evaluate \
  --metrics bleu,bertscore \
  --dataset eval/fire_safety_test.yaml
```

The combination yields a balanced view of model performance, with one metric based on surface overlap and the other on deep semantic similarity.

BLEU and BERTScore are effective metrics for evaluating quality before entering the production phase. For large-language-model operations on RHEL AI, we think about observability in terms of two execution planes that move at different speeds:

- **The Infrastructure Lifecycle**: The underlying RHEL AI image-mode nodes evolve more slowly (days to weeks) through updates like bootc image switches, firmware patches, or driver upgrades. Failures here may show up as GPU memory errors, SELinux denials, or compatibility gaps.

- **The Model Lifecycle**: Models run in production inside the Red Hat AI Inference Server or Red Hat OpenShift AI and may be swapped in or out frequently (hours to days) as part of testing or A/B deployments. Common failure signals include rising latency, KV-cache exhaustion, or accuracy drift.

To monitor effectively, both planes must be tracked together as listed in Table 6-1. If the observability fabric only watches the model layer. Still, not the host, we risk a mismatch—for example, rolling back a model without noticing a recent CUDA driver change that actually caused the performance degradation.

Table 6-1. *LLMs execution planes*

Execution Plane	Primary Runtime	Typical Cadence	"Broken" Smells
Model Lifecycle	vLLM inside Red Hat AI Inference Server	Hours–days (hot-swap, A/B)	P95 > 80 ms, KV-cache OOM, accuracy drift
Infrastructure Lifecycle	RHEL AI image-mode nodes	Days–weeks (bootc switch)	GPU ECC bursts, SELinux AVCs, firmware gap

Evaluating large language models isn't just about latency or GPU utilization—it's also about measuring output quality.

When running large language models (LLMs) in production with RHEL AI, monitoring performance is critical. Simple averages (like mean latency) are not enough to capture user experience or detect early regressions. Instead, organizations rely on a combination of latency percentiles and throughput metrics that reflect both tail performance and system capacity.

Below are the most important metrics, how they are defined, and why they matter. The following metrics[1] are considered industry standards and adopted in the famous MLPerf[2] by MLCommons.

---

[1] https://docs.nvidia.com/nim/benchmarking/llm/latest/metrics.html
[2] https://mlcommons.org/benchmarks/training/

Time to First Token (TTFT)

The interval from the submission of a request until the first output token is received. This metric evaluates the user's perceived "startup delay" prior to the model initiating its response. Its significance lies in the fact that a high TTFT results in users experiencing longer wait times before any output is visible. TTFT is influenced by factors such as request queuing, input tokenization, network latency, and prefill time associated with constructing the KV cache. The enterprise implications are notable: in interactive applications such as chatbots or logistics dashboards, minimizing TTFT enhances the perception of immediacy in responses, even if the complete output requires additional time to generate.

End-to-End Request Latency (E2E Latency)

The period from the moment a request is dispatched until the reception of the final output token. It assesses the comprehensive round-trip experience, encompassing queuing, batching, generation, and network overhead. It is significant because it accurately reflects the total duration of a complete request, and it is instrumental in evaluating Service-Level Agreement (SLA) adherence (e.g., "95% of requests complete in less than 2 seconds"). It has enterprise implications, as in API-driven systems, such as Synapse Logistics' Delivery Management System, end-to-end latency determines whether the model's performance is adequate for real-time decision-making.

Inter-token Latency (ITL)/Time per Output Token (TPOT)

The mean interval between successive tokens produced by the model, excluding the initial token. It gauges the efficacy of the decoding process (incremental token generation). ITL indicates the system's capacity to manage extended outputs effectively. Consistent ITL suggests optimal GPU memory management and efficient utilization of the KV-cache. A logistics planner requesting an extensive generated schedule (comprising hundreds of tokens) will observe suboptimal performance if TPOT escalates with sequence length.

CHAPTER 6   MONITORING AND MAINTENANCE

Percentile Latencies (P80, P95, P99)

When monitoring model or system performance, we often look at statistical percentile latency metrics instead of averages. Percentiles help describe how performance feels to *most* users, including the ones on the slower end.

- **P95 (95th Percentile Latency):** This metric indicates that 95% of requests are completed in a duration shorter than the specified value, while the remaining 5% take longer. For instance, if the P95 time per output token is 120 milliseconds, this implies that only 1 in 20 requests exceeds this duration. The P95 metric is frequently utilized as an early indicator of system stress; an increase in P95 often signifies degradation in tail-end performance, which may be attributed to GPU memory pressure, cache misses, or suboptimal query efficiency.

- **P80 (80th Percentile Latency):** This indicates that 80% of requests are completed within this duration, while the remaining 20% take longer. P80 offers a mid-tail perspective, providing insight into how the "upper-middle" segment of users experiences latency. It is less stringent than P95 but still detects performance degradation earlier than average metrics.

Why is the mean (average) not sufficient? Because averages can conceal issues. For example, if most requests take approximately 20 ms, but a few require up to 2,000 ms, the average may appear acceptable (~100 ms), yet users encountering these slow responses will likely express dissatisfaction. Percentiles such as P95 and P80 enable us to identify these outliers that significantly influence customer experience.

The time thresholds under which a given percentage of requests complete, for example:

- **P80**: 80% of requests are faster; 20% are slower.
- **P95**: 95% are faster; 5% are slower.

It measures the "tail latency" that affects a subset of users. Averages can hide outliers (e.g., most requests take 20 ms, but 1 in 20 takes 2 seconds). P95 is a common SLA target for ensuring worst-case performance remains acceptable. If our fictional company Synapse Logistics commits to "95% of ETA predictions in <750ms," that is a P95 SLA, not an average.

Tokens per Second (TPS)

Tokens per second represent the number of output tokens generated per second across all requests.

Two perspectives:

- **TPS per User**: Throughput experienced by one request
- **Total System TPS**: Aggregate throughput across concurrent users

It matters because it indicates whether GPUs are fully utilized. As concurrency increases, total TPS rises until saturation, after which latency spikes and TPS decreases. It has direct enterprise impact for batch jobs (e.g., nightly reprocessing of over 1 million shipments), and total TPS determines whether the workload can be completed within the allocated timeframe.

Requests per Second (RPS)

Requests per second represents the number of complete requests (prompt + completion) successfully processed per second. It measures the system's capacity for managing concurrent queries. Notably, the high RPS indicates that the system scales effectively with a large number of users. It is valuable for load testing multi-tenant APIs. A customer portal serving thousands of users concurrently relies on high RPS to prevent queuing delays.

Each metric highlights a different aspect of model performance:

- **TTFT**: How quickly do users see the *first* response?
- **E2E Latency**: How long before the *full* response is done?
- **TPOT/ITL**: How smooth is token generation during long completions?
- **P95/P80**: Are tail users having a bad experience?
- **TPS**: How many tokens can we serve per second?
- **RPS**: How many requests can we handle per second?

In practice, enterprises like our fictional Synapse Logistics track all of these metrics together. For example:

- **TTFT** ensures dispatch operators see immediate ETA feedback.

- **P95 E2E latency** ensures customers aren't left waiting during peak hours.
- **TPS and RPS** ensure the system scales to handle seasonal surges in shipments.

Our monitoring fabric must collaborate closely to synchronize these cadences, ensuring that an LLM rollback remains aligned with any kernel or driver modifications, and vice versa. Variations in data, concepts, and performance do not manifest simultaneously; therefore, we monitor distinct early-warning indicators for each. Beyond lifecycle monitoring, RHEL AI highlights three types of drift detection that function as early warning systems.

- **Data Drift**: When the input distribution changes. Example: seasonality in logistics demand, new slang in customer queries, or a product launch that alters usage. We track embedding distances from a known "golden baseline" to detect divergence hours to days before it impacts users.
- **Concept Drift**: When the relationship between inputs and outputs changes. Example: a regulatory update shifts compliance rules, requiring models to answer differently. A fall in safety or helpfulness scores is the early signal, with user impact appearing days to weeks later.
- **Performance Drift**: When infrastructure or software regressions slow things down. Example: a CUDA driver upgrade or a quantization change that increases token latency. By watching metrics like P95 time per output token (TPOT), we can detect issues within minutes to hours.

By treating these three drifts as first-class monitoring targets—each with its own indicators and expected timelines—enterprises can take proactive action. This prevents customer-visible problems, keeps model rollouts aligned with infrastructure changes, and maintains trust in production AI systems.

By combining latency percentiles, throughput measures, and drift detection, RHEL AI provides a holistic observability framework that aligns model reliability with enterprise business SLAs.

Real-Time Monitoring

Operating a multi-GPU large language model (LLM) back end is often compared to maintaining a jumbo jet in flight: numerous subsystems must function in perfect harmony, and even the slightest malfunction in one area—such as a clogged PCIe lane, a throttled NVLink connection, a surge in GPU ECC errors, or a decline in model performance—can propagate throughout the entire system, resulting in user-perceivable issues such as slow response times, inaccuracies, or service interruptions. Consequently, real-time observability is not merely considered a best practice but is a fundamental element of dependable artificial intelligence operations within RHEL AI. The strategy involves constructing a comprehensive monitoring framework, referred to by Red Hat as a signal chain, which encompasses every system layer: hardware, kernel, container runtime, inference runtime, and the model itself. Each layer presents unique failure modes and therefore requires instrumentation with appropriate metrics collected at suitable intervals based on their volatility. These signals are integrated into Grafana dashboards and correlated with OpenTelemetry distributed traces, enabling engineers to swiftly transition from high-level latency alerts to the exact malfunctioning subsystem, thereby reducing diagnostic duration from hours to minutes.

At the levels of accelerators and PCIe, metrics such as GPU temperature, power consumption, NVLink traffic, ECC error counts, and MIG slice utilization serve as early indicators of instability. These metrics are exported via NVIDIA Data Center GPU Manager (DCGM)[3] or AMD ROCm System Management Interface (SMI) and are collected every five seconds, given the rapid state changes under load. An increase in GPU temperature or ECC errors often signals impending performance issues well before the inference engine encounters failure. Moving higher in the stack, the kernel and operating system layers may reveal subtler yet equally consequential issues: `cgroup` resource pressure silently throttling processes, SELinux Access Vector Cache (AVC) denials obstructing critical file access, increased interrupt latency causing I/O stalls, or GPU utilization bottlenecks identified through eBPF probes. These are typically monitored using tools like node-exporter or bcc-tools, with data collected every 15 seconds to balance granularity with system overhead.

The container runtime layer introduces additional risks that can impair performance unexpectedly. Resource exhaustion events such as overlay filesystem `inode` depletion or `/dev/shm` overuse can mimic random slowdowns in inference but are, in fact, resource

---

[3] https://developer.nvidia.com/dcgm

CHAPTER 6   MONITORING AND MAINTENANCE

starvation phenomena at the container level. Metrics provided by `cri-o` and cAdvisor offer vital visibility at intervals of approximately 15 seconds, allowing operators to detect runaway processes or misconfigured containers before they compromise the inference pipeline. Above this, the inference runtime layer—powered by vLLM within RHEL AI— offers the most direct insight into user-facing performance metrics. Key indicators like `vllm_tokens_total` for throughput, `vllm_request_latency_bucket` for response time distribution, and `vllm_gpu_fragmentation_ratio` for memory health are sampled every second. This high-frequency sampling is crucial, as microscopic stalls in garbage collection or NUMA pinning errors can manifest as tail-latency spikes within milliseconds. NUMA (Non-Uniform Memory Access) refers to the organization of CPUs and memory into nodes, each with "local" memory that is faster to access than memory on other nodes. In GPU inference, misaligned NUMA placement (e.g., CPU threads bound to the wrong node) can cause additional latency and stalls; therefore, processes should be pinned to the NUMA node directly connected to the target GPU. To improve traceability, operators are encouraged to connect metrics directly from the asynchronous pipeline, with tracing spans across API server, AsyncLLM, EngineCore, and detokenizer processes linking client-facing latencies with GPU wait states and execution durations. Signals such as `vllm_engine_wait_ratio` and `vllm_step_time_seconds`, captured at one-second intervals, identify performance bottlenecks that might otherwise remain unobserved.

Wire metrics straight from the asynchronous pipeline. The Red Hat AI Inference Server splits work across two busy-loop processes:

```
Process 0    API-server   → AsyncLLM     → socket.send()
Process 1    EngineCore   → schedule()   → execute()
Process 0    AsyncLLM-out → socket.poll() → detokenizer()
```

Scrape `vllm_engine_wait_ratio` and `vllm_step_time_seconds` every second; even micro-stalls in Garbage Collection or NUMA mis-pinning surface as tail-latency spikes if our scrape window is wider than 250 ms.

Finally, the model quality-of-service layer safeguards against unnoticed degradation in model performance, which may occur even if GPU temperatures are optimal and inference throughput is high. A decline in accuracy, safety, or helpfulness adversely impacts business outcomes. To monitor this, scheduled evaluation jobs such as `ilab model evaluate` execute hourly, employing benchmarks including MMLU, MT-Bench, and GuideLLM safety and helpfulness scores. These signals serve as early warnings for concept drift—alterations in input-output mappings driven by policy or regulatory changes—and safety drift, characterized by gradual deterioration in response quality.

The true value of this multilayered observability framework lies in correlating metrics across layers in real time. For instance, an abrupt increase in end-to-end latency at the P95 percentile could be traced through Grafana to elevated TPOT values, correlated via OpenTelemetry traces with a spike in `vllm_engine_wait_ratio`, and ultimately diagnosed as a NUMA mis-pinning issue at the kernel level. Conversely, an unchanging latency profile might conceal a silent decline in GuideLLM safety scores, indicating model drift despite apparent infrastructural stability. By prioritizing observability of accelerator health, kernel integrity, container resources, inference performance, and model accuracy—each sampled at its respective volatility-based cadence—RHEL AI empowers organizations to detect and address issues proactively, often before end users experience them.

Practically, this translates into a paradigm shift whereby operating a production LLM back end becomes less about firefighting and more about ongoing assurance: ensuring that the multi-GPU inference "jumbo jet" remains airborne and operates smoothly, safely, and predictably across diverse workloads. This integrated signal chain condenses what once took hours of manual troubleshooting into mere minutes, thereby safeguarding system reliability and fostering end-user confidence.

Table 6-2 showcases the primary metrics of an end-to-end signal chain.

Table 6-2. LLMs observability signals

Layer	Signals to Collect	Recommended Exporters/Agents	Scrape Interval
Accelerator and PCIe	GPU temp/power, NVLink traffic, ECC, MIG slices	NVIDIA DCGM, AMD ROCm SMI	5 s
Kernel/OS	cgroup-pressure, SELinux AVCs, IRQ latency, eBPF `gpuutil`	node-exporter, bcc-tools	15 s
Container Runtime	overlayfs inode use, /dev/shm utilization	cri-o metrics, cAdvisor	15 s
Inference Runtime (vLLM)	`vllm_tokens_total`, `vllm_request_latency_bucket`, `vllm_gpu_fragmentation_ratio`	vLLM built-in / metrics	1 s
Model QoS	MMLU, MT-Bench, GuideLLM safety/helpfulness	`ilab model evaluate` jobs	1 h

> **Tip** Add an OpenTelemetry sidecar: client ➤ AsyncLLM ➤ EngineCore spans knit latency to GPU time into a single trace.

Service Reliability Goals

Applications built on large language models only create value if the models are consistently available and responsive. To make that reliability measurable—and to set the right expectations across both internal teams and external customers—Red Hat defines service reliability using three connected concepts:

- **Service-Level Agreement (SLA)**: The formal commitment made to customers. If the service falls short of the SLA, customers may be owed credits or other remedies.

- **Service-Level Objective (SLO)**: The internal reliability goal that keeps us comfortably within the SLA. SLOs are intentionally set stricter than the SLA, creating a safety margin.

- **Service-Level Indicator (SLI)**: The real-time metric we track that tells us whether we are meeting the SLO. Each SLO maps directly to one or more SLIs.

Regarding vLLM model serving—which provides both chat and code-completion endpoints—the primary Service-Level Objectives (SLOs) emphasize latency, availability, and resource efficiency. These targets are established so that consistent achievement over a period of 30 days ensures at least 99.9% SLA compliance concerning responsiveness and uptime. Reliability is maintained through automated alerting mechanisms: should any metric exceed 50% of its error budget within a one-hour period, alerts are promptly generated for immediate investigation. Furthermore, if the entire 30-day error budget for a specific SLO is depleted, a comprehensive post-mortem review becomes mandatory, guaranteeing that every reliability incident is thoroughly analyzed and remedied.

By conceptualizing reliability through this framework—comprising contractual SLA, operational SLO, and measurable SLI—teams can effectively align their engineering practices with business commitments. This approach provides customers with a transparent understanding of the guarantees available to them while enabling operators to utilize precise metrics and processes that ensure service quality remains predictable at scale.

CHAPTER 6 MONITORING AND MAINTENANCE

Red Hat AI Inference Server

Red Hat AI Inference Server (RHIS) is the operational core of Red Hat's AI stack, designed to make large language model (LLM) inference reliable, observable, and efficient across hybrid cloud environments. At its foundation, RHEL AI provides a hardened, GPU-optimized operating system with consistent CUDA stacks, SELinux policies, and driver versions. RHIS then layers on top of this base to deliver vLLM, packaged with tracing, metrics sidecars, and production-ready monitoring hooks.

Figure 6-1 illustrates the operation of vLLM within the RHIS, which manages model inference requests asynchronously. It efficiently coordinates CPU and GPU workloads through the use of sockets and event loops. This internal mechanism serves as the "engine room" for generating AI responses and streaming them back to users in real time. The diagram depicts how the RHIS (powered by vLLM) processes inference requests asynchronously across two processes: one dedicated to API communication and the other to GPU workload execution. It illustrates the data flow between the API Server, AsyncLLM, and EngineCore, facilitating efficient, low-latency, and concurrent model serving.

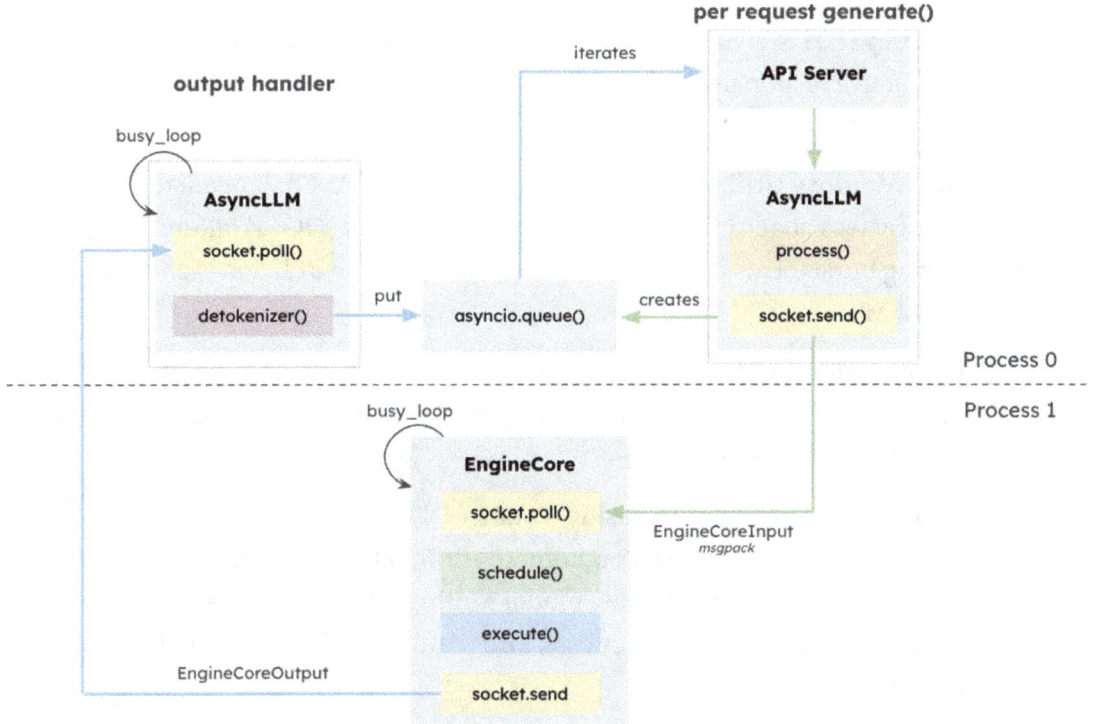

Figure 6-1. Red Hat AI Inference Server

CHAPTER 6   MONITORING AND MAINTENANCE

RHIS creates an environment where performance can be measured, tuned, and guaranteed against clear service-level objectives. Red Hat defines service reliability using three connected concepts based on the Site Reliability Engineering (SRE) paradigm:

- **Service-Level Agreement (SLA)**: The formal commitment made to customers. If the service falls short of the SLA, customers may be owed credits or other remedies.

- **Service-Level Objective (SLO)**: The internal reliability goal that keeps us comfortably within the SLA. SLOs are intentionally set stricter than the SLA, creating a safety margin.

- **Service-Level Indicator (SLI)**: The real-time metric we track that tells us whether we are meeting the SLO. Each SLO maps directly to one or more SLIs.

RHIS formalizes reliability in terms of latency, GPU utilization, engine efficiency, and data quality drift. These are not abstract goals, but measurable targets (SLIs) collected via Prometheus and visualized in Grafana:

- **Latency** (P95 $\leq$ 80 ms for chat, $\leq$ 250 ms for code): Ensures interactive responsiveness, with outliers flagged before they impact the majority of users.

- **GPU Memory Utilization** (0.75 ± 0.05): Keeps VRAM balanced; too low wastes capacity, too high risks out-of-memory (OOM) failures during bursts. This can be tuned via `--gpu-memory-utilization` in vLLM.

- **Engine Wait Ratio** (< 0.20): Monitors GPU and I/O contention. If this rises, it signals saturation or bottlenecks in upstream storage and must be investigated.

- **Embedding Drift** (≤ 0.10 cosine distance): Detects distribution shifts or poor model pushes. RHIS automates drift detection with rolling embedding centroids, shadow model routing (1% traffic to baseline for GuideLLM safety/helpfulness), and nightly MMLU/MT-Bench evaluations.

- These signals form the backbone of service reliability engineering. By binding observability to specific metrics, RHIS operators can enforce a ≥99.9% SLA for latency and availability when SLOs are consistently met.

Optimizing Models for Production

Raw performance isn't just about monitoring—it also depends on serving models efficiently. Red Hat provides the Model Optimization Toolkit (based on LLM Compressor) to shrink models through quantization, sparsity, and compression, reducing VRAM use and boosting inference throughput. For example:

- **Quantization** (e.g., INT8, FP8) reduces memory footprint with minimal accuracy loss.

- **Sparsity** (e.g., SparseGPT) zeroes out redundant weights for faster computation.

- **Hybrid compression workflows** (e.g., SmoothQuant, QuIP, SpinQuant) balance size and accuracy across CPU and GPU pipelines.

These optimizations integrate seamlessly with vLLM, enabling operators to deploy compressed Hugging Face models directly into production pipelines with lower cost per token.

At runtime, RHIS exposes vLLM server arguments to fine-tune performance:

- `--tensor-parallel-size`: Splits models across multiple GPUs for distributed execution

- `--max-model-len`: Caps context length to prevent memory blowups

- `--max-num-batched-tokens`: Controls throughput vs. latency tradeoffs in token batching

- `--gpu-memory-utilization`: Directly tunes VRAM usage for weights, KV cache, and activations

These knobs allow SREs and ML engineers to adapt deployments to **different accelerators, workload patterns, and scaling scenarios**—whether in a single GPU dev box, a multi-node OpenShift cluster, or a hybrid cloud rollout.

Table 6-3 shows the main metrics and targets for our LLMs.

CHAPTER 6   MONITORING AND MAINTENANCE

Table 6-3. *LLMs metrics and targets*

Metric (Prometheus)	Good Target	Why It Matters
`vllm_request_latency_seconds{quantile="0.95"}`	≤ 80 ms (chat)/250 ms (code)	Directly maps to user wait-time
`vllm_gpu_memory_active_bytes / total`	0.75 ± 0.05	Fragmentation high ➤ OOM risk; low ➤ wasted VRAM
`vllm_engine_wait_ratio`	< 0.20	Tells if EngineCore is starved by GPU or IO
`embedding_drift_score`	≤ 0.10	Early warning for data drift

Dashboards are stored in a **Grafana folder named after the model revision,** so data science and SRE view the same truth.

Drift Sentinels

One of the most challenging aspects of deploying large language models (LLMs) in a production environment is the ability to detect when a model begins to exhibit behavior that deviates from expectations—not due to infrastructure issues but because of shifts in data or task parameters. This phenomenon, known as drift, manifests in various forms: input data drift (such as new terminology or seasonal demand patterns), concept drift (when policy changes alter the classification approach), or performance drift (a new model version demonstrating reduced accuracy). Importantly, drift does not always become apparent through overt errors; rather, the quality of the output gradually deteriorates until it is noticed by users. To mitigate such issues, RHIS employs drift sentinels—automated early-warning mechanisms that continuously monitor the model to ensure it remains aligned with its foundational baseline. The following sentinels are built into the monitoring chain:

- **Rolling Embedding Centroid**: Track the embeddings of the last 500 prompts, compute their centroid, and compare it against the launch baseline. If the cosine distance grows beyond 0.15, it suggests the input distribution has shifted.

- **Shadow Traffic Safety Check**: Send 1% of live traffic to a shadow version of the model and run GuideLLM safety/helpfulness evaluations. This catches subtle degradations before they affect all users.

- **Scheduled Benchmarks**: Run nightly MMLU and MT-Bench evaluations, store results in Prometheus, and look for long-term accuracy or reasoning regressions.

If any sentinel fires occur, operators should investigate the root causes: Was a new model introduced? Did customer inputs change? Is a data preprocessing step broken? By treating these drift sentinels as first-class observability signals, RHIS ensures that model quality issues are caught early—well before they become SLA breaches or customer-visible failures.

Diagnose and Troubleshoot

Even with strong observability in place, large language model (LLM) inference workloads can encounter operational issues that degrade performance, consume excessive resources, or reduce output quality. These problems often surface suddenly as user-visible slowdowns, accuracy regressions, or infrastructure alerts. To accelerate resolution, RHEL AI and RHIS provide a fast triage matrix that maps common symptoms to their most likely causes, along with quick diagnostic checks and recommended fixes. This structured approach helps SREs and ML engineers move from alert → root cause → remediation with minimal downtime.

Table 6-4 is a fast triage matrix group of the most common issues we can face when dealing with inference workload (LLM models in production).

CHAPTER 6   MONITORING AND MAINTENANCE

Table 6-4. *Fast triage matrix*

Symptom	Most-Likely Root Cause	Quick Check	Fix
P95 Latency Spikes	Engine wait ratio ↑	`vllm_engine_wait_ratio` > 0.20	Increase --tensor-parallel-size or trim batch size
500 MB s⁻¹ VRAM Leak	KV-cache fragmentation	`vllm_gpu_fragmentation_ratio` > 0.25	Enable continuous batching and speculative decoding
Sudden BLEU/ Safety Drop	Data or concept drift	`embedding_drift_score` > 0.15 or GuideLLM ↓ 2 pp	Retrain quick hot-fix fine-tune via InstructLab SDG
"No Space Left on Device" During SDG	Dataset + checkpoints overflow	Check /home NVMe wear level	Add 1 TB NVMe as the hardware guide suggests
vLLM Fails After Driver Update	Driver/kernel mismatch	`dmesg	grep -i nvrm`	

Running LLM inference at scale means that failures will occur—whether due to hardware regressions, data drift, or unexpected performance bottlenecks. To minimize downtime and user impact, we can apply a structured incident resolution playbook to RHIS, standardizing the handling of alerts, identification of root causes, and deployment of fixes back into production. This is the five-step runbook:

1. Alert and Acknowledge

    - **Trigger**: PagerDuty fires when drift or performance thresholds are breached. Common triggers include

    - **Embedding drift score** beyond 0.15 (data distribution change)

    - **MMLU/MT-Bench score regression** (concept drift)

    - **Time per output token (TPOT)** spike or P95 latency breach (performance drift)

    - **Objective**: Acknowledge the alert within **five minutes** to ensure someone is actively investigating.

2. Diagnose the Issue

    - **Step 1**: Collect the last 200 prompts from production logs.

    - **Step 2**: Replay them against a canary model (known-good baseline).

    - **Step 3**: Compare Jaeger traces for AsyncLLM (API server pipeline) vs. EngineCore (GPU execution pipeline) to determine whether latency is caused by infrastructure bottlenecks (I/O, GPU, drivers) or model behavior.

    - **Objective**: Identify root cause within 30 minutes.

3. Remediate Based on Root Cause

    - **If Performance Issue**: Roll back to a previous known-good configuration. Example: `bootc status --rollback` for system images, or pin the previous Inference Server container tag.

    - **If Data/Concept Drift:**

        - Run Synthetic Data Generation (SDG) on the offending prompts.

        - Fine-tune the model using InstructLab workflows.

        - Package the updated model into an OCI image tagged `*-hotfix-YYYYMMDD`.

        - Deploy via zero-copy reload with `systemd reload`, avoiding downtime.

    - **Objective**: Restore service to within SLO thresholds as quickly as possible.

4. Post-Mortem and Continuous Improvement

    - Capture a Grafana snapshot of the incident window.

    - Attach the Git commit of configuration or model changes to the incident ticket.

    - Use findings to refine SLOs, thresholds, and automation policies to prevent recurrence.

5. Automation via Ansible

   To reduce manual effort, this entire hot-fix cycle—from SDG and fine-tuning to OCI image rebuild and zero-copy reload—can be orchestrated with Ansible Automation Platform. This eliminates the need for manual SSH sessions and ensures that fixes are applied consistently across hybrid or multi-cloud environments.

GPU Telemetry

Running LLM inference in production is not just about model accuracy—it's about keeping systems fast, reliable, and recoverable under load. RHEL AI addresses this by combining deep telemetry, immutable infrastructure upgrades, and controlled rollout strategies. Together, these ensure operators can detect issues early, upgrade safely, and roll out new models without disrupting user experience.

1. **GPU Telemetry for Early Warnings**

   The first line of defense is deep GPU telemetry. By exporting per-GPU metrics such as temperature, power draw, NVLink throughput, and ECC error rates, operators gain the ability to correlate infrastructure stress with inference performance. For example, if P95 time per output token (TPOT) begins creeping past 80 ms, dashboards can show whether the cause is thermal throttling, NVLink saturation, or simple over-utilization.
   To set this up on a RHEL AI node:

   1. Verify GPU drivers are loaded and clocks are stable (`nvidia-smi`).

   2. Run DCGM Exporter as a rootless Podman service:

      ```
      podman run --rm -d --name dcgm-exporter --net host --gpus all nvcr.io/nvidia/k8s/dcgm-exporter:latest
      ```

      This exposes metrics on :9400/metrics.

   3. Add a Prometheus scrape job for GPU metrics, and overlay them with vLLM metrics (`--metrics-port 9091`) in Grafana.

CHAPTER 6   MONITORING AND MAINTENANCE

4. Watch for correlations between GPU telemetry (e.g., DCGM_FI_DEV_NVLINK_BANDWIDTH_TOTAL) and inference latency (vllm_step_time_seconds).

This gives SREs a 5–10 minute early warning on performance regressions—before users notice latency spikes.

2. **Safe OS Upgrades with bootc**

    Hardware and driver updates can be just as risky as model drift. To manage this, RHEL AI nodes use bootc immutable images. This allows operators to switch the OS stack with a single command and roll back just as quickly if issues appear.

    - **Upgrade a node:**

      ```
      sudo bootc switch registry.redhat.io/rhelai1/bootc-nvidia-rhel9:1.5
      sudo reboot -n
      ```

    - **Rollback instantly if issues appear (e.g., SELinux AVC storms, ECC bursts):**

      ```
      sudo bootc status --rollback
      sudo reboot -n
      ```

    This approach limits OS patch risk to one reboot and one command, making driver/kernel compatibility testing a repeatable part of canary workflows.

3. **Controlled Model Rollouts (Canary → A/B → Promote)**

    Finally, upgrading models requires a strategy that balances speed, safety, and reversibility. RHEL AI can run standalone, but many enterprises deploy inference inside Kubernetes or OpenShift for scaling and CI/CD gating. In these environments, model rollout follows a canary and promotion flow:

    1. **Download the latest model build:**

       ```
       ilab model download --repository registry.redhat.io/rhelai1/granite-3.1-8b-lab-v1 --release latest
       ```

2. **Pin the model digest** in Kustomize/Helm for reproducibility.

3. **Trigger rollout:**

   ```
   oc rollout latest deployment/vllm-granite
   oc rollout status deployment/vllm-granite
   ```

4. **Verify live SLOs:**

   ```
   vllm_engine_wait_ratio < 0.20
   embedding_drift_score < 0.10
   ```

5. **Route 1% shadow traffic** to the new ReplicaSet. Auto-promote only if GuideLLM **safety/helpfulness** is ≥0.5 pp better than the current model.

6. **Rollback instantly** if drift or regressions appear:

   ```
   oc scale rs old-replicaset --replicas=<desired>
   ```

Because weights live on a read-only PVC, rollback is just a pod restart—**no multi-GB copies across the network.**

Putting It All Together

- **GPU telemetry** provides **early warnings** of performance bottlenecks.

- **bootc image management** ensures **safe infrastructure upgrades** with instant rollback.

- **Canary and A/B model rollouts** guarantee that new model versions can be tested, promoted, or reverted **without disrupting service**.

Together, these practices give RHEL AI operators the confidence to continuously upgrade both infrastructure and models while protecting latency SLAs and user trust.

You said:

longer

Red Hat Enterprise Linux AI Latest said:

Perfect—let's take the section you highlighted and expand it into a **longer, more structured narrative** that flows clearly. I'll go deeper into the **why** as well as the **how**, so the reader can appreciate the thinking behind GPU telemetry, immutable host upgrades, and canary rollouts, rather than feeling like the text is just a collection of commands.

Monitoring and Reliable Rollouts in RHEL AI

Running inference with large language models is not simply about achieving high accuracy; it is about ensuring **stable, predictable performance** in real-world environments. In production, a service outage or latency spike does not just frustrate users—it can impact business-critical workflows, trigger SLA penalties, and undermine trust in AI-driven decision-making. To prevent this, Red Hat Enterprise Linux AI (RHEL AI) emphasizes three pillars of operational reliability: **deep telemetry**, **safe host upgrades**, and **controlled model rollouts**. Together, these create a feedback loop where problems are detected early, infrastructure changes are applied safely, and new models can be introduced without jeopardizing service availability.

1. **Deep GPU Telemetry for Early Warning**

   At the heart of inference reliability lies the GPU. A single overloaded or throttled GPU can degrade performance across the entire serving stack. This is why RHEL AI recommends wiring **GPU telemetry into Prometheus and Grafana dashboards** on every node. Using NVIDIA's Data Center GPU Manager (DCGM) exporter, operators can capture per-GPU metrics such as **temperature, power draw, NVLink bandwidth, ECC error rates, and MIG slice usage**. These raw hardware signals are then overlaid with inference-layer metrics from vLLM, such as **step time per token** and **engine wait ratios**, allowing operators to directly correlate infrastructure conditions with model responsiveness.

   For example, if P95 **time per output token (TPOT)** climbs past 80 ms, telemetry might show that NVLink bandwidth has dropped, pointing to a PCIe saturation issue rather than a model bug. Similarly, rising ECC errors can foreshadow a failing GPU card before it causes a crash. With Prometheus scraping GPU signals every five seconds and vLLM latency buckets every one second, operators gain a **5–10 minute lead time** on performance anomalies before end users ever see degraded service.

   The setup process itself is simple but powerful: verify GPUs with nvidia-smi, run the DCGM exporter as a rootless Podman service, point Prometheus at the :9400/metrics endpoint, and import a

Grafana dashboard that overlays GPU and vLLM metrics. The result is a live health view where SREs can pivot from "latency alert" to "specific hardware root cause" in minutes.

2. **Safe OS and Driver Upgrades with Immutable bootc Images**

   Just as important as monitoring GPUs is managing the host environment they run on. Kernel updates, CUDA driver changes, or security patches can all introduce regressions if applied inconsistently across nodes. RHEL AI solves this by running on **bootc immutable images**, which treat the host OS like a versioned artifact rather than a mutable system.

   This means infrastructure updates are applied with a single command:

   - `sudo bootc switch registry.redhat.io/rhelai1/bootc-nvidia-rhel9:1.5`
   - `sudo reboot -n`

   A new OSTree snapshot lands on the node, and the system boots into the upgraded environment. If issues surface during canary testing—such as a spike in SELinux AVC denials or sudden GPU ECC bursts—rollback is just as fast:

   - `sudo bootc status --rollback`
   - `sudo reboot -n`

   Within a single reboot, the node returns to its previous state. This gives operators confidence to test new kernels and driver stacks on canary nodes without fear of bricking production. A rolling reboot strategy then promotes the update across the cluster, ensuring **consistent OS baselines** for all inference workloads. In practice, bootc reduces patch risk to **one reboot and one command**, replacing manual rollback gymnastics with a predictable, reversible workflow.

3. **Controlled Model Rollouts: Canary, A/B, and Rollback**

   Infrastructure stability is only half of the story—the models themselves also change. New fine-tuned builds or vendor-provided foundation model updates need to be tested in production, but blindly swapping them in risks **concept drift, safety regressions, or latency slowdowns**. To address this, RHEL AI encourages a **canary and promotion workflow** that can run either on bare metal or inside orchestrated environments like OpenShift or Kubernetes.

The process starts with downloading the new model build into the local registry cache using InstructLab CLI:

- `ilab model download \`
- `--repository registry.redhat.io/rhelai1/granite-3.1-8b-lab-v1 \`
- `--release latest`

From there, operators pin the immutable digest in configuration management (Helm, Kustomize, or Ansible) to guarantee reproducibility. The new model is then deployed as a **canary ReplicaSet**, serving only a small slice of traffic. Automated checks evaluate

- **Engine Wait Ratio (< 0.20)**: To catch GPU or I/O bottlenecks
- **Embedding Drift Score (< 0.10)**: To detect shifts in input distribution
- **GuideLLM Safety/Helpfulness Scores**: To monitor response quality and safety

If the canary passes, traffic can be gradually shifted toward the new model (A/B testing). For safety, **1% of traffic** can be forked to a shadow model to compare outputs side by side. Promotion occurs only when quality is equal to or better than baseline.

If something goes wrong, rollback is instant. Because vLLM mounts model weights from a **read-only persistent volume claim (PVC)**, reverting simply means scaling the old ReplicaSet back up—no need to copy multi-gigabyte model files across the network. In practice, rollback is measured in **a YAML edit and a pod restart**, not hours of recovery work.

4. **How These Pieces Fit Together**

   Each of these practices—GPU telemetry, bootc image management, and canary rollouts—is powerful on its own, but their real value comes from how they connect. GPU telemetry provides operators with early warnings of potential performance issues. Immutable OS snapshots ensure that infrastructure upgrades are safe and can be reversed. Canary rollouts and drift sentinels prevent bad models from poisoning production traffic. Together, they create a closed loop of monitoring, testing, and controlled change.

   This loop ensures that RHEL AI can evolve continuously—with new drivers, kernels, and models—without compromising reliability guarantees. In effect, it transforms inference operations from reactive firefighting into predictable, managed workflows where failures are expected, rehearsed, and quickly reversed.

Monitoring and Reliable Rollouts in RHEL AI

Running inference with large language models is not simply about achieving high accuracy; it is about ensuring stable, predictable performance in real-world environments. In production, a service outage or latency spike does not just frustrate users—it can impact business-critical workflows, trigger SLA penalties, and undermine trust in AI-driven decision-making. To prevent this, Red Hat Enterprise Linux AI (RHEL AI) emphasizes three pillars of operational reliability: deep telemetry, safe host upgrades, and controlled model rollouts. Together, these create a feedback loop where problems are detected early, infrastructure changes are applied safely, and new models can be introduced without jeopardizing service availability.

GPU Telemetry

At the heart of inference reliability lies the GPU. A single overloaded or throttled GPU can degrade performance across the entire serving stack. This is why RHEL AI recommends wiring GPU telemetry into Prometheus and Grafana dashboards on every node. Using NVIDIA's Data Center GPU Manager (DCGM) exporter, operators can capture per-GPU metrics such as temperature, power draw, NVLink bandwidth, ECC error rates, and MIG slice usage. These raw hardware signals are then overlaid with inference-layer metrics from vLLM, such as step time per token and engine wait ratios, allowing operators to correlate infrastructure conditions with model responsiveness directly.

For example, if the P95 **time per output token (TPOT)** exceeds 80 ms, telemetry may indicate that NVLink bandwidth has decreased, suggesting a PCIe saturation issue rather than a model bug. Similarly, rising ECC errors can foreshadow a failing GPU card before it causes a crash. With Prometheus scraping GPU signals every five seconds and vLLM latency buckets every one second, operators gain a 5-10 minute lead time on performance anomalies before end users ever see degraded service.

The setup process itself is simple but powerful: verify GPUs with `nvidia-smi`, run the DCGM exporter as a rootless Podman service, point Prometheus at the `:9400/metrics` endpoint, and import a Grafana dashboard that overlays GPU and vLLM metrics. The result is a live health view where SREs can pivot from "latency alert" to "specific hardware root cause" in minutes.

OS and Driver Upgrades

Just as important as monitoring GPUs is managing the host environment on which they run. Kernel updates, CUDA driver changes, or security patches can all introduce regressions if applied inconsistently across nodes. RHEL AI solves this by running on bootc immutable images, which treat the host OS like a versioned artifact rather than a mutable system.

This means infrastructure updates are applied with a single command:

```
sudo bootc switch registry.redhat.io/rhelai1/bootc-nvidia-rhel9:1.5
sudo reboot -n
```

A new OSTree snapshot lands on the node, and the system boots into the upgraded environment. If issues surface during canary testing—such as a spike in SELinux AVC denials or sudden GPU ECC bursts—rollback is just as fast:

```
sudo bootc status --rollback
sudo reboot -n
```

Within a single reboot, the node returns to its previous state. This gives operators confidence to test new kernels and driver stacks on canary nodes without fear of bricking production. A rolling reboot strategy then promotes the update across the cluster, ensuring consistent OS baselines for all inference workloads. In practice, bootc reduces patch risk to one reboot and one command, replacing manual rollback gymnastics with a predictable, reversible workflow.

CHAPTER 6   MONITORING AND MAINTENANCE

Model Rollouts

Infrastructure stability is only half of the story—the models themselves also change. New fine-tuned builds or vendor-provided foundation model updates need to be tested in production, but blindly swapping them in risks concept drift, safety regressions, or latency slowdowns. To address this, RHEL AI encourages a canary and promotion workflow that can run either on bare metal or inside orchestrated environments like OpenShift or Kubernetes.

The process starts with downloading the new model build into the local registry cache using InstructLab CLI:

```
ilab model download \
  --repository registry.redhat.io/rhelai1/granite-3.1-8b-lab-v1 \
  --release latest
```

From there, operators pin the immutable digest in configuration management tools (such as Helm, Kustomize, or Ansible) to ensure reproducibility. The new model is then deployed as a canary ReplicaSet, serving only a small slice of traffic. Automated checks evaluate

- **Engine Wait Ratio (< 0.20)**: To catch GPU or I/O bottlenecks
- **Embedding Drift Score (< 0.10)**: To detect shifts in input distribution
- **GuideLLM Safety/Helpfulness Scores**: To monitor response quality and safety

If the canary passes, traffic can be gradually shifted toward the new model (A/B testing). For safety, 1% of traffic can be forked to a shadow model to compare outputs side by side. Promotion occurs only when quality is equal to or better than baseline. If something goes wrong, rollback is instant. Because vLLM mounts model weights from a read-only persistent volume claim (PVC), reverting simply means scaling the old ReplicaSet back up—no need to copy multi-gigabyte model files across the network. In practice, rollback is measured in a YAML edit and a pod restart, not hours of recovery work.

Each of these practices—GPU telemetry, boot image management, and canary rollouts—is formidable in isolation; however, their true significance resides in their interconnectedness. GPU telemetry provides early warnings to operators concerning performance issues. Immutable OS snapshots guarantee that infrastructure upgrades are conducted safely and are reversible. Canary rollouts and drift sentinels prevent the deployment of substandard models from contaminating production traffic. Collectively, they establish a closed-loop system of monitoring, testing, and controlled change. This loop ensures that RHEL AI can evolve continuously—incorporating new drivers, kernels, and models—without compromising reliability guarantees. Essentially, it converts inference operations from reactive firefighting into predictable, managed workflows where failures are anticipated, rehearsed, and promptly reversed.

Patch and Upgrade

Consistent patching and updating are vital practices to maintain the security, efficiency, and currency of inference environments with the latest advancements in large language models (LLMs). These measures not only facilitate access to performance enhancements but also reduce associated risks, such as bugs, regressions, and model inversion attacks. RHEL AI incorporates integrated mechanisms for secure updates and rollbacks, allowing operators to modernize their technological stack without compromising system reliability.

Table 6-5 delineates a recommended schedule for patching and upgrading in production environments. This schedule encompasses host images, inference containers, model weights, and compression recipes, as well as strategies for rollback.

Table 6-5. Patch and upgrade cadence

Artifact	Update Method	Frequency	Safe Rollback
RHEL AI Node Image	`bootc switch ... && reboot`	Weekly (Tue 08 UTC)	`bootc status --rollback`
Inference-Server Container	`podman pull rhaiis/vllm-cuda-rhel9:<ver>`	Daily	Pin old tag in Kustomize
Model Weights	`ilab model download --release latest`	On demand/A-B test	OCI digest pin
Compression Recipe	Re-run LLM Compressor (INT4, FP8, SparseGPT)	When latency/cost target changes	Keep prior `.safetensors`

All images and containers might enable Sigstore[4] cosign signatures; validate at pull time to stop supply-chain tampering. This is the best signature in the market, as traditional SHA and MD5 signature algorithms do not provide sufficient protection against supply chain attacks.

Optimization and Cost-to-Serve

Running LLM inference at scale means balancing performance against cost. GPUs are the most expensive part of the stack, so tuning how models are compressed, distributed, and utilized can make the difference between efficient service and wasted spend. The following three techniques provide a practical workflow to reduce cost-to-serve without sacrificing quality.

Compression

Optimize the utilization of larger models on existing GPUs and reduce inference latency by selecting an appropriate precision format. Begin with the full-precision baseline (FP16 or BF16) to determine reference latency using

```
ilab model chat --model <path> --metrics-port 9091
```

Subsequently, quantize the model to INT4 and FP8 variants utilizing the Red Hat Model Optimization Toolkit, based on the LLM Compressor framework. Deploy each variant under operational load and monitor the vllm_step_time_seconds metric.

Evaluate the outcomes:

- If VRAM capacity is the limiting factor, INT4 will reduce memory consumption by approximately half, enabling the deployment of more models per node.

- If latency is the primary concern, FP8 on H200 or newer GPUs may surpass INT4 performance owing to tensor-core throughput.

Select the precision format that offers the lowest cost per request within your CI/CD pipeline. It is imperative to benchmark both INT4 and FP8 on the target hardware prior to making a final decision.

---

[4] https://www.sigstore.dev/

Parallelism Tuning

Ensure large models fully utilize available GPUs without experiencing idle resources or synchronization overhead.

Determine your hardware configuration, including the number of GPUs per node and total nodes.

Configure the parallelism flags in vLLM based on the following matrix:

- **Single 8× H100 Node**: `--tensor-parallel-size 8`

- **Two 4-GPU Nodes**: `--pipeline-parallel-size 2 --tensor-parallel-size 4`

- **Mixture-of-Experts (MoE) Model with 32 Experts**: `-expert-parallel-size 4 --data-parallel-size 2`

Conduct load testing using prompts that resemble production scenarios. Monitoring Indicators:

- `vllm_engine_wait_ratio`: Should remain below 0.20

- `vllm_request_latency_seconds{quantile="0.95"}`: Must stay within the specified Service-Level Agreement (SLA)

Recommended action to integrate the optimal parallelism flags into your container specifications or systemd unit configurations to ensure consistent and repeatable scaling.

Utilization Guard

Prevent expenditure on underutilized GPUs by dynamically adjusting the pool size to mitigate GPU waste.

Implementation Guidelines include monitoring the `vllm_engine_wait_ratio` within Prometheus. A sustained ratio below 0.05 over a six-hour period indicates underutilization of GPUs.

Initiate an automated reduction in scale:

- For bare metal systems, release GPUs by decreasing the number of model replicas.

- In Kubernetes or OpenShift environments, reduce deployment replicas accordingly:

  ```
  kubectl scale deployment/vllm --replicas=<N>
  ```

CHAPTER 6   MONITORING AND MAINTENANCE

Should the workload increase subsequently, revert the scaling via the cluster autoscaler or Ansible automation workflows.

A recommended action is to integrate utilization thresholds into your alerting protocols and automation systems to ensure GPUs scale in response to actual demand.

Implement compression levers to diminish the size and latency associated with service delivery. Utilize parallelism tuning to optimize GPU throughput. Enforce a utilization guard to reduce scale during periods of low demand. Collectively, these methodologies establish a closed loop, whereby cost, latency, and reliability are persistently balanced.

Automated Lifecycle Controls

In a production inference environment, reliability cannot depend solely on manual oversight. Models evolve quickly, infrastructure components receive frequent patches, and user inputs shift unpredictably over time. Left unmanaged, these changes can introduce instability, degrade response quality, or even violate service-level objectives. To keep inference both safe and efficient at scale, RHEL AI relies on automated lifecycle controls—guardrails that enforce consistency, detect regressions, and trigger rollbacks or promotions without requiring constant human intervention.

These controls operate across the infrastructure, model, and quality layers:

- **Immutable Host Images (bootc)**: Bootc image streams are built nightly. Continuous Integration (CI) systems validate each new snapshot and automatically block promotion if Red Hat Insights flags a known-bad driver/kernel combination. This ensures that GPU nodes only ever run trusted, tested baselines.

- **Shadow Traffic for Model Validation**: A small portion of production traffic (typically 1%) is routed to the next candidate model. If drift checks show that the candidate achieves at least 0.5 points higher GuideLLM safety/helpfulness score than the current model, it is promoted automatically, avoiding manual A/B approval delays.

- **Quality Budget Enforcement**: Models are allowed a limited "error budget" for drift. For example, the system permits up to 90 minutes per day where the `embedding_drift_score` exceeds **0.10**. Grafana dashboards display a real-time burn-down of this budget, giving operators immediate visibility into whether drift is trending toward a breach.

By codifying these controls into CI/CD pipelines and monitoring dashboards, RHEL AI shifts model operations from reactive firefighting to predictable, policy-driven automation. This not only reduces operational burden but also ensures that upgrades and model improvements happen faster—while protecting user experience and service-level guarantees.

Backups and DR

In an LLM-centric platform, backups and disaster recovery (DR) address different but complementary problems. A backup is a consistent point-in-time copy of everything that constitutes our model's state—large weight files, fine-tuning checkpoints, prompt libraries, container manifests, vector-index snapshots, and the telemetry that indicates how it all performed. These copies are stored in versioned, immutable storage options such as cross-region S3, Azure Blob, or an on-prem Ceph bucket, enabling us to revert to "yesterday's mindset" whenever corruption, poor tuning, or accidental deletion occurs. DR, on the other hand, is a runbook that presumes an entire site or cloud region vanishes and asks: "How do we resurrect the whole service quickly enough that users barely notice?" For an LLM stack, this typically involves booting fresh GPU nodes from bootc OSTree images mirrored to object storage, retrieving geo-replicated vLLM container images from Quay, restoring the latest model weights from a versioned bucket, and redirecting Grafana and Thanos to a secondary metrics store—all under automation (GitOps, Argo CD, `oc rollout latest`) to ensure the components come up in the correct sequence.

Two levers govern how aggressive we need to be. Recovery Point Objective (RPO) is the maximum age of data we are willing to lose. In practice, we set it per artifact: we might settle for a 24-hour RPO on immutable OS images, 12 hours on container layers, 2 hours on model checkpoints that evolve during fine-tuning, and 5 minutes on traces and metrics that let us reconstruct the root cause of an incident. Recovery Time Objective (RTO) is the ceiling on downtime before customers or regulators complain. It is the sum of data-copy time, container or VM re-deployment, load-balancer failover, and GPU warm-up. Bootc's zero-copy node rebuilds, pre-provisioned standby GPUs, and scripted redeployments compress RTO dramatically, often to a few minutes for stateless services and a bit longer for heavyweight model weights.

Because telemetry is our flight recorder, the first step in any architecture is to scrape metrics and embeddings continuously; if the data was never collected, the incident effectively never happened. Once observability is in place, we can diagnose events by evidence instead of intuition, track phenomena like embedding drift quantitatively, and patch confidently by keeping the operating-system image, runtime container, and model weights on three independent, reversible tracks. Treat those three lenses—observability, precise RPO/RTO targets, and modular patching—as a discipline, and our Red Hat-based AI estate will remain auditable, resilient, and optimized, no matter what failure mode or compliance surprise tomorrow brings.

Table 6-6. *RPO for key LLM components*

Item	Target	RPO	Restore
Bootc OSTree	S3 and on-prem mirror	24 h	`bootc install --stateroot prod`
vLLM Containers	Quay geo-replica	12 h	`oc rollout latest`
Weights/ Checkpoints	S3 (versioned)	2 h	`ilab model download --digest ...`
Metrics/Traces	Thanos object storage	5 min	Point Grafana at new store

This is the bottom line that we should always keep in mind:

- **Set Up Telemetry First**: If it isn't scraped, it never happened.
- **Diagnose via Data, Not Hunches**: Embedding drift + trace spans makes root cause measurable.
- **Patch with Zero-Copy and Image-Mode**: Keep OS, runtime, and model on independent, reversible tracks.

Follow the three lenses above, and our Red Hat AI stack stays observable, resilient, and optimized—ready for the next surprise our users (or regulators) throw at it.

Conclusion

This chapter concentrates on the supervision and upkeep of AI systems, particularly within RHEL AI. It underscores the significance of observability at both the infrastructure and model layers through metrics such as BLEU and BERTScore to evaluate output quality. Principal performance indicators, including latency percentiles (P95), tokens per second, and requests per second, are monitored alongside drift detection (encompassing data, concept, and performance) to sustain model reliability.

CHAPTER 6　MONITORING AND MAINTENANCE

Additionally, the chapter outlines a multitiered monitoring framework that utilizes tools such as Grafana and Prometheus, along with structured incident response procedures and safe deployment strategies, to ensure system robustness and continuous operation.

In the next chapter, you will learn how to apply RHEL AI in real-world use cases and follow best practices for integrating retrieval-augmented generation and fine-tuning techniques.

CHAPTER 7

Use Cases and Best Practices

Introduction

Chapter 7 shifts its focus from individual features to the broader perspective of how enterprise AI components—such as retrieval-augmented generation, vector databases, fine-tuning pipelines, agent frameworks, and model registries—collaborate on Red Hat platforms. Rather than advocating a single "correct" approach, it introduces various use case patterns, ranging from using different teacher model models to RAG implementation, and shares best practices, including integrating third-party libraries within virtual environments, pinning OSTree images for reproducibility, configuring OpenAI-compatible APIs, and automating processes via Ansible. The chapter also provides deployment snippets to help practitioners develop portable, auditable, and adaptable solutions.

Retrieval-Augmented Generation

Retrieval-augmented generation (RAG) is a technique that enhances a language model's performance by injecting external knowledge at inference time. Instead of permanently altering the model's internal weights, RAG retrieves relevant documents from an indexed corpus (vector database) and appends them to the model's prompt—giving it the context it needs to answer accurately.

Think of it as adding a "library" next to the model: the model doesn't "remember" everything internally, but it knows how to look up answers in a trusted reference. The full end-to-end pipeline is illustrated in Figure 7-1, while Figure 7-2 explains the complete user interaction.

CHAPTER 7 USE CASES AND BEST PRACTICES

On a RHEL AI system, setting up RAG involves

1. **Creating embeddings** from our documents using a transformer model
2. **Storing those embeddings** in a vector store such as Chroma
3. **Retrieving top-k matching documents** at query time and appending them to the model's input
4. **Generating a response** using our base LLM (e.g., a Granite model) served via `ilab model serve`

The model itself stays frozen—we can swap in new documents without retraining.

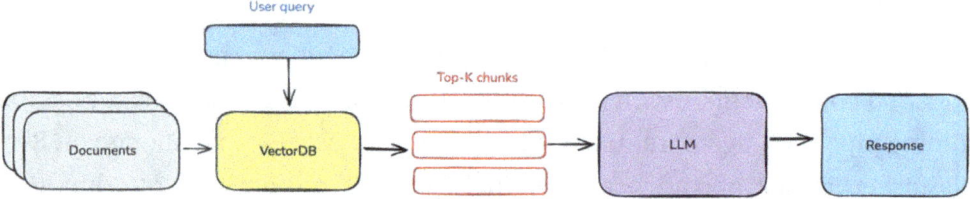

Figure 7-1. Basic RAG pipeline

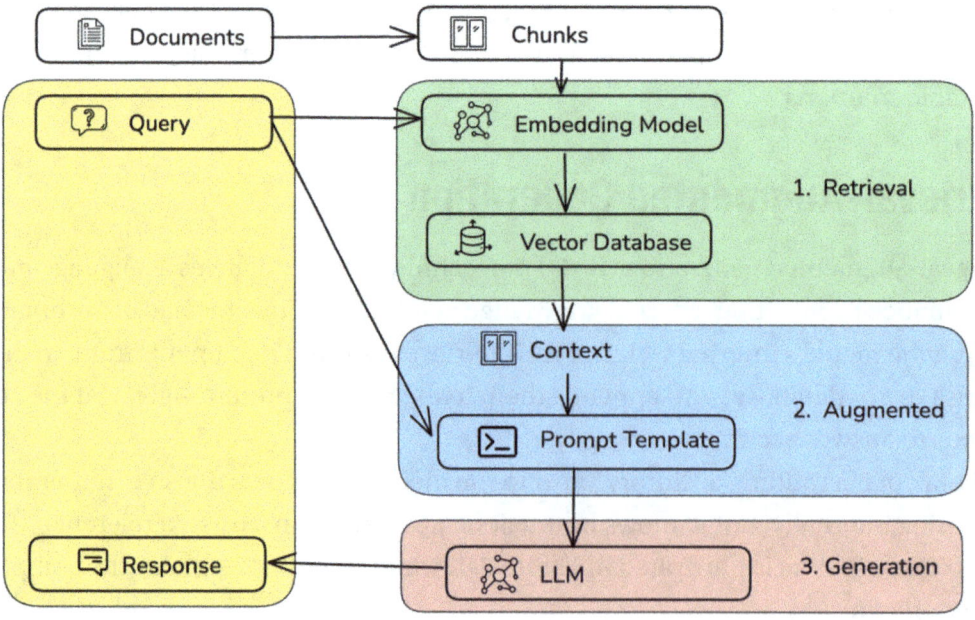

Figure 7-2. RAG schema

When enhancing a model's domain knowledge, teams usually choose between fine-tuning (integrating knowledge into the model's weights) or using retrieval-augmented generation (RAG)—adding relevant context at runtime. Each approach has advantages depending on our latency, traceability, and maintenance requirements. The following section compares these two methods across technical, operational, and strategic dimensions, helping us determine which path fits our RHEL AI use case—or whether a hybrid strategy might offer the best of both.

Real-World Analogy

When enhancing a model's knowledge, teams usually face a key design choice: Should we embed knowledge directly into the model's weights through retraining, or should we keep the model frozen and use RAG to fetch knowledge at runtime? Both approaches have advantages, and in practice, many enterprises use a hybrid strategy.

Brain Surgery

Retraining or fine-tuning writes knowledge directly into the model. Think of it like a brain surgery operation: we are modifying the model's memory so it "knows" new information internally.

- **How It Works**: You create seed Q&A pairs in taxonomy/.../qna.yaml, generate synthetic data (SDG), fine-tune the model via the LAB workflow, and serve the new checkpoint.

- **Best For**: Knowledge that rarely changes and must always be present (e.g., compliance rules, JSON formatting, domain-specific business processes).

- **Performance**: Once retrained, inference is fast—no extra steps are needed.

- **Cost**: Requires GPUs and training time up front, but inference is standard afterward.

- **Traceability**: Harder to audit—since knowledge is "baked in," the model cannot cite sources.
- **Deployment Fit**: Ideal for edge environments, air-gapped systems, or latency-sensitive applications.

Librarian

RAG leaves the base model untouched but gives it the ability to look things up at runtime. Think of it like a librarian fetching the right reference on demand.

- **How It Works**: Documents are embedded and stored in a vector database (e.g., Chroma). At query time, the system retrieves the most relevant passages and appends them to the prompt, which the model then uses to answer.
- **Best For**: Evolving knowledge bases, wikis, support tickets, or multilingual document sets.
- **Performance**: Slightly slower than retraining because of the vector search step (milliseconds to seconds).
- **Cost**: Light inference load; vector DB can run on CPUs or GPUs.
- **Traceability**: High—responses can cite retrieved documents directly.
- **Deployment Fit**: Cloud, on-prem, or hybrid setups where knowledge changes frequently.

Retraining generally results in a low risk of hallucination regarding topics on which it was fine-tuned. Still, the risk becomes significantly higher if the query extends beyond its training domain. RAG typically presents a lower risk of hallucination because it retrieves relevant documents; however, retrieval errors may still lead to incorrect or incomplete answers.

Updates and maintenance in a retraining scenario necessitate an additional fine-tuning cycle when knowledge is revised. In contrast, RAG for updating involves re-embedding new documents, thereby eliminating the need for retraining.

In practical RHEL AI implementations, numerous teams initially employ RAG to enhance agility and ensure content currency. Over time, they analyze which question-and-answer pairs or documents are retrieved most frequently, subsequently refining those into the model. This methodology reduces latency and GPU expenses while ensuring that long-tail knowledge remains current and verifiable.

RAG vs. Retraining

When deciding how to extend an LLM with domain knowledge, two common strategies are available: retraining or fine-tuning and RAG. Each approach has its strengths and trade-offs, and the choice depends on the type of knowledge, its frequency of change, and the deployment environment.

Core Idea and Analogy

- **Retraining/Fine-Tuning**: Knowledge is stored directly in the model's parameters. This is like **brain surgery**, where information is injected into the model's "memory."

- **RAG**: Knowledge is stored externally, and the model looks it up on demand. This is like a **librarian**, fetching relevant source material when asked.

How It Works

- **Retraining**: Create Q&A seeds in taxonomy/.../qna.yaml, generate synthetic data using Synthetic Data Generation (SDG), fine-tune the model using the LAB workflow, and then serve the new checkpoint.

- **RAG**: Keep the base model unchanged. Instead, embed documents into a vector database (such as Chroma). At query time, retrieve the top-k relevant passages and append them to the model's prompt.

Best Use Cases

- **Retraining**: Works best for knowledge that **rarely changes** or skills that must be embedded permanently, such as compliance rules, formatting requirements (like JSON output), or domain-specific expertise.

- **RAG**: Ideal for **large and evolving document sets**, such as wikis, support tickets, or knowledge bases, and for scenarios where answers must include **citations**.

Performance and Latency

- **Retraining**: Fast inference—no extra steps are needed at runtime since the knowledge is already inside the model.

CHAPTER 7   USE CASES AND BEST PRACTICES

- **RAG**: Slightly slower, since each query requires a vector search. The additional latency is usually in the range of **milliseconds to seconds**, depending on the size of the document set and the search back end.

Hardware and Cost Considerations

- **Retraining**: Requires GPUs and compute resources during fine-tuning, but inference afterward is standard and efficient.
- **RAG**: Light on GPU needs—only embeddings require GPU support; the vector database and retrieval step can run on CPUs.

Updating Knowledge

- **Retraining**: Updating requires a new fine-tuning cycle whenever knowledge changes.
- **RAG**: Simply re-embed the updated documents into the vector store—no model retraining required.

Traceability and Auditing

- **Retraining**: Harder to audit—the model "knows" the information but cannot cite its sources.
- **RAG**: High traceability—responses can cite the specific documents retrieved, making it easier to explain and validate outputs.

Hallucination Risk

- **Retraining**: Low risk on topics included in fine-tuning, but high risk if the model is asked about topics outside its training scope.
- **RAG**: Generally lower hallucination risk, since answers are grounded in retrieved documents. However, hallucinations can still occur if retrieval fails or retrieves irrelevant content.

Deployment Fit

- **Retraining**: Suited for edge environments, air-gapped systems, or applications with strict low-latency SLAs.
- **RAG**: Well-suited for cloud, on-prem, or hybrid deployments where content changes frequently and where multilingual support or evolving knowledge is required.

Hybrid Strategy

In practice, many Red Hat AI deployments start with RAG for agility and freshness, then fine-tune frequently retrieved Q&A pairs into the model over time. This hybrid approach reduces latency and GPU costs while maintaining knowledge that is both up to date and auditable.

Use Case

Every organization maintains critical safety procedures, such as fire safety manuals, evacuation steps, and compliance rules. These documents are usually written in long PDF manuals or wikis, making them hard for staff to quickly reference during emergencies or drills. Instead of expecting employees to search through static pages, we can automate these procedures with RAG. As this procedure might vary quickly, we prefer to use the RAG instead of retraining practice.

In this example, we will

- Store the fire safety manual as text in a vector database.
- Serve a Granite-based LLM via the Red Hat Inference Server (RHIS) with vLLM.
- Connect the LLM to the vector database using LangChain.
- Allow employees (or automated systems) to ask natural-language questions such as
    - *"Summarise section 4.3 of the fire-safety manual."*
    - *"What should we do if the main exit is blocked during evacuation?"*
    - *"List all fire extinguisher locations on the second floor."*

This setup not only delivers fast, grounded answers but also provides traceability—the model cites the section of the manual it used, reducing hallucination risk and supporting compliance. Below is the step-by-step guide for building this system on a fresh RHEL AI machine.

CHAPTER 7   USE CASES AND BEST PRACTICES

Vector Database

In RAG workflows, a vector database stores document embeddings, allowing for the retrieval of relevant text chunks at inference time. This example uses Chroma, a lightweight, developer-friendly vector store that runs entirely in-process—ideal for RHEL AI users who want minimal setup, no external services, and full control over storage (e.g., local disk or NVMe). Chroma uses DuckDB and Parquet under the hood, which makes it fast and portable without requiring a running server.

For large-scale or distributed deployments, alternatives like Weaviate offer advanced features such as built-in hybrid search, cloud hosting, or persistent clusters. But Chroma is a strong default for single-node experiments, edge cases, or containerized microservices—especially when our goal is to quickly prototype RAG pipelines without adding infrastructure complexity.

Below is a practical, end-to-end recipe that sets up a vector database on a fresh RHEL AI machine, loads embeddings using Hugging Face models, and prepares the stack for RAG queries. Chroma is not shipped in the base image, so install it inside a user virtual environment.

The following provides a detailed, step-by-step instruction for the setup of RHEL AI and ChromaDB:

1. Create a Python environment

    ```
    python -m venv ~/venvs/rag
    source ~/venvs/rag/bin/activate
    pip install chromadb langchain sentencepiece
    ```

    This ensures your vector store dependencies are isolated and survive image upgrades.

2. Initialize embeddings and vector store in Python

    Create rag_index.py:

    ```
    from pathlib import Path
    from langchain.embeddings import HuggingFaceEmbeddings
    from langchain.vectorstores import Chroma
    from chromadb.config import Settings
    # Use a Hugging Face embedding model
    embed = HuggingFaceEmbeddings(model_name="thenlper/gte-large")
    ```

CHAPTER 7   USE CASES AND BEST PRACTICES

```
# Create a Chroma collection backed by DuckDB + Parquet
vect = Chroma(
    collection_name="docs",
    embedding_function=embed,
    client_settings=Settings(chroma_api_impl="duckdb+parquet")
)
```

This sets up Chroma[1] with a DuckDB[2] plus Parquet[3] back end, which is fast, portable, and requires no database server.

3. Load documents and generate embeddings

   Prepare a directory, e.g., ~/corpus/, and place our fire safety manual (split into .txt sections if possible).

   ```
   for path in Path("corpus").glob("*.txt"):
       text = path.read_text()
       vect.add_texts([text], metadatas=[{"source": path.name}])
   print("Fire safety manual indexed.")
   ```

   This loop ingests all text files in a local corpus/ directory, embeds them with the chosen Hugging Face model, and stores both embeddings and metadata in Chroma.

   Run it:

   ```
   python rag_index.py
   ```

4. Persist and optimize storage

   By default, Chroma stores data under ~/.chroma. For larger projects, move this folder to an NVMe-backed directory for faster reads/writes:

   ```
   mv ~/.chroma /mnt/nvme/chroma
   export CHROMA_DB_DIR=/mnt/nvme/chroma
   ```

---

[1] https://www.trychroma.com/
[2] https://duckdb.org/
[3] https://parquet.apache.org/

CHAPTER 7   USE CASES AND BEST PRACTICES

5. Query your vector store

    Once documents are embedded, you can issue similarity searches from within LangChain or directly from Chroma. These retrieved chunks can then be passed into RAG prompts for your base model.

Note   Always test with real business documents, not generic prompts, to confirm retrieval is actually grounding responses.

The result is a fully working, local vector database on RHEL AI that can be used for RAG experiments or production pipelines. Chroma's simplicity makes it perfect for rapid iteration. Milvus is a high-performance vector database built for large-scale, production-grade similarity search, while ChromaDB is a lightweight, developer-friendly vector store ideal for rapid RAG prototyping and local experimentation.

For large-scale or distributed deployments, we may consider alternatives such as Weaviate or Milvus. These are the benefits of adopting Weaviate for our RAG implementation:

- **Hybrid Search**: Weaviate combines vector similarity search with traditional keyword filtering (e.g., finding reviews about "flight delays" with negative sentiment from specific time periods).

- **Multimodal Data Support**: Native support for text, images, and structured data that can reflect the full spectrum of customer interactions.

- **RAG-Optimized**: Purpose-built for retrieval-augmented generation workflows, with native support for context injection and prompt engineering.

- **Real-Time Performance**: Sub-second query responses even with tens or hundreds of millions of vectors, making it suitable for real-time decision support systems.

- **Built-in Vectorization**: Automatic text embedding generation using a range of state-of-the-art models.

- **Cloud-Native Scalability**: Horizontal scaling capabilities that grow with enterprise data volumes and query loads.
- **Enterprise Security**: Role-based access control, API key management, ISO27001 certified.

RAG

With our documents embedded in Chroma, the next step is to wire retrieval to the running model endpoint. Red Hat AI Inference Server (vLLM) exposes an OpenAI-compatible REST API, and LangChain's OpenAI client can talk to it directly. When we run a query through the RetrievalQA pipeline, the workflow follows four clear steps:

1. **Embed the Query**: The user's input is converted into a vector representation using the same embedding model that was used to index the documents.
2. **Retrieve Top-k Chunks**: The system searches the Chroma vector store and selects the most relevant document chunks based on vector similarity.
3. **Append to the Prompt**: The retrieved chunks are added to the original query, forming an augmented prompt that provides the model with domain-specific context (e.g., fire safety procedures).
4. **Generate the Answer**: The augmented prompt is sent to vLLM through its OpenAI-compatible API, and the model produces a grounded response.

This sequence ensures that answers are not only fluent but also contextually accurate and tied to your knowledge base, reducing hallucination risk and improving traceability.

The following `rag_query.py` script builds a RetrievalQA chain that (a) queries Chroma with MMR search to fetch the top-k relevant passages and (b) sends those passages to the Granite model via the vLLM endpoint, producing an answer that's grounded in our own content. This is how we turn a static fire safety manual into a searchable assistant without retraining.

CHAPTER 7 USE CASES AND BEST PRACTICES

We use the OpenAI library to connect to vLLM because it speaks the OpenAI specification created by LangChain. Create rag_query.py:

```
from langchain.chains import RetrievalQA
from langchain.llms   import OpenAI

llm   = OpenAI(openai_api_base="http://127.0.0.1:8000/v1",
            openai_api_key="none",
            model_name="granite-7b-custom")

qa = RetrievalQA.from_chain_type(
        llm        = llm,
        chain_type = "stuff",
        retriever  = vect.as_retriever(search_type="mmr", k=5)
    )
```

We assume: (1) vLLM is running at http://127.0.0.1:8000/v1, (2) your Chroma collection vect is already populated with the same embedding model used at query time, and (3) you want answers that cite the sources the model was given. After creating rag_query.py, run a targeted question (e.g., *"Summarise section 4.3 of the fire-safety manual"*) to verify that results are retrieved, appended, and generated through the OpenAI-compatible vLLM endpoint.

```
print(qa("Summarise section 4.3 of the fire-safety manual"))
```

This ensures that RAG is not only returning chunks but also grounding the LLM's output in your intended knowledge domain (e.g., safety procedures, compliance rules, or internal documentation).

REST API

Up to this point, we've built a RAG workflow that takes a user query, looks up relevant chunks from our fire safety manual, and generates a grounded response with vLLM. This workflow is often called a "pipeline" because it connects several steps together:

1. User submits a question.

2. The system embeds the query and retrieves the most relevant document chunks from Chroma.

3. Those chunks are appended to the user's query to form an augmented prompt.
4. The augmented prompt is sent to vLLM, which generates the final answer.

That's great for testing in Python, but in the real world, we want to make this accessible to other applications—chat UIs, compliance dashboards, mobile apps, or even automation scripts. The easiest way to do this is to wrap the pipeline in a REST API, which acts as a simple HTTP service that accepts questions and returns answers in JSON format. Once every single component of our RAG pipeline is set up and responding to queries, the final step is to expose it as a simple web service. This makes it easy to integrate with chat UIs, internal tools, or downstream automation. Using FastAPI and Uvicorn, we can stand up a minimal REST endpoint in just a few lines—without needing a full web framework or heavy infrastructure. First, install the required packages:

```
pip install fastapi uvicorn
```

The example below wraps our RetrievalQA chain in an HTTP POST interface that listens for questions and returns generated answers in JSON format using a FastAPI app (api.py):

```
from fastapi import FastAPI
from pydantic import BaseModel
class Question(BaseModel):
    question: str
app = FastAPI()
@app.post("/ask")
async def ask(q: Question):
    return {"answer": qa(q.question)}
```

Run the server on port 9000; listen for every interface on the host:

```
uvicorn api:app --host 0.0.0.0 --port 9000
```

Now, you can send queries with an HTTP client like our browser, a test program like Postman or Bruno, or a simple command line curl or from any HTTP client:

```
curl -X POST "http://localhost:9000/ask" -H "Content-Type: application/json" -d '{"question":"Summarise section 4.3 of the fire-safety manual"}'
```

This returns a JSON object with the grounded answer.

We can run the `uvicorn` using the systemd service `ragapi.service` file like the one below:

```
[Unit]
Description=Fire Safety RAG API Service
After=network.target
[Service]
User=raguser
Group=ragruser
WorkingDirectory=/home/youruser/rag
Environment="PATH=/home/youruser/venvs/ragapi/bin"
ExecStart=/home/youruser/venvs/ragapi/bin/uvicorn api:app --host 0.0.0.0 --port 9000
Restart=always
RestartSec=5
[Install]
WantedBy=multi-user.target
```

Reload systemd and enable the service:

```
sudo systemctl daemon-reload
sudo systemctl enable ragapi.service
sudo systemctl start ragapi.service
```

By exposing the RAG workflow as a REST API:

- Users and apps can query the fire safety manual in natural language.

- Internal tools (dashboards, chatbots) can integrate the assistant without duplicating logic.

- Automation systems (e.g., incident response workflows) can call the API to fetch safety instructions in real time.

On RHEL AI, this approach is lightweight and container-friendly and requires no additional infrastructure beyond FastAPI and Uvicorn.

Our finished stack now looks like Figure 7-3.

CHAPTER 7 USE CASES AND BEST PRACTICES

Figure 7-3. *RAG implementation*

Figure 7-3 illustrates the full workflow of our RAG system, showing how a user's simple question flows through several components before coming back as a grounded answer. The process begins with the client, which could be anything from a chatbot UI to a web form or automation tool, where a user enters a query such as *"Summarise section 4.3 of the fire-safety manual."* This query is then sent to FastAPI, which acts as the lightweight REST gateway, accepting the request and passing it into the pipeline without the user needing to understand the underlying logic. From there, the request is handled by LangChain's RetrievalQA chain, which manages the key retrieval steps: embedding the query into a vector representation, searching the vector database for relevant matches, and constructing an augmented prompt that combines the user's question with supporting context. The supporting knowledge comes from ChromaDB, the vector store where documents like manuals or policies are stored as embeddings; when queried, it returns the top-k most relevant chunks that can help answer the question. Finally, the augmented prompt is sent to the vLLM inference server running on RHEL AI or Red Hat AI Inference Server, which generates a fluent response that incorporates both the user's input and the retrieved passages. This answer is then returned through FastAPI back to the client in JSON format. The result is an end-to-end system where the model doesn't just "guess" based on its training but grounds its answers in real organizational knowledge, making outputs more accurate, up to date, and auditable. In effect, the figure shows how different layers—client interface, REST API, retrieval logic, vector database, and inference runtime—fit together to turn static documents into an intelligent assistant.

LangChain

Sometimes we don't need a full-blown platform or orchestration system—we just want a simple chat API that connects to our model and lets other tools (like web UIs, Slack bots, or scripts) interact with it. This setup is ideal for POCs, demos, or integrating with frontend tools like Gradio or Slack bots. This is where LangChain + FastAPI + Uvicorn makes an excellent combination:

- **LangChain** provides the retrieval and LLM orchestration logic.

- **FastAPI** is a modern, high-performance Python web framework designed for building APIs with minimal boilerplate.

- **Uvicorn** is a lightning-fast ASGI (Asynchronous Server Gateway Interface) server, optimized for running FastAPI applications in production.

We can also integrate in a graphical front end like LibreChat[4] that looks like the look and feel of ChatGPT.

Together, these let us stand up a working chat endpoint in under five minutes.

Step 1: Activate Your Python Virtual Environment

Always run this in a user-level environment so upgrades to RHEL AI don't overwrite your libraries.

```
source ~/venvs/aiapps/bin/activate
```

Step 2: Install Required Packages

We'll need LangChain (to connect to the model), OpenAI (to talk to vLLM's OpenAI-compatible endpoint), FastAPI (for the API framework), and Uvicorn (to serve it).

```
pip install langchain openai fastapi uvicorn
```

Step 3: Create the FastAPI Application

Save the following as app.py:

```
from fastapi import FastAPI
from langchain.llms import OpenAI
# Connect to the locally running vLLM inference server
llm = OpenAI(
    openai_api_base="http://127.0.0.1:8000/v1",
    openai_api_key="none",           # vLLM doesn't need a real key
    model_name="granite-7b-custom"   # label for our Granite model
)
# Create a FastAPI app
app = FastAPI()
# Define a /chat endpoint
```

---

[4] https://www.librechat.ai/

```python
@app.post("/chat")
async def chat(prompt: str):
    return {"answer": llm(prompt)}
```

This small app does the following:

1. Defines a connection to the vLLM server (127.0.0.1:8000/v1).

2. Wraps that connection in a FastAPI application.

3. Exposes a **/chat** endpoint where clients can post a prompt and get an answer.

Step 4: Run the Service with Uvicorn

Start the service using Uvicorn:

```
uvicorn app:app --host 0.0.0.0 --port 9000
```

Here's what happens:

- `app:app` means *"look inside app.py and run the app object."*
- `--host 0.0.0.0` makes the service listen on all network interfaces.
- `--port 9000` chooses the port where the service will be available.

Step 5: Test the Endpoint

You can now send a query using curl or any HTTP client:

```
curl -X POST "http://localhost:9000/chat" -H "Content-Type: application/json" -d "\"What is the fire evacuation procedure?\""
```

Expected response:

```
{"answer":"According to the fire safety manual, the procedure begins by..."}
```

With just these steps, you've deployed a minimal LLM chat service. It can be called from other apps, integrated into a chatbot front end, or expanded with additional logic (like RAG or multi-turn memory).

CHAPTER 7   USE CASES AND BEST PRACTICES

Third-Party Integrations

RHEL AI provides a robust foundation out of the box: Python 3 for extensibility, InstructLab CLI for workflow automation, vLLM for high-performance inference, DeepSpeed and PyTorch Fully Sharded Data Parallel (FSDP) for distributed training, and IBM's Granite family of models as the default building blocks. These components are hardened and supported by Red Hat, giving enterprises a stable and secure baseline. But in practice, many organizations need to go further—whether that's introducing RAG, adopting alternative model families with specialized reasoning skills, or deploying lightweight serving runtimes that can run efficiently on laptops and edge devices. In this book, we show how to extend the base RHEL AI platform in a clean, composable way by layering additional tools on top using virtual environments, containerized workflows, and Red Hat's automation patterns. The philosophy here is additive: the base RHEL AI image remains untouched, while third-party integrations are applied in the user space or orchestrated via automation frameworks like Ansible Automation Platform.

The snippet below shows how to set up our `aiapps` venv and make it persist across reboots.

```
# Inside RHEL AI
python -m venv ~/venvs/aiapps
source ~/venvs/aiapps/bin/activate     # prompt → (aiapps)
pip install --upgrade pip wheel
pip install langchain==0.2.* chromadb gradio fastapi uvicorn sentencepiece
```

This makes upgrades safe, because extensions survive bootc image switches, container restarts, and model updates without requiring a rebuild of the base system. It also aligns with Red Hat's principle of immutable infrastructure—the underlying substrate is stable and supportable, while innovation happens in layers above it. The AI ecosystem is evolving rapidly, and several emerging technologies pair particularly well with RHEL AI deployments:

1. **Long-Term Memory with Chroma**: RAG has become the standard for keeping models fresh without costly retraining. Chroma, now widely adopted in enterprise stacks, is a lightweight but high-performance vector database that integrates seamlessly into LangChain workflows. It runs fully in-process, supports Parquet/DuckDB back ends, and can scale from local NVMe

storage on a developer laptop to distributed clusters for production. In a fire safety automation example, Chroma allows staff to query updated procedures without retraining Granite each time the manual changes, as we just demonstrated in the previous section.

2. **Alternative Model Families** (DeepSeek R1-70B): While Granite remains the recommended baseline for enterprise workloads, newer open-source families like DeepSeek R1-72B have shown state-of-the-art performance in multilingual reasoning, particularly across English and Chinese. With Red Hat's support for OCI-compliant model containers, deploying these third-party models on RHEL AI is straightforward. You can pull the container, register it with InstructLab, and run inference side-by-side with Granite, choosing the best model per workload. This hybrid model strategy gives enterprises flexibility without lock-in.

3. **Lightweight Local Serving** (Ollama): For developers, field engineers, and edge deployments, serving large models is often impractical. Tools like Ollama, now widely used, allow GGUF quantized models to run on consumer hardware with minimal configuration. By integrating Ollama into RHEL AI workflows, teams can prototype locally, sync pipelines with production Granite or DeepSeek deployments, and validate updates before rolling them out cluster-wide.

Accelerate Training

Training large language models (LLMs) is one of the most resource-intensive workloads in AI. While inference can often be optimized through quantization and model compression, training requires careful distribution of compute, memory, and communication across multiple GPUs. RHEL AI integrates tightly with both DeepSpeed[5]

---

[5] https://www.deepspeed.ai

and Fully Sharded Data Parallel[6] (FSDP), two of the most widely adopted training frameworks in 2025, enabling enterprises to train or fine-tune models at scale on heterogeneous hardware.

At a high level, these tools solve the same core problem—how to fit models with billions of parameters across available accelerators without running out of memory or sacrificing throughput—but they take different approaches. DeepSpeed is tuned for extremely large models and uses advanced techniques like ZeRO-3 partitioning, activation checkpointing, and CPU/NVMe offload to push memory limits beyond a single GPU. FSDP, built into PyTorch, shards both model parameters and optimizer states across GPUs, reducing redundant copies and delivering excellent efficiency on clusters with fast interconnects. Both are first-class citizens in the RHEL AI stack and can be invoked directly via the **InstructLab CLI.**

Training with DeepSpeed on NVIDIA A100

DeepSpeed remains the gold standard for NVIDIA clusters, especially those equipped with A100 or H100 GPUs. It is particularly effective when training dense transformer models like Granite-13B or 70B. With ZeRO Stage 3, parameters, gradients, and optimizer states are partitioned across GPUs, allowing near-linear scaling. Train Granite on 4× NVIDIA A100 GPUs using DeepSpeed:

```
ilab model train --strategy lab-multiphase --trainer deepspeed --deepspeed-stage 3 --gpus 4
```

In this configuration:

- `--strategy lab-multiphase` runs the recommended RHEL AI workflow: pretraining ➤ fine-tuning ➤ evaluation.

- `--trainer deepspeed` selects DeepSpeed as the back end.

- `--deepspeed-stage 3` enables full parameter sharding, the most memory-efficient mode.

- `--gpus 4` specifies the number of available A100 GPUs on the node.

---

[6] https://pytorch.org/blog/introducing-pytorch-fully-sharded-data-parallel-api/

With this setup, training can scale beyond what fits in GPU memory by using NVMe offload, and users can tune batch sizes without hitting out-of-memory (OOM) errors.

Training with FSDP on AMD MI300X or Mixed Hardware

While DeepSpeed is heavily optimized for NVIDIA CUDA stacks, many enterprises are adopting AMD MI300X accelerators, valued for their high memory capacity and ROCm support. For these systems—or when mixing vendors—FSDP is often the preferred choice because it is framework-native, hardware-agnostic, and tightly integrated with PyTorch. Train Granite on AMD MI300X or mixed GPU hardware using FSDP:

```
ilab model train --trainer fsdp --fsdp-shard-size 4
```

The command:

- `--trainer fsdp` selects the FSDP back end.
- `--fsdp-shard-size 4` divides model states into four shards, distributing them across available GPUs.

This approach maximizes utilization on high-bandwidth interconnects (e.g., AMD's Infinity Fabric or NVLink) while keeping memory balanced across devices. For MI300X systems with 192 GB per GPU, FSDP allows training models that would otherwise require dozens of smaller GPUs. Mixed hardware or AMD MI300X:

```
ilab model train --trainer fsdp --fsdp-shard-size 4
```

Tune vLLM

Fine-tuning our model is only half the battle—serving it efficiently is the other. This section shows how to adjust vLLM's memory usage, context size, and retry behavior, especially for cutting-edge GPUs like GH200. These config tweaks can dramatically improve startup stability and response times.

We edit `~/.config/instructlab/config.yaml` to look like the following:

```
serve:
  vllm:
    vllm_args:
      - --max-context-size
```

```
    - "8192"
    - --gpu-memory-utilization
    - "0.90"
max_startup_attempts: 1200
```

Restart:

```
ilab model serve --model-path <checkpoint_dir>
```

The impact of the Tune vLLM configuration is focused on improving stability and performance when serving large language models using vLLM, especially on high-end GPUs like the NVIDIA GH200. Here's a breakdown of what each change does and its overall effect:

Context Size (--max-context-size "8192")

- **Effect**: Increases the maximum token context window to 8192 tokens
- **Impact**: Allows the model to handle much longer inputs or conversations, making it suitable for complex tasks like summarization or multi-turn chat without losing earlier context

GPU Memory Utilization (--gpu-memory-utilization "0.90")

- **Effect**: Tells vLLM to use up to 90% of GPU memory
- **Impact**: Maximizes memory usage efficiency, allowing for larger batch sizes or more concurrent requests, leading to faster inference and better throughput, while still avoiding out-of-memory errors

Startup Attempts (max_startup_attempts: 1200)

- **Effect**: Increases the number of retries during model startup.
- **Impact**: Crucial for **cutting-edge GPUs like GH200**, which may have variable startup behavior. This reduces failure risk during deployment and ensures the model starts reliably, even under less predictable hardware initialization states.

Command (ilab model serve --model-path <checkpoint_dir>)

- **Effect**: Starts serving the fine-tuned model using the new settings
- **Impact**: Applies all the above optimizations in practice, leading to faster response times, fewer startup issues, and better memory handling during live inference

Bring Our Own Teacher

Do we need to use a different foundation model—like LLaMA or DeepSeek—for training or synthetic data generation? RHEL AI makes it easy. Download the model, plug it into our workflow, and point to our preferred student. This section shows how to swap in custom GGUF or Hugging Face (HF) models with minimal effort. The AI models are usually in GPT-Generated Unified Format (GGUF[7]), which is a file format that streamlines the use and deployment of LLMs. GGUF is the most recent development that builds upon the foundations laid out by its predecessor, the file format GGML,[8] developed by Georgi Gerganov, a high-performance tensor library. GGUF is specially designed to store inference models and perform well on consumer-grade computer hardware. Because it's compatible with various programming languages, such as Python and R, GGUF has contributed to the format's popularity. It also supports fine-tuning, allowing users to adapt LLMs to specialized applications, and stores prompt templates for model deployments across various applications. While GGML is still in use, its support has been superseded by GGUF.

Let us implement the teacher–student paradigm by referring to the knowledge distillation strategy outlined in Chapter 3. For instance, replace the IBM Granite model with the Meta Llama model. The subsequent example utilizes Llama 3.3 70B as the SDG teacher from the Red Hat container registry:

```
ilab model download --repository docker://registry.redhat.io/rhelai1/
llama-3.3-70b-Instruct
```

Downloads the LLaMA 3.3 70B Instruct model container from Red Hat's registry. This model acts as the teacher for synthetic data generation. By downloading it via Docker, RHEL AI ensures secure, reproducible model packaging. It enables using high-performing foundation models without manual setup or file conversion.

```
ilab data generate --pipeline llama --gpus 8
```

Launches the data generation pipeline using the downloaded LLaMA model and assigns 8 GPUs for the task. Generates high-quality, instruction-following synthetic data from the teacher model, which is later used to train a student model. Using multiple GPUs speeds up the process and supports larger batch sizes, crucial when working with a 70B parameter model.

---

[7] https://huggingface.co/docs/hub/en/gguf
[8] https://ggml.ai/

Swap the student by specifying the name of the model with the parameter --model-name, pointing to any GGUF or HF repository.

This approach empowers users to optimize their AI training pipeline by selecting the most suitable teacher model while maintaining ease of use and compatibility. It promotes customization, performance efficiency, and hardware accessibility—critical factors for enterprise and specialized AI deployments.

Automate with Ansible

Manually running ilab commands works fine for quick experiments, but in production, you want automation. This is where Red Hat Ansible Automation Platform comes in. With Ansible, you can turn every step of the model lifecycle into a repeatable, automated workflow—from downloading the baseline model, to generating synthetic data, to training on GPUs. This ensures that your fine-tuning jobs are consistent, auditable, and resilient to human error. RHEL AI integrates with Ansible through two collections:

- **infra.ai**: Handles infrastructure provisioning (e.g., spinning up GPU nodes on bare metal or cloud)
- **redhat.ai**: Provides modules for running InstructLab commands (ilab model download, ilab data generate, ilab model train, etc.) in a declarative way

In this section, we'll build an **end-to-end fine-tuning playbook** called fine_tune.yml and run it with the ansible-playbook command.

From your Ansible control node, create a new file called fine_tune.yml.

```
---
- name: End-to-end fine-tune workflow
  hosts: rhelai
  collections:
    - redhat.ai
  tasks:
    - name: Download Granite 7B starter model
      redhat.ai.model_download:
        repository: registry.redhat.io/rhelai1/granite-7b-starter
    - name: Generate synthetic data
```

```
    redhat.ai.data_generate:
      sdg_scale_factor: 20
  - name: Fine-tune model with DeepSpeed
    redhat.ai.model_train:
      trainer: deepspeed
      gpus: 4
```

Let's break down what each part does:

1. **Hosts: rhelai**

   - This playbook targets the inventory group `rhelai`. These hosts are provisioned by the `infra.ai` collection and should have GPUs available.

2. **Collection: redhat.ai**

   - We're using the `redhat.ai` Ansible collection, which wraps InstructLab commands into easy-to-use modules.

3. **Task 1: Model Download**

   - Pulls the Granite 7B starter model from Red Hat's registry (`registry.redhat.io/rhelai1/granite-7b-starter`).
   - This serves as the baseline model that will be fine-tuned.

4. **Task 2: Synthetic Data Generation (SDG)**

   - Runs SDG with a 20× scaling factor. This step amplifies our dataset by generating diverse instruction–response pairs.

5. **Task 3: Model Training**

   - Starts fine-tuning using DeepSpeed on 4 GPUs. DeepSpeed handles sharding and memory efficiency, enabling the training of larger models with fewer resources.

Once saved, run the workflow with

`ansible-playbook fine_tune.yml`

This will automatically

1. Download the model
2. Generate synthetic data
3. Fine-tune using DeepSpeed

All three steps run in sequence, providing a fully automated and reproducible fine-tuning pipeline.

By formalizing the workflow within Ansible, several advantages are obtained:

- **Repeatability**: The ability to execute the same procedure across various environments (development, staging, production).

- **Auditability**: The YAML playbook serves as a precise documentation of the model training process.

- **Automation**: Eliminates manual command input, with the playbook managing sequencing and error handling.

- **Scalability**: Integrates with infra.ai to automatically provision GPU nodes and conduct large-scale fine-tuning.

Custom Image Layers

Sometimes, it is necessary to go beyond the default RHEL AI image; perhaps you require your own utilities, model packages, or pinned dependencies. By utilizing Kickstart and bootc, you can construct reproducible, bootable images that incorporate your custom layers. This methodology is effective even on air-gapped hosts, thereby guaranteeing consistency throughout development, staging, and production environments.

Step 1. Add Your Container to a Kickstart File

Kickstart controls how the image is built. You extend it with the ostreecontainer directive pointing to your container image:

```
ostreecontainer --url quay.io/acme/my-rhelai:latest
```

Here:

- quay.io/acme/my-rhelai:latest is your custom container image (replace with your registry + tag).

- The container gets layered on top of the RHEL AI base during image creation.

Step 2. Respin the ISO

Once your Kickstart file is ready, rebuild the bootable ISO:

```
mkksiso rhelai-bootc.ks rhelai-1.5.iso rhelai-custom.iso
```

What's happening here:

- `rhelai-bootc.ks`: Our Kickstart file with the container layer defined
- `rhelai-1.5.iso`: The base RHEL AI installer ISO
- `rhelai-custom.iso`: The new, layered ISO that you can boot from

This creates a self-contained bootable image with your customizations baked in.

Step 3. Boot or Switch to the Custom Image

You now have two options:

- **Fresh Install**: Boot a new system from the rhelai-custom.iso.
- **Switch on an Existing Host**:

  ```
  sudo bootc switch quay.io/acme/my-rhelai:latest
  ```

The bootc switch command pivots an already running system to your new container image, applying the custom layer in place.

The significance of this approach lies in its reproducibility: each ISO is anchored to a container digest. Portability: Compatible even within air-gapped networks (physical media can be used to transport the ISO). Containers are capable of being versioned and signed, thereby providing a clear audit trail. Developers and operations teams can construct once and execute universally with consistent components, gaining flexibility.

GPU Profiles

Not all GPUs are created equal. The list below summarizes the status and tuning requirements for common accelerator profiles—such as NVIDIA H200, Grace Hopper (GH200), and AMD MI300X—to help identify the optimal configuration for a given hardware setup. For more detailed options, see Chapter 4.

CHAPTER 7   USE CASES AND BEST PRACTICES

- **NVIDIA H200**: Use h200_xN profile.
- **Grace Hopper GH200**: Set max_startup_attempts: 1200.
- **AMD MI300X**: Use mi300x_xN profile.

Updates and Maintenance

Keep our environment healthy and current with this quick checklist for updating the OS, models, and Python packages. Back up config files, version our YAML, and use bootc and ilab commands for seamless upgrades without breaking reproducibility.

For the OS and container use:

```
sudo bootc upgrade --apply
```

To update the base model (IBM Granite and others):

```
ilab model download -update
```

For each external library, rely on the PIP package manager update mechanism:

```
source ~/venvs/aiapps/bin/activate
pip list --outdated              # extra libs
```

Always back up config.yaml before rerunning ilab config init.

Storage

AI workloads require fast and reliable storage for housekeeping information. We suggest these few simple practices: mount datasets on XFS volumes, relocate checkpoints to NVMe, and set ILAB_HOME to offload artifacts—all helping our training runs stay clean and performant.

Add 1 TB NVMe storage under /home for datasets and checkpoints. Another alternative is to set ILAB_HOME=/mnt to relocate InstructLab artifacts. Mount external datasets on an XFS partition labeled "ilab-data".

CHAPTER 7 USE CASES AND BEST PRACTICES

Preflight Checklist

Prior to initiating the process of fine-tuning, deployment, or constructing a custom image, it is best practice to pause and conduct validation of the setup. The following checklist is intended to identify common misconfigurations at an early stage, thereby preventing upgrade failures, automation errors, or reproducibility issues later on. Consider this as a "preflight" review—ensure each item is confirmed before proceeding.

1. **Virtualenv**

    Ensure that your Python virtual environment is located on a persistent volume. This safeguards it from being lost during container restarts or node reboots. All necessary packages should be documented in a requirements.txt file stored within your Git repository. This facilitates others in recreating the environment and guarantees consistency across builds and deployments.

2. **config.yaml**

    Your configuration file should be checked into version control. This provides traceability and makes it possible to roll back to known-good states. Pay special attention to the GPU profile defined in `config.yaml`, as selecting the wrong accelerator settings (e.g., H200 vs. MI300X) can lead to runtime failures or degraded performance.

3. **Ansible Secrets**

    Any sensitive variables, such as API keys or database credentials, should never be hard-coded. Instead, store them in Ansible Vault or within an Automation Execution Environment (AEE). This approach reduces the risk of accidental leaks and ensures compliance with security best practices.

4. **bootc Image**

    When referencing container images, it is advisable to pin them by digest (sha256:...) rather than by a mutable tag such as latest. Tags are subject to change without notice, which may lead to the introduction of unforeseen updates into your environment. Pinning by digest ensures that the same binary image is utilized across all deployments.

5. **Models**

    When deploying AI models, specify a particular release hash using the `--release <sha>` parameter. This measure prevents unintended divergence resulting from upstream updates, thereby ensuring that your fine-tuned model operates on the same foundational version on which it was originally validated.

By executing these procedures, we establish a reproducible and auditable foundation. Whether you are initiating the development of a custom image, evaluating a fine-tuned model, or preparing for a production deployment, the checklist offers a systematic approach to prevent common errors and ensure your environment adheres to established best practices.

Troubleshooting Quick Reference

When things go wrong, don't panic—most errors in the RHEL AI stack trace back to a small set of predictable causes. Below are the most common problems you might encounter, why they occur, and what you can do to fix them.

1. **Out of Memory Errors**

    Symptom: ValueError: failed to allocate…

    Cause: The selected model exceeds the available GPU VRAM.

    Resolution: Reduce the quantization level (e.g., switch from Q4 to Q3) so the model uses less memory, or spread the model across multiple GPUs using `--tensor-parallel-size 4`.

2. **Empty Results from Chroma**

    Symptom: Chroma returns an empty list after a query.

    Cause: The embedding model used during query time does not match the one used during data ingestion.

    Resolution: Always use the same embedding model for both indexing and querying steps. A mismatch guarantees poor or empty retrievals.

3. **LangChain Timeout with Ollama**

    Symptom: LangChain queries stall or return timeout errors.

    Cause: The Ollama API is listening on a different port than expected.

    Resolution: Verify the `openai_api_base` setting. For Ollama, the correct value is

    ```
    openai_api_base="http://localhost:11434/v1"
    ```

4. **vLLM Stalling on Grace Hopper (GH200)**

    Symptom: The vLLM server hangs or stalls on startup.

    Cause: GH200 GPUs require longer startup attempts due to initialization delays.

    Resolution: Increase the retry limit by setting:

    ```
    max_startup_attempts: 1200
    ```

When to Escalate

Most issues can be resolved with configuration changes, but some symptoms point to deeper infrastructure problems that need escalation:

- **Persistent OOM Errors Even After Reducing Model Size**: May indicate driver misconfiguration, incorrect CUDA runtime, or faulty GPU hardware.

- **Chroma Returns Inconsistent or Corrupted Results**: Could be a database-level corruption; escalate to your DBA or storage team.

- **LangChain or Ollama Timeouts on the Correct Port**: May be a networking or firewall issue; involve your sysadmin or platform engineer.

- **vLLM Repeatedly Stalls Despite Raising** `max_startup_attempts`: Could signal GPU firmware/driver incompatibility or kernel issues; escalate to Red Hat support or GPU vendor.

CHAPTER 7   USE CASES AND BEST PRACTICES

When in doubt, document the steps you've tried, gather logs, and involve the appropriate support channel as early as possible. This prevents wasted cycles chasing infrastructure-level problems with application-level fixes.

AI Agents

Sometimes one LLM just isn't enough. That's where crewAI comes in—a lightweight, open-source framework that lets multiple AI agents work together on complex tasks like planning, drafting, and fact-checking. Think of it as building a small team of specialists, each with a clear role and goal, all powered by our local LLM (like Granite running through vLLM). crewAI is an open-source framework for orchestrating multiple LLM "agents." Getting started is simple: install it in our existing Python virtual environment, wire it up to our RHEL AI stack, and assign roles like "planner," "writer," and "checker." We will be surprised how quickly these agents can tackle multistep tasks—especially when packaged behind FastAPI for easy deployment using the same automation tools we are already using. To keep our system clean and reproducible, install crewAI inside our `aiapps` virtual environment. This keeps dependencies isolated from the base RHEL AI image and ensures smooth upgrades later.

```
source ~/venvs/aiapps/bin/activate
pip install crewai
```

After installing CrewAI, we can define a crew of three agents, for example, each backed by our local vLLM instance running a Granite model. Each agent is assigned a role and a clear goal—like planning steps, drafting text, or checking facts.

Step 1. Import the Required Libraries

```
from crewai import Crew, Agent
from openai import OpenAI
```

- **crewai**: Used to define agents and organize them into a collaborative workflow
- **openai**: Provides the large language model back end that powers each agent

CHAPTER 7 USE CASES AND BEST PRACTICES

Step 2. Configure the Language Model

```
llm = OpenAI(
    base_url="http://127.0.0.1:8000/v1",
    api_key="none",
    model_name="granite-7b-custom"
)
```

- base_url points to your local model endpoint.
- api_key is set to "none" because a local deployment doesn't require authentication (unlike OpenAI's hosted API).
- model_name specifies which model to use—here, a custom granite-7b-custom.

Step 3. Define the Agents

```
plan  = Agent(role="planner", goal="break the problem into ordered steps", llm=llm)
write = Agent(role="writer",  goal="draft the answer", llm=llm)
check = Agent(role="checker", goal="verify factual accuracy", llm=llm)
```

Each agent has a role, what it represents, and a goal, what it tries to achieve.

- **Planner**: Breaks down the problem into a logical sequence of steps
- **Writer**: Generates the draft content based on the plan
- **Checker**: Reviews the draft for accuracy

All agents use the same language model, but their goals guide how they respond.

Step 4. Assemble the Crew

```
crew = Crew([plan, write, check])
```

The Crew object organizes agents into a workflow. Here, the order is: planner ➤ writer ➤ checker.

Step 5. Run the Workflow

```
print(crew.run("Draft a 2 page executive summary of climate risk insurance."))
```

When `run()` is called:

1. The planner receives the request and outlines the steps.
2. The writer takes that outline and produces a draft.
3. The checker reviews the draft for factual accuracy and consistency.
4. The crew returns the final output, which is then printed.

This approach permits the segmentation of complex tasks into smaller, specialized subtasks, reduces errors through the introduction of a "checker" stage, and facilitates experimentation with various workflows by adding or removing roles.

crewAI is not solely intelligent but also highly practical. This elucidates why numerous teams incorporate it into their RHEL AI toolkit. The primary advantage of agentic artificial intelligence is its capacity for automatic delegation: each agent is responsible for a specific goal and tool set. It is compatible with OpenAI standards, utilizing the same REST schema as vLLM and Ollama—eliminating the need for a proxy. Furthermore, it is reproducible, with agent definitions and prompts stored in Git alongside the RHEL AI `config.yaml` file.

Tip Package our crew behind FastAPI and deploy with the same infra.ai/redhat.ai Ansible collections shown earlier.

Model Registry

Picking the right model registry is one of those deceptively small decisions that can either grease—or gum up—our entire MLOps pipeline. A registry sits at the center of the model lifecycle: it versions every artifact, records lineage, enforces approvals, and is often the last checkpoint before a model hits a production endpoint. Because teams have wildly different constraints—on-prem vs. cloud, GitOps vs. point-and-click, regulated vs. experimental—registries have diversified into three broad camps:

1. **Open-source and self-hosted** options like *MLflow*, *DVC Studio*, and *Red Hat OpenShift AI* favor portability and deep platform integration, letting us run the same workflow anywhere from a laptop to a Kubernetes cluster.

CHAPTER 7   USE CASES AND BEST PRACTICES

2. **Cloud-provider registries**—AWS SageMaker, Azure ML, and Google Vertex AI—fold the registry into a larger managed MLOps stack, trading ultimate portability for frictionless deployment and first-party services.

3. **Specialist SaaS/enterprise platforms** such as *Weights & Biases*, *Neptune.ai*, *Comet*, and *Verta* layer rich UIs, governance features, and turnkey monitoring on top of the core registry function, ideal for teams that prize time-to-value and auditability.

The Hugging Face Model Hub already functions as a de facto model registry: every model lives in its own Git-backed repository, so we get immutable version tags, branches, rich metadata/model cards, and full lineage "for free." Enterprise and Team plans layer on private repos, SSO, audit logs, granular access-control "gating," and token management, so organizations can keep models behind a firewall while still pushing and pulling via the same API and UI. Where it differs from purpose-built MLOps registries is workflow opinion: the Hub doesn't enforce staged transitions (e.g., *Staging ➤ Production*) or approval rules out-of-the-box—we have to wire those in with external CI/CD or the Hub's webhooks. In short, for many teams, the Hub already covers 80% of registry needs (secure storage, versioning, discoverability, and distribution), and with more than 1.4 million models hosted as of March 2025, it doubles as the world's largest public catalogue too, but if we need tight governance gates or deployment automations, we may still wrap additional tooling around it.

Tables 7-1, 7-2, and 7-3 break down why teams choose each model registry, outline the typical fit, and spotlight recent feature highlights—giving us a quick way to map our needs to the right tool.

Open-Source and Self-Hosted

When we need full control over where—and how—our models live, open-source, self-hosted registries are the go-to. The three options in Table 7-1 span the major ways teams run production ML today: a Databricks-friendly workhorse (MLflow), a Git-native registry that slips neatly into any CI/CD pipeline (DVC Studio), and a Kubernetes operator built for enterprise clusters (Red Hat OpenShift AI). Together, they cover everything from a lone GPU server to a namespaced OpenShift fleet, all while keeping licensing costs at zero.

Table 7-1. Open-source model registries

Registry	Why Teams Like It	Typical Fit
MLflow Model Registry	Simple API, stage transitions ("Staging → Production"), native in Databricks, huge community	When we want something we can run anywhere or inside Databricks without extra cost logit.io
DVC Studio Model Registry	Git-native: every model version is a Git tag; easy to integrate with CI/CD; works even on-prem	When we already keep data/code in Git and prefer GitOps workflows dvc.org
Red Hat OpenShift AI Model Registry	Kubernetes-native operator that lets us spin up multiple, namespaced registries on any OpenShift/ROSA/ARO cluster. Handles model metadata, versioning, approval workflow, and one-click deploy to KServe; stores artifacts in OCI image repos or external MySQL and plugs into OpenShift Pipelines. Still Tech Preview as of v2.15–2.16	

Cloud-Provider Registries

When our models are already being trained, stored, and served inside a major cloud, the path of least resistance is the registry native to that ecosystem. Table 7-2 compares the built-in offerings from AWS, Azure, and Google—each one tightly coupled to its provider's MLOps stack so we can hop from versioning and approvals straight to a managed endpoint without ever leaving the console.

Table 7-2. Cloud model registries

Cloud	Registry Feature Set	Good to Know
AWS SageMaker Model Registry	Versioning, lineage, approvals, direct one-click deploy to SageMaker Endpoints	Now tracks lineage automatically
Azure Machine Learning Registry	Central registry decoupled from workspaces; promotes models across dev ➤ test ➤ prod; fine-grained RBAC	Helps when we need strict network/subscription isolation yet shared models
Google Vertex AI Model Registry	Central repository, aliases per version, deploy straight to endpoints; supports AutoML and BigQuery ML models	Last major update of June 2025 added richer search and aliasing

Specialist SaaS/Enterprise

When we would rather "rent than run" our registry—and want enterprise niceties out-of-the-box—specialist SaaS platforms are the sweet spot. Table 7-3 profiles four leaders that wrap hosted storage in rich UIs, lineage graphs, CI/CD hooks, and policy controls: W&B for teams already steeped in its experiment tracker, Neptune for lightweight Git-friendly projects that may self-host later, Comet for organizations that need granular approval gates, and Verta for heavily regulated setups demanding end-to-end traceability.

Table 7-3. SaaS model registries

Registry	Stand-out Capabilities	When It Shines
Weights & Biases (W&B) Model Registry	Tight link to W&B Artifacts; lineage graphs, CI/CD web-hooks, rich UI	Teams already using W&B for experiment tracking and reports docs.wandb.ai
Neptune.ai	Lightweight registry plus experiment tracking; flexible metadata schema	SMEs that want a hosted option but can self-host later neptune.ai
Comet Model Registry	Workspace-level registry, built-in approval workflow, Slack/webhook automation	Organizations that need fine-grained approval before deploy comet.com
Verta AI	Registry tightly coupled with model deployment and monitoring; policy-based governance	Regulated industries that need end-to-end traceability (listed among top registry tools) neptune.ai

Frequently Asked Questions

Below is a curated list of frequently asked questions gathered from real-world Red Hat AI deployments, training sessions, and customer engagements. These answers draw on a decade of hands-on experience in model fine-tuning, data synthesis, and enterprise-scale AI operations—particularly within RHEL and OpenShift AI environments. Use this section as a quick reference for common setup challenges, model behavior, and best practices.

Which model are we going to train on?

Answer: A general advice is to start with the *granite* model as our foundation, then bring in *melonite* later for training; the download step we see now is loading those two quantized models so they fit on a laptop. If we need more precision, we can move to the Llama family of large language models.

Are the YAML Q-and-A files the output of the synthesizer?

Answer: No. They are *inputs* that we write by hand to guide the synthesizer. Each file gives short "context" excerpts plus three Q-and-A pairs; the teacher model then reads our full PDF/Markdown and generates the rest of the synthetic dataset from that seed.

CHAPTER 7   USE CASES AND BEST PRACTICES

How many Q-and-A pairs do we need per context, and how many variants will the system create?

Answer: Exactly three Q-and-A pairs per context are required. During synthesis, the teacher model produces 50 variations of *each* pair by default, but we can lower that to 5, 10, 100, etc.

Can the whole context-and-Q-and-A preparation be automated?

Answer: Technically yes, but fully automated extraction is still poorer than a domain expert writing a *small*, high-quality seed set. Manual curation up front yields better downstream accuracy, even though the synthesizer finishes the bulk work.

Does the pipeline support multiple languages (e.g., German, French, Dutch, Italian, Chinese)?

Answer: It will work in any language **only if** *both* our foundation model *and* our teacher/synthesizer model already support that language. Mixing an English-only teacher with a different German, French, Dutch, Italian, and Chinese-capable base model is not recommended.

Can the model do more than generate text—e.g., run shell commands?

Answer: A bare LLM only predicts the next token, but we can wrap it in an "agentic" layer that calls external APIs. Red Hat does this with tooling such as *Lightspeed* and an upcoming open-source project (LAMAS-tech) so the model can inspect logs, call a ticketing system, etc.

What happens if the base model and my fine-tuned dialect both know an answer?

Answer: Fine-tuning *overrides* conflicting knowledge. Our "dialect" becomes the preferred answer, while everything else the base model knew remains intact.

How can we detect if the synthesizer missed parts of the document?

Answer: Maintain an evaluation question set that represents the knowledge we expect. After every training run, ask those questions; gaps or regressions tell us what still needs coverage. This iterative evaluation can be automated in an MLOps pipeline.

Is quality assurance manual or automated?

Answer: Both. OpenShift AI bundles *Trusty AI*[9] and guardrail models to test mathematics, logic, reasoning, safety, and misuse automatically. We still configure the criteria and can add human review, but the execution is repeatable and largely automated.

---

[9] https://github.com/trustyai-explainability

After training, how many contexts will the system create? Is that configurable?

Answer: The teacher model tries to cover the entire source document on its own. There is no fixed limit; we can throttle or enlarge it, but by default, it keeps adding contexts until the document is fully represented.

Why does the model sometimes "make things up"?

Answer: That behavior is called *hallucination*. We can mitigate it by lowering the temperature, adding guardrail models, or instructing the model to respond with "I don't know" below a certain confidence threshold. Enterprises usually deploy such guardrails in production.

Conclusion

This chapter examines practical strategies for integrating and expanding RHEL AI within real-world enterprise contexts. It compares RAG and fine-tuning, elucidating optimal scenarios for each methodology and how to synergistically combine them to enhance agility and precision. The chapter provides detailed, step-by-step instructions for setting up RAG pipelines using ChromaDB, LangChain, and FastAPI. It discusses automation via Ansible, options for model registries, and GPU optimization techniques. It concludes by emphasizing the importance of extensibility, automation, and governance practices that ensure RHEL AI deployments are reproducible, auditable, and adaptable across diverse environments.

In the next chapter, you will learn about the future trends shaping RHEL AI, including explainable AI, model governance, edge deployments, and sustainability innovations.

CHAPTER 8

Future Trends in RHEL AI

Introduction

Orchestrating models, pipelines, and infrastructure has taught me that an enterprise AI platform must grow on three concurrent timelines: hardware acceleration, software architecture, and governance. RHEL AI's foundation—bootable container images carrying the InstructLab toolchain, Python, and Granite LLMs—already removes operating-system friction for data scientists and MLOps teams. However, the next decade will not be won through abstractions alone. Explainability, ubiquitous edge inference, responsible governance, quantum-inspired optimization, hybrid topologies, and sustainable operations will determine whether enterprise AI is merely functional or genuinely transformative. Below, I outline those trends with specific capabilities I expect—and in some cases already see—inside the RHEL AI ecosystem.

Disclaimer

The procedures, insights, and forward-looking statements described here reflect my personal research and experience with RHEL AI. They have NOT been reviewed, endorsed, or officially approved by Red Hat. Use them at your own discretion and always consult Red Hat's published documentation and support channels for authoritative guidance.

Explainable AI (XAI)

The open-source ethos behind RHEL AI encourages inspecting, remixing, and improving every layer, from dataset recipes to LoRA adapters. RHEL AI was born with an open-source ethos: every piece of the pipeline—bootable OS image, `ilab` CLI, Granite

CHAPTER 8 FUTURE TRENDS IN RHEL AI

base models, tuning datasets—can be inspected, forked, and improved. Still, most teams treated model decisions as a black box, but this is coming to an end soon. I am a strong believer that the next wave of RHEL AI, therefore, hard-bakes explainability into the workflow instead of bolting it on later.

These are the most interesting expansions that we might see soon:

- **Embedded Attribution Pipelines**: Future releases will likely ship with a lightweight attribution engine integrated into the `ilab model evaluate` workflow, emitting token-level attention heat-maps alongside BLEU- or BERT-score metrics (refer to Observability in Chapter 6). The same multiphase training loop that today auto-selects top checkpoints can record gradients for saliency post-processing with negligible overhead.

- **Native SPDX Lineage**: RHEL AI already relies on Git-based taxonomies; extending commit metadata to include SPDX-like facts about provenance will let auditors trace every parameter back to the exact YAML example that influenced it.

- **"Rust-Level" Introspection**: Because all inference is served through vLLM, explainability hooks can be added at the middleware layer instead of inside model weights, allowing pluggable explanation formats (e.g., JSON-L, Counterfactual Records). The fundamental principle is straightforward: if a decision holds significance, the developer must have the capacity to reproduce and challenge it.

- **Retrieval Attribution**: This is the process of showing which documents or text chunks from a vector database influenced an LLM's answer, often with scores that indicate their relevance. In RHEL AI, this is evolving into saliency maps, which visually highlight the exact passages or tokens that shaped the model's response, making outputs more transparent and auditable. A saliency map is a visualization that highlights which words or passages in the input had the greatest influence on an LLM's output, making the model's reasoning more transparent.

Native SPDX Lineage

SPDX[1] (Software Package Data Exchange) is an open standard used to describe the contents and provenance of software packages in a structured, machine-readable way. At its simplest, think of it as a nutrition label for software, listing ingredients (files, dependencies, licenses, authorship) so you can trace exactly where everything came from. In traditional software supply chains, SPDX helps security teams verify that binaries and libraries match their declared sources, making audits faster and reducing the risk of hidden vulnerabilities or licensing issues. Bringing this concept into RHEL AI, SPDX lineage means applying the same traceability to model development. Every time we generate synthetic data, fine-tune a model, or push a checkpoint, the system can automatically attach metadata describing *what data was used, which configuration was applied, and which YAML examples shaped the final parameters.* Instead of having a black-box model, enterprises get a structured record—almost like a Git commit history—that links model weights back to the precise training inputs. The benefit for AI teams is enormous: auditors can confirm that a deployed model was fine-tuned only on approved data; SREs can trace quality regressions back to a specific SDG batch or taxonomy change; and compliance teams can prove to regulators that no sensitive or unlicensed data was introduced during training. In other words, SPDX lineage turns model evaluation and deployment from an act of faith into an auditable, reproducible process.

RHEL AI already stores all user skills and knowledge in a Git-hosted taxonomy tree. Extending each commit with SPDX-style metadata—*who* authored the YAML, *when* it entered the tree, and the exact license—creates a cryptographically linked chain from raw text to the final weight. During audit, we might be able to therefore point to any parameter and answer: "This was influenced by `compositional_skills/writing/editing/qna.yaml`, commit `abc123` from 17 May 2025, licensed CC-BY-4.0."

Four Pillars

In XAI for enterprises, RHEL AI is built on four key pillars that ensure models are not only robust but also auditable, interpretable, and easy to maintain. These pillars address the primary challenges of traditional LLM infrastructures and demonstrate how RHEL AI effectively addresses these issues to meet enterprise needs.

---

[1] https://spdx.dev/

CHAPTER 8   FUTURE TRENDS IN RHEL AI

1. **Regulatory Audit and Compliance**

    Traditional LLM architectures significantly complicate regulatory audits. Teams frequently depend on ad hoc notebooks and disconnected scripts to demonstrate compliance with frameworks such as the EU AI Act or NIST Risk Management Framework (RMF). This method is fragile and inconsistent, resulting in potential gaps that auditors may scrutinize. Every model artifact in RHEL AI is tied to SPDX lineage metadata and stored in an immutable container image, providing "explainability as an artifact." In other words, the model carries its own audit trail—making compliance checks faster, repeatable, and defensible.

2. **Debugging Model Predictions**

    When a model produces an incorrect prediction, traditional debugging methods often involve reviewing logs through "grep" and reliance on conjecture, attempting to trace an output back to the influencing inputs. With token-level saliency maps in RHEL AI, developers can directly click on a model's output and accurately trace it back to the specific training example that had the greatest influence on its gradient. This capability enables engineers to understand the rationale behind the model's response, thereby reducing root cause analysis from hours to minutes.

3. **Monitoring Model Drift**

    Over time, models experience degradation as inputs evolve, new terminology appears, or concepts undergo changes. Conventional frameworks typically identify this drift solely during periodic benchmarking, which may overlook subtle yet detrimental degradations. By monitoring attribution deltas, RHEL AI identifies areas where knowledge has diminished—even if superficial metrics such as accuracy or F1-score remain unchanged. This proactive strategy provides operators with early warnings before drift impacts users.

4. **Multi-team Collaboration**

   In large organizations, multiple teams contribute taxonomies, YAML prompts, or fine-tuned datasets. Without version control, disputes turn into finger-pointing ("he-said/she-said blame games") over who caused a regression. Because RHEL AI builds everything on Git-backed taxonomies, every change is tracked like a software commit. Teams can immediately see which YAML file or prompt update shifted the probability distribution of a disputed output, making collaboration transparent and accountable.

   Collectively, these four pillars guarantee that RHEL AI transcends merely being a model-serving platform; it constitutes an enterprise-ready explainability system. Regulatory authorities obtain auditable lineage, engineers acquire debuggable predictions, operators receive early drift signals, and teams benefit from collaborative version control. These capabilities fundamentally convert AI from a black box into a trusted business instrument.

A Day in the Life of a Developer

Imagine you're an AI engineer working at Synapse Logistics, and the marketing team comes to you with a problem: the company chatbot keeps telling customers that the new product SupraFlex X2 is available in *red*, when the official spec sheet clearly lists the color as *crimson*. They want to know why the model is getting it wrong—and they want it fixed quickly.

1. **Reproduce the Query**

   The first thing you do is run the same query the marketing team tried, to confirm the issue:

   ```
   ilab model chat --prompt "What color is SupraFlex X2?"
   ```

   Sure enough, the model responds with "red."

2. **Fetch an Explanation**

   Every model response in RHEL AI is traceable. The CLI provides a unique identifier (UUID) for the session. Using that, you can pull an explanation of the model's decision-making process:

The CLI prints a UUID:

`ilab explain get <uuid>`

The JSON output shows the top three tokens by gradient influence: ["red", "color", "shade"]. This tells you the model's confidence was strongly biased toward *red*.

3. **Trace Lineage**

   Now you want to know *why* the model latched onto *red*. Using lineage tracing, you can go directly from the influenced parameter back to the training data that shaped it:

   `ilab lineage param layer.8.mlp.w2`

   The output reveals that the relevant parameter weights were influenced by an entry in the `marketing_materials/q3_2024/qna section.yaml`, specifically at commit `f0e1d2c`.

4. **Patch the Data**

   We inspect that YAML file and see the mistake: the training example incorrectly listed the product color as red. You fix the entry to crimson, add SPDX headers for provenance, and commit the change.

5. **Retrain and Evaluate**

   With the data corrected, you retrain the model and immediately run evaluation benchmarks to ensure no regressions:

   `ilab model train && ilab model evaluate --benchmark mt_bench`

This time, the attribution report shows that the token *"crimson"* dominates the explanation, precisely as it should. The total time of this story takes approximately 45 minutes. The audit trail is completely verifiable, the model has been corrected, and the marketing team is satisfied. More importantly, we now possess a transparent and explainable chain of evidence that demonstrates how the error was introduced, how it was corrected, and how the system guarantees reproducibility.

Governance Meets Engineering

In traditional information technology (IT) systems, governance has historically involved establishing policies, supervising compliance, and producing evidence of adherence. For instance, access control policies regulate user login permissions, while audit logs document that only authorized actions have been performed. However, in the era of AI-driven decision-making, governance must extend beyond infrastructural measures to include the behavior of the models themselves. Merely stating, "we secured the GPU nodes," is no longer sufficient; organizations must also be capable of demonstrating that "our model never produced a prohibited response."

This is where explainability functions as the enforcement mechanism for governance. Beyond serving as a reassurance feature for developers, attribution and explainability provide essential signals that facilitate the implementation of policy-as-code. With RHEL AI, upcoming governance features will enable teams to define compliance rules in structured YAML files, which can then be automatically enforced within Continuous Integration/Continuous Deployment (CI/CD) pipelines. An illustrative example is provided below:

```yaml
policies:
  prohibited_tokens:
    - sex
    - political_extremism
  max_saliency_for_prohibited: 0.05
```

This policy delineates two primary measures: firstly, it explicitly forbids outputs containing specific tokens, such as sexual content and extremist political terminology. Secondly, it establishes a saliency threshold, indicating that even in the absence of direct token generation, if attribution signals demonstrate a significant reliance on such tokens during the generation process (exceeding 0.05 influence), the evaluation will be considered unsuccessful.

In practice, this converts compliance from a reactive audit process—such as quarterly PDF reports reviewed manually—into a proactive, automated gate through Continuous Integration/Continuous Deployment (CI/CD) pipelines that impede pull requests in cases of governance rule violations. This represents the distinction between identifying issues weeks after deployment and preventing their occurrence from reaching the production environment.

CHAPTER 8   FUTURE TRENDS IN RHEL AI

From a customer perspective, this approach builds trust. End users no longer need to take a vendor's word that the model "behaves safely." Instead, they get assurance that every model version has passed through automated gates designed to prevent harmful, biased, or noncompliant outputs. This aligns with rising expectations under the EU AI Act, NIST AI Risk Management Framework, and emerging corporate policies on responsible AI.

From a regulatory perspective, this approach creates machine-readable compliance evidence. Instead of scattered notes or static reports, every model build carries its own audit trail: SPDX lineage proving the data it was trained on, explainability logs showing token-level influence, and governance manifests declaring what policies were applied. If challenged by a regulator, enterprises can point to a reproducible pipeline and say: *"This model was trained on this dataset, with this policy manifest, and evaluated with these explainability thresholds."*

In the enterprise world, AI adoption often stalls not because the technology is incapable but because stakeholders cannot trust it. CIOs worry about regulatory fines, compliance officers fear reputational risk, and business leaders don't want opaque black-box systems making customer-facing decisions. Governance manifests in RHEL AI bridge this gap by making explainability actionable.

- **For Security Teams**: They can define prohibited tokens and enforce saliency thresholds just as they would firewall rules.

- **For Compliance Officers**: They can point auditors to machine-readable manifests instead of manually compiling quarterly evidence.

- **For Developers**: They get immediate feedback during pull requests if their fine-tuned model drifts into noncompliance.

- **For Executives**: They gain confidence that AI systems align with corporate values and external regulations, without slowing innovation.

Governance in artificial intelligence (AI) extends beyond merely stating "don't do bad things." It involves integrating policy enforcement directly into the model lifecycle, thereby ensuring that compliance becomes a continuous, automated, and auditable process. In this context, RHEL AI redefines the concept of explainability, not merely as a dashboard feature but as the fundamental basis of enterprise trust. By incorporating compliance checks into CI/CD pipelines, RHEL AI guarantees that each model version deployed into production is safe, explainable, and compliant with regulatory standards from the outset.

Developer Tooling for Explainability

RHEL AI use cases are not only focused on serving and training and serving models; it also emphasizes making explainability accessible to developers by integrating it into the tools already used by engineers. Looking ahead, several enhancements are on the horizon that will provide practitioners with direct, intuitive insights into their models' behavior. Envision debugging a fine-tuned checkpoint in the same manner as debugging code. A future extension for Visual Studio Code could display inline heatmaps adjacent to generated outputs, illustrating token importance at a glance. Instead of sifting through JSON logs, developers would visually discern which tokens the model assigned the greatest weight to during response generation. For interactive workloads, explainability is expected to become as seamless as utilizing SQL EXPLAIN plans. With live saliency streaming, developers could observe token influence in real time as they input queries into a chat session. This facilitates a deeper understanding of why a model tends toward a specific answer even before the final output is produced. When comparing two checkpoints—such as before and after fine-tuning—it can be challenging to detect subtle behavioral shifts. A cross-model diffing feature will simplify this process, enabling users to identify which tokens have experienced the most significant attention shifts, thereby pinpointing where the fine-tuning has impacted the model's internal reasoning. As sustainability emerges as a primary concern, RHEL AI is progressing toward energy-aware explanations. By incorporating GPU energy metadata directly into attribution reports, teams will be able to evaluate the carbon footprint associated with generating answers relative to their quality. This approach allows organizations to optimize not only for accuracy but also for efficiency and ecological sustainability. The commitment of RHEL AI to open tooling naturally extends to open reasoning. By embedding attribution, provenance, and middleware-level introspection into the same ilab verbs used for training and deployment, explainability is elevated to a first-class artifact rather than an afterthought. When every answer can be replayed, traced, and contested, AI transforms from a black box into a transparent technology, fulfilling the promise of open source: trust through visibility of its inner workings.

CHAPTER 8 FUTURE TRENDS IN RHEL AI

Edge AI

Every release of RHEL AI broadens its hardware support. The latest version of RHEL AI, at the time of writing this book, includes NVIDIA H200, Grace Hopper GH200 (TP), and AMD MI300X accelerators. That signals two long-term trajectories:

1. **High-density inference farms** in clouds and data-centers, powered by powerful GPUs like 8× H100/H200 nodes delivering multi-tenant throughput.

2. **Peripheral micro-edges**—factory servers, field-deployed vehicles, even retail kiosks—powered by single-GPU or even CPU-quantized versions of the same mode, like a quantized "little brothers" embedded in smartphones, vehicles, kiosks, and OT gateways.

Most AI projects require instant responses, usually with uptime constraints that often involve sub-100 ms SLA requirements. Moving part of the compute graph to edge profiles is crucial. Expect future `ilab config init` profiles named edge_x1 or similar, pretuned for 16-GB edge cards and capable of hot-swapping LoRA layers over the wire.

Container-native Update-of-Weights (UoW) workflows—an extension of the current `boot switch` mechanism used for OS layers—will enable OTA model patching without rebooting the edge device.

In conversational commerce, factory quality control, and mixed-reality dashboards, response times rarely exceed **100 ms**. Sending every prompt to a remote data center introduces additional hops, jitter, and privacy concerns. The solution is *edge inference*: running the latency-sensitive part of the model directly on the same rack—or even the same circuit board—that produces the data.

Table 8-1. Matching silicon profile to workload

Deployment Tier	Typical Hardware	Aggregate VRAM	Use Case Focus
Cloud Megacluster	8 × H100 or 8 × H200	640–1,128 GB	Multi-tenant chat, vector DB retrieval
Regional POP	2 × H100 or 1 × MI300X	80–192 GB	Personalization, low-latency scoring
Micro-edge	1 × L4/L40S or CPU-INT8	24–48 GB	Vision + language fusion, on-device RAG

RHEL AI's hardware requirements guide confirms that the same image boots everywhere, from 8 × H100 racks down to a single L4 card. That single-image guarantee means you ship *one* container artifact and let `ilab` choose the right kernel, driver, and scheduler toggles at install time.

Edge-Optimized Profiles

The `ilab config init` command already tailors YAML to **h100_x8** or **mi300x_x4** rigs. Expect forthcoming *edge_* profiles tuned for 1×16 GB–48 GB devices:

`ilab config init --profile edge_x1`

Profile traits:

- 4-bit or 8-bit quantization using QLoRA adapters.
- KV-cache offload to system RAM when VRAM is scarce.
- Dynamic LoRA hot-swap: Edge nodes can pull a new adapter over TLS, load it in-process, and start responding with *zero downtime*—crucial for 24/7 kiosks.

Container-Native Update-of-Weights (UoW)

One of the primary challenges in deploying AI at scale—particularly in edge or industrial settings—revolves around maintaining up-to-date models without disrupting ongoing operations. Traditional methods of upgrades frequently necessitate downtime, significant file transfers, or complete container rebuilds. RHEL AI addresses this issue through a concept known as the container-native UoW, which builds upon the immutable operating system philosophy employed in boot environments. Similar to how a bootc environment switch can swap an entire kernel or container image atomically, UoW concentrates on updating solely the model weights, thereby preserving the runtime environment. For instance, implementing a new Low-Rank Adaptation (LoRA) package involves the following straightforward procedure:

`sudo bootc switch registry.redhat.io/rhelai1/edge-lora-pack:v2`

Key benefits of UoW:

- **Atomic Updates**: If a transfer is interrupted (e.g., network drop, power cut), the system automatically keeps the old model in place. This prevents corruption and ensures the node never gets stuck in an unusable state.

- **Reversible Rollbacks**: If the new model introduces regressions, a single command instantly restores the previous version:

    ```
    sudo bootc rollback
    ```

The rollback completes in seconds, making it practical for mission-critical edge deployments.

- **Audit-Ready Lineage**: Every switch operation is logged with a cryptographic digest that ties the updated weights back to the same lineage database already used for tracking code and datasets. This ensures full traceability and makes compliance audits straightforward.

By decoupling weight updates from the heavier runtime stack, RHEL AI enables continuous model security patching in environments where downtime is unacceptable. Field robots, factory PLCs, or medical devices can receive LoRA fine-tune updates without needing off-hours maintenance windows or bulky container rebuilds. In effect, UoW delivers the best of both worlds: the immutability and safety of bootc with the flexibility of rapid model iteration.

As AI shifts toward real-time decision-making at the edge, RHEL AI might enable ultra-low-latency inference—often under 100 milliseconds—by bringing intelligence closer to where data is generated. Instead of relying solely on cloud models, RHEL AI might become a platform to enable edge nodes into self-sufficient AI endpoints that can host vLLM, mount LoRA adapters, and recover automatically after power interruptions. Using advanced design patterns like split-graph inference (processing encoders locally and attention layers regionally), warm-cache routing (reusing cached user context for faster responses), and LoRA-per-tenant isolation (ensuring model security between clients), the RHEL AI platform might deliver cloud-grade governance with on-site speed. Together, these innovations might make it possible to deploy intelligent, compliant, and resilient AI workloads anywhere—from factory floors and field robots to delivery fleets and retail kiosks—without sacrificing performance or control.

Governance and Ethics

In the near future, governance in RHEL AI might move from static compliance checklists to continuous, built-in assurance. Every deployed model already runs inside an immutable, signed container image, anchored by RHEL and the InstructLab toolchain. Building on that foundation, Red Hat is extending the stack to automatically collect model lineage, attribution, and usage metadata in real time. Each prediction can be tied to its source data, versioned code, and policy manifest, creating a living audit trail that satisfies evolving standards such as the EU AI Act, NIST AI Risk Management Framework, and U.S. Executive Order 14110. Beyond compliance, this direction reflects a deeper ethical principle: trust through verifiability. Governance is no longer an external process—it becomes part of the model's runtime, enforcing fairness thresholds, bias alerts, and provenance validation as part of every inference cycle. RHEL AI's road map points toward a future where governance isn't a burden on innovation but an enabler—a system that allows teams to deploy faster precisely because every decision, dataset, and model update is provably accountable.

Runtime Attestation

One of the biggest challenges in deploying AI responsibly is proving that the model running in production is exactly the one we intended to deploy. Regulators, auditors, and even internal security teams want assurance that the model weights in memory haven't been tampered with and that they match a known, trusted version. RHEL AI might address this with runtime attestation, an approach that extends the same principles of SBOMs[2] (Software Bills of Materials) to model serving. Think of it as a "live SBOM for AI"—a continuous record of exactly which weights are being used at any point in time.

In upcoming RHEL AI releases, every vLLM shard might include a remote-attestation daemon that verifies its runtime integrity in three key steps:

1. **Digest Calculation on Boot**

    When a shard starts, it computes a SHA-256 digest (cryptographic fingerprint) of both the container image and the model weight files it has loaded. This ensures that even a single-bit change in the weights will produce a different fingerprint.

---

[2] https://www.cisa.gov/sbom

2. **Trusted Signing and Reporting**

   The digest is signed by the node's TPM (Trusted Platform Module) or HSM (Hardware Security Module), hardware devices that provide tamper-proof cryptographic keys. The signed digest might be sent to Red Hat Insights, alongside the standard OS-level CVE scans that are already part of RHEL's patching workflow.

3. **Automated Response to Revoked Models**

   If Insights detects that a digest corresponds to a revoked or vulnerable model (e.g., one found to contain privacy-violating training data), it triggers an automated response. The affected service might immediately be isolated by systemd, and the load balancer stops routing traffic to that shard—typically within minutes.

The result is a runtime environment where you can always answer the critical question:

☞ *"Which exact model parameters are currently processing user prompts?"*

This has major implications for compliance and trust:

- **For Regulators**: You can prove with cryptographic evidence that no unauthorized model has ever served user queries.

- **For Security Teams**: You can detect and quarantine compromised weights before they impact production.

- **For Operations Teams**: You gain the same rollback and incident-handling patterns you already use with OS and container vulnerabilities, but now extended to the model layer.

In short, runtime attestation brings supply chain security into the world of AI, making model serving not just faster and scalable but also provably trustworthy.

Differential Privacy

Fine-tuning with private data used to require a bespoke Opacus[3] or JAX pipeline.[4] RHEL AI might soon expose a native option to handle it. This is a possible use case for the healthcare industry:

```
ilab model train \
  --dataset path/to/medical_records \
  --dp-epsilon 2.5 \
  --dp-delta 1e-6 \
  --dp-max-grad-norm 1.2
```

Because the differential privacy[5] (DP) parameters might live in the *same* YAML manifest shown above, each experiment's privacy budget is traceable and immutable.

In DP, the goal is to train or query a model in a way that limits how much any single individual's data can influence the final output. To describe that limit mathematically, we use two parameters—epsilon (ε) and delta (δ)—which together define the model's privacy budget.

- **Epsilon (ε)** represents the *privacy loss bound*. A smaller ε means *stronger privacy* (less influence from any single record), while a larger ε allows *weaker privacy but higher model accuracy*. For instance, ε = 2.5 is moderate privacy—the model learns useful patterns but keeps individual data contributions obscured.

- **Delta (δ)** is the *probability that the privacy guarantee might fail*. It accounts for rare edge cases where the noise added by the DP algorithm doesn't fully protect an individual's data. Typical values are very small (e.g., δ = 1e-6), meaning such failures are virtually negligible.

Together, these parameters form a measurable contract between data scientists and auditors: the privacy budget. In future versions of RHEL AI, when you specify --dp-epsilon and --dp-delta in an `ilab model train` command, those values could be logged automatically in the training journal and surfaced in the Insights dashboard—so that regulators or compliance teams can see not just *what model was trained* but *how much privacy was consumed*.

---

[3] https://opacus.ai
[4] https://github.com/sanchit-gandhi/whisper-jax
[5] https://pydp.readthedocs.io/

CHAPTER 8   FUTURE TRENDS IN RHEL AI

Agentic AI

Agentic AI represents the latest advancement in technology, expanding the traditional capabilities of LLMs by facilitating systems that can reason, plan, act, and reflect autonomously within designated enterprise policies. Instead of merely reacting to prompts, future implementations of agentic models in RHEL AI are anticipated to function as goal-driven entities capable of deconstructing complex tasks into actionable steps, invoking external tools or APIs, and enhancing their outputs through iterative self-assessment.

Within the Red Hat ecosystem, this agentic capability arises from collaboration among various Red Hat products that support programmable APIs. Developers may soon be able to define agentic workflows using YAML, encoding not only knowledge but also reasoning strategies and decision hierarchies. This enables models to learn how to perform actions, consult domain-specific data sources, and adapt dynamically based on intermediate results. Through integration with the Ansible Automation Platform and OpenShift AI, agentic models can initiate real-world workflows, such as infrastructure provisioning, incident remediation, and data pipeline orchestration, based on natural language intent. This approach transitions agentic AI from a purely theoretical concept to a governed execution framework, wherein self-directed AI agents operate autonomously while adhering to enterprise policies, version control standards, and compliance requirements. Such developments may mark a shift from AI merely generating answers to AI that plans, makes decisions, and acts responsibly within the secure and open foundation of Red Hat's enterprise ecosystem.

Quantum AI

Quantum processing units (QPUs) remain exotic, but their trajectory resembles GPUs circa 2010. In the coming decade, I foresee two overlap zones with RHEL AI:

1. **Quantum-Inspired Classical Algorithms**: Techniques such as Tensor-Network Factorization or QAOA-like circuit simulators can already compress embedding layers; integrating them as *optional back ends* inside DeepSpeed or FSDP (both already packaged in the image) will yield model-size reductions of 30–50% without new hardware.

2. **Tensor-Network Factorization**: Recent work shows Matrix-Product States compress sequence models while retaining accuracy, cutting parameter counts by *30–50%* on MNIST and CIFAR tasks.[6] A *Nature* study extended the approach to NLP, demonstrating interpretable tensor networks for long-range dependencies.[7]

3. **Hybrid Execution Paths**: Picture a training script where forward passes run on GPUs, while gradient-descent-heavy optimization of sparse attention heads is off-loaded to a cloud QPU via gRPC. The container image model of RHEL AI makes it plausible to ship a QPU stub today and redirect calls to a quantum service as it matures.

The strategic implication: RHEL AI must stay *hardware-agnostic but quantum-ready*—abstracting silicon diversity behind the same CLI verbs (`ilab model train`, `ilab model serve`).

To turn quantum acceleration from a research novelty into a drop-in performance tier, RHEL AI must treat qubits as just another execution target—no different, conceptually, from adding a new GPU SKU. The matrix below distills that mindset into four design principles that guide every layer of the stack, from the `ilab` CLI down to container packaging and audit logs, ensuring that quantum functionality slots into existing workflows without retraining teams, bloating images, or breaking compliance trails, as shown in Table 8-2.

---

[6] https://arxiv.org/html/2503.05535v2
[7] https://www.nature.com/articles/s41598-024-84295-2

Table 8-2. Design principles

Principle	Practical Mechanism	Benefit
Hardware-Agnostic CLI Verbs	`ilab model train/serve/evaluate` already hide CUDA vs. ROCm; extend the same pattern to qpu	Zero retraining of data science teams
Back-End Plugs, Not Forks	Ship tensor-network, QAOA, and QPU drivers as *optional* RPM layers	Avoids container image sprawl
Stateless gRPC Sidecars	Optimizers and solvers run in off-process daemons	Keeps the main training loop deterministic
Provenance and Audit Parity	SPDX lineage already tags YAML -> weights; include QPU job-IDs in that chain	Regulators can replay the quantum step, too

Quantum AI will not replace GPUs; it will **augment** them, just as GPUs augment CPUs. By keeping its CLI verbs stable, container images immutable, and provenance transparent, RHEL AI positions itself as the **control plane** where tomorrow's qubits and today's teraflops meet. Whether through tensor-network compression that slashes model size 40%[8] or hybrid optimizers that offload gnarly Hessians to cloud QPUs,[9] enterprises can adopt quantum acceleration incrementally—without rewriting pipelines or re-training staff. The mission for the coming decade is clear: **be hardware-agnostic but quantum-ready.**

Hybrid AI

RHEL AI's installation guides already document workflows for bare metal, AWS, IBM Cloud, Azure, and GCP. In practice, enterprises are increasingly co-locating training on cloud clusters and inference on-premises for data sovereignty or latency reasons. Next-gen enhancements that Red Hat might consider:

- **Federated `ilab` Contexts**: Rather than separate deployments, the CLI will gain a `--context` flag pointing at remote clusters over SSH or REST, letting a developer invoke `ilab model train` in the cloud and `ilab model serve` locally from one terminal.

---

[8] https://arxiv.org/html/2503.05535v2
[9] https://arxiv.org/html/2405.00252v2

- **Ansible Automation Platform Collections**: The RHEL AI release notes already preview Ansible collections (`infra.ai`, `redhat.ai`) for provisioning and workload management; expect playbooks that orchestrate a *single* hybrid pipeline—spinning up transient cloud GPUs for multiphase training, then snapshotting weights into on-prem object storage.

- **Unified License Metering**: Red Hat's subscription skews will very likely move to an elastic count of "AI core-hours," automatically reconciled whether consumed on bare metal or hyperscale.

Hybrid AI is not a compromise; it is the architecture that lets enterprises keep sensitive data inside firewalls while renting exascale compute only when the gradient truly calls for it.

Sustainable Development

Sustainability in AI isn't just about big data centers—it's about making every watt of power and every byte of storage count. Even a single RHEL AI workstation can consume terabytes of high-speed storage during model training, so every small efficiency gain adds up.

1. **Adaptive Mixed Precision**

   The current RHEL AI inference stack already leverages optimized kernels, such as bfloat16 or INT4, on GPUs like the AMD MI300X, to provide high-performance capabilities. In the foreseeable future, precision levels are anticipated to become adaptive: the system may automatically reduce to INT8 during periods of low GPU utilization, thereby optimizing accuracy and energy consumption in real time. This process can be considered analogous to dynamic voltage and frequency scaling (DVFS), but applied to tensors rather than transistors.

2. **Carbon-Aware Scheduling**

   Future releases may also incorporate carbon-aware automation into routine workflows. The system could allocate the workload to a Kubernetes cluster in a region powered by renewable energy.

This "green orchestration" approach builds on patterns already used by major cloud providers, where Kubernetes clusters can query real-time carbon intensity data through APIs (like Google Cloud's Carbon-Free Energy Percent[10] or AWS's Clean Energy Region[11] metadata). In practical terms, this means RHEL AI jobs could soon decide when and where to run—choosing cleaner energy windows or greener data centers—without manual intervention.

The idea mirrors CI/CD time-of-day build pipelines, but with a sustainability twist: the system treats carbon as a first-class scheduling metric, right alongside CPU, GPU, and memory. In large distributed training or data generation pipelines, even a 10–15% shift toward low-carbon windows can translate into significant reductions in CO_2 emissions without sacrificing performance.

3. **Open Measurement and Reporting**

   Every Synthetic Data Generation (SDG) execution within RHEL AI currently produces comprehensive JSONL logs, including GPU type and duration. The inclusion of an "energy-used" metric would constitute a logical subsequent enhancement. Future Red Hat Insights dashboards could potentially display metrics such as "grams of CO_2 per megatoken trained," thereby transforming sustainability from a conceptual notion into a quantifiable metric. Ultimately, the most sustainable computation is the one we never perform. That's why pruning, sparsity, and intelligent edge caching will continue to play a crucial role in maintaining the power and efficiency of AI.

---

[10] https://cloud.google.com/sustainability/region-carbon
[11] https://aws.amazon.com/blogs/architecture/how-to-select-a-region-for-your-workload-based-on-sustainability-goals/

Conclusion

This chapter examines potential emerging trajectories that may shape the future generation of RHEL AI. It underscores explainable AI (XAI) as a fundamental element, featuring integrated attribution maps, SPDX lineage, and policy-driven governance to ensure transparent and auditable model conduct. The chapter elaborates on advancements such as edge AI, hybrid deployments, runtime attestation, quantum-ready processing, and differential privacy—all of which are targeted at scalable, secure, and ethically responsible AI operations. The future of RHEL AI lies in the integration of transparency, sustainability, and hybrid orchestration, thereby ensuring that enterprise AI remains both trustworthy and efficient in an evolving hardware and regulatory environment.

In the next chapter, you will learn how to engage with the RHEL AI community, access official support, pursue certifications, and contribute to open-source development.

CHAPTER 9

Community and Support

Introduction

This chapter explores the vibrant ecosystem of community engagement and official support that underpins RHEL AI. As organizations integrate RHEL AI into their infrastructure, understanding the available support channels, training opportunities, and collaborative resources becomes essential. This chapter provides practical guidance on accessing technical assistance, developing professional skills, contributing to the open-source community, and participating in Red Hat-led events and workshops. Whether you are a system administrator, developer, or data scientist, this chapter equips you with the tools to become a confident and connected RHEL AI user.

Official Support Channels

RHEL AI empowers enterprises with tools like InstructLab and synthetic data generation to develop and deploy AI workloads. Beyond the technology, Red Hat provides robust support and a thriving community ecosystem to help users navigate and optimize their RHEL AI environments. Red Hat offers several official support options to ensure that organizations can operate RHEL AI reliably:

- **Customer Portal**: The primary destination for support access, documentation, and updates. Users can manage subscriptions, open support cases, and access updates through access.redhat.com.

- **Support Lifecycle Policy**: RHEL AI follows a defined lifecycle, with versions under "Full Support" until 30 days after the general availability of the next RHEL AI version. During this phase, customers receive security updates, critical fixes, and advisory guidance.

CHAPTER 9   COMMUNITY AND SUPPORT

- **Service-Level Agreements (SLAs)**: Red Hat offers enterprise-grade SLAs, ensuring timely response and resolution for technical support requests, aligned with the severity and business impact.

To begin exploring or resolving issues:

1. Visit Red Hat Support (https://access.redhat.com/support/).
2. Navigate to the RHEL AI section.
3. Access guides, log support tickets, or download updates relevant to our deployment.

These are the three knowledge resources currently available:

- **Documentation**: Comprehensive technical documents cover installation, CLI commands, hardware requirements, updating, and custom model generation (available via the Red Hat Customer Portal).
- **CLI Reference Guide**: For hands-on users, the RHEL AI CLI guide provides detailed command usage, including `ilab config`, `ilab model train`, and other related commands.
- **Release Notes**: Stay informed on new features, supported hardware, and enhancements through regularly updated release notes.

We can connect to these two community engagements:

- **Red Hat Community Forums**: Engage with other users and Red Hat experts to share insights, ask questions, and collaborate on troubleshooting.
- **InstructLab Project**: Contribute to the open-source initiative that enhances LLMs through taxonomy-guided data generation. InstructLab welcomes community contributions and makes AI accessible to a broader audience.

InstructLab Community Collaboration Spaces

A vibrant, collaborative community powers the RHEL AI ecosystem through the open-source InstructLab project. Whether you're new to the platform or an experienced contributor, InstructLab offers numerous ways to connect, share, and grow. If we are just getting started with InstructLab, we recommend joining the Discord (`https://instructlab.ai/discord`) or Slack (`https://github.com/instructlab/community/blob/main/InstructLab_SLACK_GUIDE.md`) channels. These real-time workspaces are ideal for asking questions, getting setup help, and chatting with project maintainers and fellow contributors. For broader project updates or feedback, the email lists (`https://groups.google.com/a/instructlab.ai/g/users`) provide structured communication channels.

These are the regular community meetings:

- **Weekly All-Community Meeting**: Tuesdays at 14:00 UTC—for project updates, community Q&A, and onboarding

- **Weekly CLI Meeting**: Thursdays at 14:00 UTC—dedicated to InstructLab CLI development and road map discussions

- **Biweekly Taxonomy Meetings**: Mondays and Thursdays—ideal for contributors focused on skills and knowledge YAMLs

- **Monthly UI Team Meeting**: First Wednesday of each month at 17:00 UTC—for those interested in the InstructLab GUI

Subscribe to the InstructLab Project Calendar to stay up-to-date on all upcoming meetings.

These are the recommended community channels:

- **GitHub Discussions**: Used for collaborative debugging and quick community problem-solving across repositories.

- **Hugging Face**[1]: Where you can explore and download community-built LLMs.

- **Social Media**: Stay informed through LinkedIn,[2] Twitter/X,[3] Mastodon,[4] Reddit,[5] and YouTube.[6]

---

[1] `https://huggingface.co/instructlab`
[2] `https://www.linkedin.com/company/instructlab`
[3] `https://twitter.com/instructlab`
[4] `https://mastodon.social/@InstructLab`
[5] `https://reddit.com/r/instructlab`
[6] `https://www.youtube.com/@InstructLab`

CHAPTER 9   COMMUNITY AND SUPPORT

Do you have a tutorial, blog post, or demo? The community encourages sharing! You can file an issue in the InstructLab Community Repo[7] or email the community mailing list[8] to showcase your contribution.

Training Resources for RHEL AI

As organizations adopt RHEL AI for advanced machine learning and large language model (LLM) workloads, acquiring the right skills becomes essential. Red Hat provides a range of training resources to help developers, data scientists, and IT administrators become proficient in deploying, configuring, and optimizing RHEL AI environments.

Red Hat's official documentation is the cornerstone for understanding and using RHEL AI. Key documents include

- **Getting Started Guide**: Introduces the RHEL AI architecture, core components like InstructLab, and how to begin a project

- **CLI Reference**: Offers detailed command-line syntax and usage for tools such as `ilab config`, `ilab model train`, and `ilab data generate`

- **Custom LLM Guide**: Walks through creating custom language models using synthetic data generation (SDG), training, and evaluation workflows

These materials are freely available via the Red Hat Customer Portal (https://access.redhat.com/).

The *InstructLab on the RHEL* platform on Red Hat Developers[9] includes guided exercises that walk users through

- Installing and configuring `ilab`
- Downloading and serving models
- Creating skills and knowledge YAML files
- Generating synthetic data
- Chatting with and fine-tuning models

---

[7] https://github.com/instructlab/community/issues
[8] https://groups.google.com/a/instructlab.ai/g/community
[9] https://developers.redhat.com/products/rhel-ai/instructlab

244

These tutorials are ideal for self-paced, practical learning.

Red Hat offers instructor-led and self-paced courses tailored to meet the needs of enterprise environments. While general courses on Red Hat OpenShift and Linux are applicable broadly, specialized content for RHEL AI is often bundled under emerging technology or AI streams. Check Red Hat's training portal for upcoming offerings.

The InstructLab GitHub repository (`https://github.com/instructlab`) contains source code, examples, and contribution guidelines. It's a valuable resource for developers looking to extend RHEL AI capabilities or contribute back to the community.

Through the Customer Portal, users can access curated knowledge base articles, troubleshooting tips, and case studies. These complement the formal documentation and offer solutions to real-world issues.

Certifications

With the rise of enterprise-grade AI platforms like RHEL AI, professionals across IT and data science are looking for ways to validate their skills. While RHEL AI-specific certifications are still evolving, several Red Hat certifications and complementary credentials can help us establish credibility and prepare for AI-centered roles in the enterprise.

Red Hat Certified Engineer (RHCE)

The RHCE is a cornerstone certification for Linux system administrators. It provides a solid foundation in managing Red Hat Enterprise Linux systems—skills essential for deploying and maintaining RHEL AI environments. RHCE certification validates

- Linux system management and automation
- Networking and storage configuration
- Shell scripting and troubleshooting

Recommended For: System administrators and infrastructure engineers supporting RHEL AI deployments

CHAPTER 9   COMMUNITY AND SUPPORT

Red Hat Certified Specialist in OpenShift Administration

RHEL AI often runs on Red Hat OpenShift, especially in containerized or hybrid cloud environments. This certification focuses on

- Managing OpenShift clusters
- Deploying containerized applications
- Implementing security and role-based access

Recommended For: Professionals deploying RHEL AI in Kubernetes-based environments or integrating with OpenShift Data Science.

AI and Data Science Learning Paths

While there is no dedicated RHEL AI certification yet, Red Hat offers emerging technology courses through Red Hat Training and Learning Subscription platforms. These include

- Courses on OpenShift Data Science and MLOps
- Lab-based training on container orchestration and AI workflows
- Early-access content tied to evolving RHEL AI capabilities

Recommended For: Data scientists, ML engineers, and architects building AI pipelines using Red Hat technologies.

External Certifications

To round out our RHEL AI expertise, consider external AI/ML certifications:

- **TensorFlow Developer Certificate** (Google)
- **Certified Kubernetes Administrator (CKA)** (CNCF)
- **NVIDIA Deep Learning Institute** certifications
- **Linux Foundation AI certifications** (https://training.linuxfoundation.org/ai-machine-learning/)

These can complement Red Hat credentials and demonstrate a comprehensive AI skill set.

CHAPTER 9   COMMUNITY AND SUPPORT

As RHEL AI matures, Red Hat is expected to introduce more tailored certifications specific to InstructLab, synthetic data workflows, and LLM customization. Stay updated through Red Hat Training and the Red Hat Customer Portal.

Contributing to the Open-Source Community

RHEL AI is more than just a robust AI platform—it's a product of collaborative innovation between Red Hat, the open-source community, and partners like the MIT-IBM Watson AI Lab. At the heart of this ecosystem is InstructLab, the open-source project that drives RHEL AI's ability to customize large language models (LLMs) through synthetic data generation and taxonomy-based contributions.

Contributing to RHEL AI's open-source community allows developers, researchers, and organizations to

- Enhance foundational LLMs with domain-specific knowledge
- Influence the direction of enterprise AI tooling
- Improve the accessibility and diversity of AI use cases
- Collaborate with a global network of AI professionals

Areas to Contribute:

- **Skills**: Procedural know-how (e.g., "how to file a patent").
- **Knowledge**: Factual content (e.g., "What is the Higgs boson?").
- **Taxonomy Structure**: Improve classification for more straightforward navigation.
- **Documentation and Tutorials**: Help others onboard quickly.

Community Resources:

- **InstructLab GitHub**: github.com/instructlab.
- **Red Hat Customer Portal**: Official docs and support channels.
- **Forums and Discussions**: Engage with other contributors via community.redhat.com or `https://github.com/instructlab/instructlab/discussions`.
- **Events**: Participate in open-source summits, webinars, and hackathons.

Red Hat's open-source projects adhere to a Contributor Covenant Code of Conduct (https://www.contributor-covenant.org/). Contributors are expected to engage respectfully, provide actionable feedback, and support inclusivity in the AI space.

Webinars, Workshops, and Conferences

As enterprises adopt RHEL AI to accelerate AI innovation, staying current with best practices, tooling updates, and community-driven developments becomes essential. Red Hat offers and participates in a variety of webinars, hands-on workshops, and industry conferences to help users and organizations maximize the impact of RHEL AI and its InstructLab-powered ecosystem.

Red Hat routinely hosts live and on-demand webinars that cover

- RHEL AI architecture and deployment
- Customizing LLMs with InstructLab
- Synthetic data generation and evaluation workflows
- Real-world use cases in industries like finance, healthcare, and manufacturing

These sessions are ideal for both technical audiences and IT decision-makers. They often include demos, expert Q&A sessions, and guidance on integrating RHEL AI into existing enterprise infrastructures.

Visit Red Hat Webinars (https://www.redhat.com/en/events/red-hat-webinars) and search for "AI" or "InstructLab" for upcoming sessions.

Hands-On Workshops

Red Hat offers **instructor-led and virtual workshops** that provide hands-on experience with

- Installing and configuring RHEL AI
- Using `ilab` CLI commands for model training and data generation
- Developing and contributing knowledge and skills in YAML
- Fine-tuning and serving models for specific use cases

These workshops often utilize the *InstructLab on the RHEL* training environment, enabling users to build, test, and refine LLMs in real time.

Who should attend: developers building AI features into enterprise apps, system administrators managing AI workloads on RHEL or OpenShift, and data scientists looking to enhance LLMs with proprietary knowledge.

Conferences

RHEL AI and InstructLab are regularly showcased at major Red Hat and open-source events, including

- **Red Hat Summit**: The flagship annual conference, often featuring RHEL AI demos, road map sessions, and customer success stories.
- **Open-Source Summit**: Events co-hosted with the Linux Foundation highlight InstructLab's role in open-source AI.
- **KubeCon + AI Day**: Focus on deploying and managing AI workloads in Kubernetes environments, with RHEL AI as a central player on OpenShift.

Conference sessions often include in-depth discussions on RHEL AI performance tuning, multi-node deployments, and integration with enterprise MLOps platforms.

To find upcoming events and recordings:

- Subscribe to Red Hat Events
- Follow Red Hat's official YouTube and LinkedIn channels
- Join mailing lists through the Red Hat Customer Portal or the developer community

Webinars, workshops, and conferences are key to gaining practical knowledge and strategic insights into RHEL AI. Whether we are new to the platform or managing production-grade deployments, these events provide direct access to Red Hat experts and the broader AI community.

CHAPTER 9 COMMUNITY AND SUPPORT

Happy Hacking!

As you reach the end of this book, remember that the RHEL AI journey doesn't stop here—it's only just beginning. Whether you're customizing large language models, sharing your skills through InstructLab, or innovating at the edge of AI-powered infrastructure, your contributions matter. The Red Hat AI community thrives on openness, collaboration, and continuous improvement.

We look forward to seeing the incredible things you build with RHEL AI. Don't be a stranger—share your breakthroughs, ideas, and feedback with the community. And above all, keep exploring, keep building, and...

Happy hacking!

Conclusion

This chapter underscores the ecosystem of collaboration, education, and technical assistance that forms the foundation of RHEL AI. It details how users may access official support through the Red Hat Customer Portal, documentation, and Service-Level Agreements (SLAs) while engaging with the open-source InstructLab community via GitHub, Slack, and weekly meetings. Furthermore, the chapter discusses training resources, certifications, and practical workshops designed to assist professionals in mastering RHEL AI tools and workflows. Ultimately, it emphasizes Red Hat's culture of open collaboration, encouraging users to contribute, share knowledge, and continuously innovate within the RHEL AI ecosystem.

Index

A

Accelerate training
    DeepSpeed, 198, 199
    distribution, 197
    FSDP, 199
Access vector cache (AVC), 151
AEE, *see* Automation execution environment (AEE)
Agentic AI, 7, 234
    characteristics, 10
    defined, 10
    examples, 10
    use cases, 10
AGI, *see* Artificial general intelligence (AGI)
AI, *see* Artificial intelligence (AI)
Amazon Web Services (AWS)
    defined, 40
    failed launch, 45
    launch, 44
    launch instance, 44
    limitations, 40
    marketplace, 41, 42
    operators, 103
    specifications, 40
    subscription, 42
    virtual machine sizes, 43
AMD ROCm System Management Interface (SMI), 151
Ansible, 139, 202–204
    collection, 106, 107
    event-driven automation, 112
    execution time, 111
    infrastructure provisioning and lifecycle operations, 106
    inventory layout, 108
    outcome-oriented automation patterns, 112, 113
    playbook, 109–111
    roles, 110, 111
    trained model, 111
Artificial general intelligence (AGI), 11
Artificial intelligence (AI)
    adoption, 226
    agents, 210–212
    configuration and customization, 76
    defined, 1
    design document
        baseline model, 121–127
        bootstrap InstructLab, 119, 120
        business context, 116
        business drivers, 117
        capability statement, 116
        checklist, 117
        curate domain knowledge, 127–129
        ilab config init, 120
        infrastructure, 118, 119
        operationalization, 118
        SDG, 130–135
        serving, chatting and integrating, 136, 137
        success criteria, 117
        taxonomy tree, 130
        template, 116

INDEX

Artificial intelligence (AI) (cont.)
  governance, 226
  hype cycle, 5
  lifecycle, 13
  model training and uploading, 77
  tasks, 6
  types, 6, 7
ASGI, see Asynchronous Server Gateway Interface (ASGI)
Asynchronous Server Gateway Interface (ASGI), 194
Asynchronous z-stream, 102
AVC, see Access vector cache (AVC)
Audit trail, 226
Automated alerting mechanisms, 154
Automatic delegation, 212
Automation execution environment (AEE), 207
AWS, see Amazon Web Services (AWS)

B

Baseline model
  datatypes, 121
  domain specialization, 122
  embedded/constrained environments, 121
  high-performance inference runtime, 125
  IBM Granite models, 121, 123
  interactive chat session, 127
  interactive shell, 125
  Merlinite, 124
  open-source model, 122
BERTScore, 144–146
Bilingual evaluation understudy (BLEU), 144
Black-box model, 221

BLEU, see Bilingual evaluation understudy (BLEU)
Bootable container (bootc), 101, 102
Bootc immutable images, 166
Bootstrap InstructLab, 119, 120
Bootstrapping, 98
Brain surgery, 181

C

Canary ReplicaSet, 167
Carbon-aware automation, 237
Certifications
  AI and data science learning paths, 246
  external, 246, 247
  OpenShift administration, 246
  RHCE, 245
Chatting, 78–80
CI/CD, see Continuous integration/continuous deployment (CI/CD)
Cloud Object Storage (COS), 55
Command-line tool (ilab), 27, 28
Community channels, 243
Community engagements, 242
Community resources, 247
Compliance
  implications, 232
  static checklists, 231
  YAML files, 225
Compound annual growth rate (CAGR), 6
Compression, 172
Concept drift, 150, 158, 167, 170
Conduct load testing, 173
Conferences, 249
Container-native UoW, 228–230
Continuous integration/continuous deployment (CI/CD), 137, 225

crewAI, 212
COS, *see* Cloud Object Storage (COS)
Custom AI model, 115, 116
Customer portal, 241
Custom image layers, 204, 205

D

Data Center GPU Manager (DCGM), 165, 168
Data drift, 150, 158
Data generation pipeline, 201
Deep learning (DL), 1
DeepSpeed, 84–86, 90, 91, 101, 197–199
Delivery management system (DMS), 116
Differential privacy (DP), 233
Disaster recovery (DR), 175, 176
Domain adaptation, 126
Drift detection, 150
Drift sentinels, 158, 159
Dynamic voltage and frequency scaling (DVFS), 237

E

Edge AI
    container-native UoW workflows, 228–230
    high-density inference farms, 228
    inference, 228
    peripheral micro-edg**es**, 228
    profile traits, 229
    uptime constraints, 228
EE, *see* Execution environments (EE)
End-to-end request latency (E2E latency), 147
Ethical principle, 231

Execution environments (EE), 108
Explainable AI (XAI), 19
    developer problem, 223, 224
    developer tooling, 227
    expansions, 220
    governance, 225–227
    issues
        debugging model predictions, 222
        monitoring model drift, 222
        multi-team collaboration, 223
        regulatory audit and compliance, 222
    SPDX lineage, 221
Extremist political terminology, 225

F

FastAPI, 191, 194
Fast triage matrix, 159, 160
Fictional synapse logistics, 149
Fine-tuning, 25, 83, 98, 121, 126, 127, 129, 133, 175, 181, 199, 227, 233
Fully sharded data parallel (FSDP), 139, 198, 199

G

GCE, *see* Google Compute Engine (GCE)
GCP, *see* Google Cloud Platform (GCP)
GCS, *see* Google Cloud Storage (GCS)
GenAI, *see* Generative AI (GenAI)
Generation process, 225
Generative AI (GenAI), 6, 7
    characteristics, 8
    examples, 8
    tools, 9
GGUF, *see* GPT-Generated Unified Format (GGUF)

INDEX

Google Cloud Platform (GCP)
    advantages, 51
    errors, 53
    GPU VM sizes, 54
    launch, 52, 53
    marketplace, 51
    product details, 52
    virtual machine, 52
Google Cloud Storage (GCS), 52
Google Compute Engine (GCE), 51
Governance, 219
    access control policies, 225
    audit process, 225
    customer perspective, 226
    and ethics, 231–233
    example, 225
    explainability actionable, 226
    features, 225
    framework, 64, 65
    policy measures, 225
    regulatory perspective, 226
    security, 99, 100
GPT-Generated Unified Format (GGUF), 201
GPU acceleration, 28, 29
    AI applications, 60
    AI performance, 87
    baseline performance, 86, 87
    cloud platforms, 61
    comparison, 86
    DeepSpeed, 84–86
    foundation model, 83
    HBM, 83
    HPC performance, 87
    physical servers, 60
    pipeline engineering, 88–92
    scale-out topologies, 92, 93
    training and inference, 84
    verification, 61, 62
    workflow, 100
GPUaaS, *see* GPU-as-a-Service (GPUaaS)
GPU-as-a-Service (GPUaaS), 16
GPUs, *see* Graphics processing units (GPUs)
Granite-7B, 124
Granite LLMs, 13
Graphics processing units (GPUs), 29, 84
    profiles, 205
    telemetry, 162–168
Green orchestration approach, 238

H

Hardware acceleration, 219
Hardware Security Module (HSM), 232
HBM, *see* High bandwidth memory (HBM)
High bandwidth memory (HBM), 83
HSM, *see* Hardware Security Module (HSM)
Hugging face, 88, 89
Hugging face models, 186
Hybrid AI, 236, 237
Hybrid execution paths, 235

I, J

IBM Cloud
    CLI, 55, 57, 58
    default user account, 58, 59
    GPU instance alternatives, 59
    image, 55, 56
    inference workloads, 55
iLab, 74–76
Infrastructure lifecycle, 145
Infrastructure stability, 166, 170

InstructLab, 4, 13, 27
    base model, 73
    bootstrap, 119, 120
    community collaboration spaces, 242–244
    defined, 69
    SDG, 72
    structured taxonomy, 71
    synthetic data creation, 69, 70
    workflow, 74, 137
Inter-token latency (ITL)/time per output token (TPOT), 147

K

Kickstart, 30, 37–40
Knowledge distillation, 67, 68, 122, 201
Knowledge resources, 242
Knowledge training, 133

L

LangChain, 139, 193–195
Large language models (LLMs), 3, 4, 9, 13, 17, 25, 69, 84, 118, 197, 247
    diagnose and troubleshoot, 159–162
    downloading and management, 75
    execution planes, 146
    metrics and targets, 157, 158
    monitoring performance, 146
    observability signals, 153
    training, 121
Latency-sensitive applications, 119
Latency slowdowns, 167, 170
LLMs, *see* Large language models (LLMs)
Low-rank adaptation (LoRA)
LoRA, *see* LoRA-per-tenant isolation, 230
Low-rank adaptation (LoRA), 229, 230

M

MaaS, *see* Model-as-a-Service (MaaS)
Machine learning (ML), 1
MCP, *see* Model Context Protocol (MCP)
Merlinite-7B, 123
Microservices, 186
Microsoft Azure
    configuration, 46
    deployment, 47
    guided approach, 46
    installation, 45
    launch instance, 48
    manual conversion process, 50
    marketplace, 45, 46
    resources, 50
    types, 45
    virtual machine, 48, 49
    VM sizes, 46, 47
    workloads, 45
Milvus, 188
Mixture of Experts (MoE), 17
ML, *see* Machine learning (ML)
MoE, *see* Mixture of Experts (MoE)
Model-as-a-Service (MaaS), 16
Model Context Protocol (MCP), 16
Model lifecycle, 146
Model performance, 149
Model registry
    camps, 212
    cloud-provider registries, 214, 215
    functions, 213
    lifecycle, 212
    open-source and self-hosted, 213, 214
    SaaS/enterprise, 215, 216
    workflow opinion, 213

INDEX

N

Natural language processing (NLP), 5, 143
NestedFP, 92
Neural network, 67
NLP, *see* Natural language processing (NLP)
Non-uniform memory access (NUMA), 152
NUMA, *see* Non-uniform memory access (NUMA)
NVIDIA Data Center GPU Manager (DCGM), 151

O

Observability
    BERTScore, 144–146
    BLEU, 144
    defined, 143
    E2E latency, 147
    ITL/TPOT, 147
    LLMs, 153
    percentile latencies, 148
    RPS, 149, 150
    TPS, 149
    TTFT, 147
OpenShift AI
    architecture, 15
    benefit, 15
    configurations, 15
    defined, 14
    deployment, 16
    features, 14
    interface, 14
    MLOps capabilities, 14
    observability metrics, 16
    platforms, 15
Open-source community, 247, 248
Operational technology (OT), 20
Operator-assistive systems, 5
OT, *see* Operational technology (OT)

P

P80 (80th percentile latency), 148
P95 (95th percentile latency), 148
Parallelism tuning, 173
Performance drift, 150, 158
PostgreSQL, 138
Predictive AI, 8
Predictive maintenance models, 5

Q

QPUs, *see* Quantum processing units (QPUs)
Quantization, 121, 122
Quantum AI
    design principles, 235, 236
    implications, 235
    overlap zones, 234
    tensor-network compression, 236
Quantum-inspired classical algorithms, 234
Quantum processing units (QPUs), 234

R

RBAC, *see* Role-based access control (RBAC)
Read-only persistent volume claim (PVC), 167
Real-time monitoring, 151–153
Recovery point objective (RPO), 175, 176
Recovery time objective (RTO), 175

Red Hat, 2, 3
Red Hat AI, 11
Red Hat AI Inference Server
    (RHIS), 17, 155
  defined, 155
  diagram, 155
  drift sentinels, 158, 159
  fine-tune performance, 157
  measurable targets, 156, 157
  optimizing models, 157
  SRE paradigm, 156
  vLLM operation, 155
Red Hat Certified Engineer (RHCE), 245
Red Hat container registry, 201
Red Hat Enterprise Linux AI (RHEL AI)
  additional storage, 62, 63
  advantages, 81
  applications, 4
    finance, 19
    government and defense, 23, 24
    healthcare, 18
    manufacturing, 20, 21
    retail, 21, 22
    telecommunications, 22, 23
  architecture, 85
  automation, observability, and
      lifecycle, 100, 101
  certifications, 245–247
  cloud GPU offering, 97, 98
  cloud providers, 40–59
  command-line tool, 27, 28
  compliance, 12
  configuration, 96
  data gravity, 99
  defined, 1
  deployment, 4
  distributed training, 98
  domains, 7

download, 30–32
features, 3, 4, 13
governance, 99, 100
GPU acceleration support, 28, 29
GUI installation, 37
industry-standard libraries, 12
Kickstart installation, 37–40
libraries, 27
license, 32, 33
model swap, 102
monitoring and rollouts
  automated lifecycle controls,
    174, 175
  backups and DR, 175, 176
  compression, 172
  GPU telemetry, 168
  model rollouts, 170, 171
  optimization and cost-to-serve, 172
  OS and driver upgrades, 169
  parallelism tuning, 173
  patching and updating, 171, 172
  utilization guard, 173, 174
multi-tenancy, 104
vs. OpenShift AI, 15
open-source ethos, 219
operational reliability, 165, 168
performance, 3
performance optimization, 12
personal research and experience, 219
preflight checklist, 207, 208
repositories, 34–36
security, 12, 99, 100, 105, 106
steps, 12
storage, 99, 206
system requirements, 29, 30
third-party libraries and tools, 138–141
tools, 3
training and inference, 82, 83

Red Hat Enterprise Linux AI
  (RHEL AI) (*cont.*)
  training resources, 244, 245
  trial, 33
  updates and maintenance, 206
  updating guide, 102
  upgrade, 104, 105
  use cases, 4–6, 9, 10
  verification, 60
  version, 25, 26
Red Hat Enterprise Linux (RHEL), 2
Red Hat OpenShift Data Science, 14
Requests per second (RPS), 149, 150
Resource exhaustion events, 151
REST API, 190–193
Retrieval-augmented generation (RAG)
  advantages, 181
  analogy, 181
  brain surgery, 181
  defined, 179
  frameworks, 138
  implementation, 193
  librarian, 182
  OpenAI library, 190
  pipeline, 180, 190, 191
  vs. retraining
    deployment fit, 184
    hallucination risk, 184
    hardware and cost
      considerations, 184
    hybrid strategy, 185
    idea and analogy, 183
    performance and latency, 183
    traceability and auditing, 184
    updating knowledge, 184
    use caes, 183
    working principles, 183
  schema, 180

  setting up, 180
  steps, 189
  workflow, 192, 193
RHCE, *see* Red Hat Certified
  Engineer (RHCE)
RHEL, *see* Red Hat Enterprise
  Linux (RHEL)
RHEL AI, *see* Red Hat Enterprise Linux AI
  (RHEL AI)
RHIS, *see* Red Hat AI Inference
  Server (RHIS)
Role-based access control (RBAC), 23
RPO, *see* Recovery point objective (RPO)
RTO, *see* Recovery time objective (RTO)
Runtime attestation, 231, 232

S

Safety regressions, 167, 170
SBOMs, *see* Software bills of
  materials (SBOMs)
Scalable AI, 94
  cost-efficiency, 95
  deployment, 94
  GPU instances, 94
  tooling, 94
SCAP security guide (SSG), 103
SDG, *see* Synthetic data generation (SDG)
Security hardening, 103
SELinux, 23, 101
Service-level agreement (SLA), 147, 154,
  156, 242
Service-level indicator (SLI), 154, 156
Service-level objective (SLO), 143,
  154, 156
Service reliability, 154
Serving models, 77, 78
Sexual content, 225

INDEX

Site reliability engineering (SRE), 156
Skill training, 133
SLA, *see* Service-level agreement (SLA)
SLI, *see* Service-level indicator (SLI)
SLO, *see* Service-level objective (SLO)
Software architecture, 219
Software bills of materials (SBOMs), 231
Software package data exchange (SPDX), 221
SPDX, *see* Software package data exchange (SPDX)
Split-graph inference, 230
Support lifecycle policy, 241
Sustainability, 227, 237, 238
Synthetic data generation (SDG), 9, 69, 72, 119, 121, 183, 238
    completion, 135
    defined, 130
    documents, 132
    generated data, 133, 134
    higher-quality teacher model, 132
    logistics domain, 130
    output files, 131
    timestamp, 131
    training set, 130

T

Tail latency, 148
Teacher models, 67, 122, 130, 179
Tensor-network factorization, 235
Tensor processing units (TPUs), 84
Terraform, 96, 97
Third-party integrations, 196, 197
Time per output token (TPOT), 165, 169
Time to first token (TTFT), 147
Tokens per second (TPS), 149
TPS, *see* Tokens per second (TPS)
Troubleshooting, 208–210
Trusted Platform Module (TPM), 232
Trusty AI, 217
TPM, *see* Trusted Platform Module (TPM)
TPOT, *see* Time per output token (TPOT)
TPS, *see* Tokens per second (TPS)
TPUs, *see* Tensor processing units (TPUs)
TTFT, *see* Time to first token (TTFT)
Tune vLLM, 199, 200

U

UoW, *see* Update-of-weights (UoW)
Update-of-weights (UoW), 228–230
User-perceivable issues, 151
Uvicorn, 191, 194, 195

V

Vector database, 186–189
Virtual environment (venv), 141

W

Warm-cache routing, 230
Weaviate, 138, 188
Webinars, 248
Wire metrics, 152
Workshops, 248

X, Y, Z

XAI, *see* Explainable AI (XAI)

GPSR Compliance
The European Union's (EU) General Product Safety Regulation (GPSR) is a set of rules that requires consumer products to be safe and our obligations to ensure this.

If you have any concerns about our products, you can contact us on

ProductSafety@springernature.com

In case Publisher is established outside the EU, the EU authorized representative is:

Springer Nature Customer Service Center GmbH
Europaplatz 3
69115 Heidelberg, Germany

www.ingramcontent.com/pod-product-compliance
Lightning Source LLC
LaVergne TN
LVHW081537070526
838199LV00056B/3698